Women Living Change

IN THE SERIES

Women in the Political Economy
edited by Ronnie J. Steinberg

Women Living
Change

*Edited by Susan C. Bourque
and Donna Robinson Divine*

TEMPLE UNIVERSITY PRESS
Philadelphia

Temple University Press
Philadelphia 19122
© 1985 by Temple University
All rights reserved
Published 1985
Printed in the United States of America

Library of Congress Cataloging in Publication Data
Main entry under title:

Women living change.

   (Women in the political economy)
   Includes index.
   1. Women—Social conditions—Cross-cultural studies.   2. So-
cial change—Cross-cultural studies.   3. Women—Psychology—
Cross-cultural studies.   4. Feminism—Cross-cultural studies.
I. Bourque, Susan Carolyn, 1943–   .   II. Divine, Donna Robin-
son, 1941–   .   III. Series.
HQ1154.W88385 1985   305.4   84-25277
ISBN 0-87722-369-6

In memory of
Lillian G. Robinson
Carolyn Wood-Sherif
Jeanne McFarland

Contents

CONTENTS

viii

Acknowledgments

The essays in this volume come from work undertaken at the Smith College Research Project on Women and Social Change. This multidisciplinary team was created in 1978 with the generous support of the Andrew W. Mellon Foundation. At Smith, the Project constitutes the center for encouraging research on the lives and experiences of women. Over the course of the past several years, the principal investigators have pursued individual research while simultaneously constructing frameworks for interdisciplinary explorations.

Our joint work has taught us that broad political and economic changes need to be understood by probing the particular and individual. Conversely, our studies of the emotional and intellectual development of women indicate how carefully we must look at the impact of political and social contexts on individual psychologies. Our goal has been to create a lively intellectual environment, in which finely textured case studies can be related to overarching theoretical questions. As the essays in this volume illustrate, this approach has led us to revise our understanding of social change.

An undertaking of this magnitude requires sustained scholarly and institutional support, which we have received in abundance. First and foremost, our thanks to Jill K. Conway, President of Smith College from 1975 to 1985, whose fund-raising efforts on behalf of the Project have been essential and successful.

From the Project's inception, we have also received enthusiastic encouragement from the distinguished scholars who have served on our Board of Advisors. They have challenged us, intellectually and institutionally, and have always been there when we needed them. Serving in this capacity at the Project's inception were Herbert Gutman, Frances Fox Piven, and the late Carolyn Wood Sherif. Our very special thanks to the current Board, Joan Wallach Scott, Thomas Pettigrew and Carolyn Heilbrun, who have been both stalwart advocates and marvelous colleagues.

Our profound thanks go to the women whose lives are the basis of these studies. Clearly, without their collaboration in sharing their experience this undertaking would have been impossible. We would also like to acknowledge here the many scholars who have joined us at Smith and shared in our ongoing discourse in one of the many Project-sponsored forums: Summer Post-doctoral Workshops, Works-in-Progress Seminars, Faculty Development Seminars, and Lectures. The presence of these scholars—from throughout the United States, Europe and the Third World—on the Smith campus inspired sudents and faculty alike, and created an awareness of the richness of current research on gender. It would be premature to offer a final evaluation on the Project's impact; but one measure of its success is the ever increasing range of Smith and Five College consortium faculty who contribute to Project activities, challenging us with new perspectives, questions and insights.

At Smith, we are indebted to the Project staff, particularly to Carol Smith, who has taken enormous time with the manuscript, and to Kathleen Thayer, our administrative assistant. Also to Gale McClung who helped edit many of the essays.

We are particularly grateful to the Temple University Press, and to Michael Ames and Ronnie Steinberg for their acute intellectual insight and their efforts to bring this project to a speedy and successful completion.

Introduction

Women and Social Change

Revolution, modernization, social disintegration, revitalization, and cultural breakdown—all are labels we use to describe the processes of change and to convey its scope. These terms emphasize the collective impact of historical events, yet they frequently obscure important differences in experience and meaning for individuals who share similar histories. In this volume we focus on both differences and similarities, as we examine the interplay of change in broader social systems and in individual lives. Fundamental to our study is the idea that, through contextualized case studies of women who have lived through distinctive political, social, and economic upheavals, we will understand more fully the significance and complexity of social change. Thus, the contributions to this volume were written with the joint goals of (a) identifying the forces that shape change and (b) tracing the cultural constructions of gender in the midst of change.

Change is often seen by social scientists from the administrative perspective of the policymaker or bureaucrat. This book looks instead at persons who are in the mainstream yet, as are most of us, often outside the formal decision-making structures of the modern state. These women are not the government's authorized agents; but they are definitely affected by government policies and, depending on the circumstances, may seek to support, modify or subvert policies. One of the central puzzles we examine is why some women, at given times, transform their views of their social place, reassessing their societies and the larger forces shaping their lives. To understand why some women actively embrace change, we must also attempt to discern why others, apparently similarly situated, do not. We need to identify the elements in individual and group experience that lead some women to an involvement in and a desire for change, while others eschew, reject, and even organize against it. To examine these issues is to avoid, from the onset, the common pitfalls of treating *women* as an undifferentiated group; treating gender as if it were always the primary determinant of behavior; and treating change as if it were inherently good or evil.

When the current generation of feminist scholars drew our attention to a population missing from histories, omitted from the social sciences, and systematically devalued in the humanities, they did so with a call not only for the incorporation of women as proper subjects for sustained and serious study, but also for the revision of the academic disciplines themselves. The necessity for re-examining history, rethinking politics, rewriting literary criticism and, more extremely, re-creating language is an argument that has been powerfully presented. Critiquing the scholarly arts and sciences has been the point of departure for much painstaking and creative research. Again and again, the question "what was the impact on women . . ." has been asked and variously answered. While the substance of good empirical research on women is rapidly developing, we need to cast that substance into adequate comparative forms.

At this point, no single overarching theory has been able to explain the divergent experiences of women. There is merit to an argument contending that to employ a singular analytical framework reduces the richness of women's lives, thereby conveying a distorted picture of their historical past and their political present. Just as there is no one experience of womanhood that transcends history and culture, there has been no uniform experience of subordination, and no single path to change. In fact, the individual essays in this volume demonstrate the range of contemporary theories which are useful—and others which merit thorough critiques and rejection—for the study of gender and change. The essays also reflect the multidisciplinary nature of the research network at the Smith Project on Women and Social Change.

To understand women more fully, we see special advantages in multidisciplinary approaches which draw together the structural analyses of the social sciences with the insights of humanists and psychologists. From the social and political sciences, we have learned to ask what events precipitate the creation of movements demanding changes in women's political, social, or economic position. Psychology raises questions about the roles of siblings, parents, spouses, children, friends, peers, mentors, and teachers in women's responses to change. Psychologists have also related age, life-cycle, and generation to attitudes and values. From the perspective of the humanities, we focus on forms of expression in literature, ritual, and song. All of these perspectives have informed the essays in this volume. Addressing change from a variety of disciplines avoids an array of ecological fallacies that tend to obscure the broader, fundamental forces shaping individual behavior. Rather than explaining responses to change solely on the basis of individual psyches, our approach seeks the links between the micro perspective and the contextual factors at the macro levels.[1]

Do multiple theoretical frameworks and multidisciplinary approaches make comparisons between societies and historical periods impossible? We would suggest that one can develop a comparative language that highlights similar processes and patterns, yet avoids distortions and simplifications of the richness and variability of particular times and places. The best comparative perspective would address the lives of women, not simply as reactive to their environment, but rather as proactive with it. It would assume that lives are informed by history, which is inherited; but that history is mitigated in particular ways by the relative positions and subjective judgments of individuals. Moreover, the assimilation of that history would be shown to be influenced by the nature of the vehicle through which it is transmitted— through folktales, myths, and memory or through records and books.

Central to the comparative language we advance for this anthology is the notion of *context*. Women belong to many contexts, affiliate with many institutions, and consequently must be considered within many social categories. Different contexts may well have their own distinct sets of values, distributions of power, and norms for interaction. The fact that women, like men, are placed simultaneously in a number of different contexts affirms that social purposes are served in and through multiple relationships and activities. Effective comparisons, which successfully maintain a sense of social process, should allow for the possibility that individuals negotiate multiple, mutually exclusive goals, and accommodate many contradictory aims.

We suggest that context, itself, consists of three components: *structure, relationship,* and *consciousness.* Each of these components presupposes the other two and must be defined in terms of its connection with the others; it is, nevertheless, important to highlight the distinctiveness of each. The most striking of these components is, perhaps, structure: the families, villages, nations, schools, and clubs in which women might find themselves. Structures foster their own traditions, generating rules sometimes autonomously and sometimes in symmetry with the rules of other structures. These traditions open up some opportunities and foreclose others, thus indicating that while men and women do not necessarily act in fully prescribed ways, neither are they totally autonomous beings. A second component, relationship, arises often but not necessarily as a consequence of structure, because structure promotes interaction that results in emotional bonding of varying intensity. Structures and relationships inspire and make inevitable a domain of intellectual activities—musing, questioning, reflecting, and reasoning—and we incorporate these activities in our final component of consciousness.[2]

Considered together, the recognition of these components makes the study of women a less difficult problem. These categories help us to understand how the emphasis among contexts can shift. Such shifts help women strike a balance between obligations, responsibilities, and burdens on the one hand and desires, interests, and self-fulfillment on the other. They also identify moments of change.

Our emphasis on context further highlights the capacity of men and women to alter the facts, the importance and the meaning of their multiple placements. When institutions appear to *obstruct* the capacity of some segment of society to meet its needs or realize its goals, that segment can create or use other institutions for its collective and individual development. Over time, it is also possible to alter the activities of different contexts, as well as to change the meaning attributed to existing relationships and behavioral patterns.[3] Of course, the range of adoptive and transforming behavior corresponds not only with individual needs and sensibilities but also with the conditions—political, social, and economic—of the historical moment.

The fact of sexual subordination creates the need for, and powerfully affects the frequency of, this kind of institution building and trading. We are not suggesting that men and women *necessarily* develop different interests and perspectives. We are suggesting, rather, that the patterns of relations between the sexes in a particular society—given the contexts in which they find themselves—may lead each sex to encounter the world in significantly different ways. These encounters often occur in distinct contexts that define the possibilities available to each gender. Because the contexts for women—and the traditions from which they have been drawn—deny much more than they grant, women are forced to seek their own institutional outlets, deploy their own languages, and set their own priorities in accordance with their experiences and calculations.

This argument also implies that, as women enter into structures similar to those of men and find themselves in comparable relationships, aspects of their behavior may change. Their calculations, too, will derive from their movement into new contexts. Our approach stresses variability even as it acknowledges class, ethnicity, and gender. Because ours is not a single variable model, we interpret the outcome of a change in structure or relationship in conjunction with other contextual elements. For instance, the movement of women into the paid work force—a structural change—will not tell us much until we can link the impact of that change to personal relationships, family dynamics, and individual consciousness.

The focus on context helps us elaborate the multiplicity of factors affecting women's lives. In looking at the structural component, we must necessarily assess the economic realities. Clearly women's economic roles, expectations, and the opportunities and limits of their access to resources are central to their reactions to change. Similarly the political structure—both formal and informal—contains some of the relevant arenas where choices are made and strategies and options developed.

Context, as we have used it, will be defined initially by the women whose lives we are examining. We are looking for the factors these women identify as relevant. We want to learn their sense of place within their societies. By building upon these individual responses, we are able to determine the factors that tend to unite women; the causes and consequences of change; and the ways in which those experiences are communicated and shared. We argue that there is a discernible relation between a woman's understanding of her placement in society and her political consciousness. Again this suggests a dynamic interpretation of women's lives, with shifting assessments in response to changing environments. Moments of insight and changed perceptions can become central elements of concern, from which new possibilities can emerge.

7

Our approach does not deny the possibility of self-deception; nor does it necessarily tell us if the choices women make are the best ones or the only ones available to them. It does, however, encourage us to take seriously the notion that some women may accept subordination because the prospects for change are both too limited and too costly. We believe our approach encourages scholars to discover the ways in which women, themselves, understand and negotiate their social, political, economic, and cultural placements.

Feminist scholarship has advanced our understanding of the complexity of the issue of subordination. Starting from reports of its apparent universality and its overwhelming nature, this scholarship has refined the concept of subordination. It includes a much fuller appreciation of the *complexity* of the circumstances in which women find themselves and the *variety* of ways in which the impact of subordination is mitigated.

Women may be subordinated by the same mechanisms that potentially serve as a means for their advancement. And, despite the intensity and injustice of sexual subordination, women are often able to put resources into service for their own interests and their own needs. The experiences of sexual subordination—and other social divisions such as race and class—provide the material out of which structures, relationships, behavior, and languages are shared and meanings are developed.

Evidence suggests that changes in economies, polities and cultures, which have often entailed great insecurities for women, have also activated hitherto suppressed human capacities. As the introduction of a cash economy made the lives of many peasant women more economically vulnerable, it also expanded their capacity to determine their own occupations and to insist on an education for their daughters. Because of their increased dependence on cash, and often on a male wage earner, peasant women became more aware of the importance of formalizing their sexual relationships; and of the law as an instrument for their own protection. In terms of suffering, the losses in economic security may have outweighed the gains in autonomy or in raised consciousness; but the immediate hardships were not without potential for enhancing the position of women in later generations.

Stifled by domestic seclusion, middle-class, nineteenth-century American women sought and established rich and rewarding friendships with other women. These relationships, rather than their marriages, frequently served as the center of their emotional lives. If the economy is an arena unequal to the task of meeting women's interests or wishes, the histories of ritual, literature, and female networks suggest that some possibilities commensurate with need or ambition may be found or created. Women have long transformed acts of religious devotion into settings in which economic linkages are established, political alliances forged, and social contacts amplified. While the processes of state expansion and the erosion of communities have presented women with serious challenges, and the major transformations of modern societies have often destroyed the socioeconomic supports upon which women rely, the studies in this book demonstrate not only the scope of women's responses but also the range of their capacities to cope.

Clearly there are many routes to consciousness. For some women, a re-evaluation of their identities or situations may be experienced as a struggle to restructure primary relationships. For others, re-evaluations may result from organizational involvements directed at liberating other oppressed sectors of society. By distinguishing between individual and collective action and by identifying the mechanisms propelling women to personal and collective change, we can move toward comparative observations of why some women respond, in whatever form, to change while other women do not.

In studying how women organize, live, and seek to change their lives, we are looking at a flexible set of experiences through which women adapt, survive, and seek to make gains. The scholarly issue is not the disparity in power between men and women, but the ways in which the disparity is understood and used. The subordination of women has been properly understood as confining women and severely qualifying the originating powers they possess as individuals. When certain avenues for development are closed, however, individuals seize others, frequently with determination and ingenuity. Women weigh the advantages and disadvantages derived from maintaining, strengthening, or weakening particular patterns of relationships; a particular institutional focus; or a specific set of activities. Even without necessarily altering their behavior, men and women have enormous scope for changing the meaning they attribute to their own activities. Through these activities, either in response to situations imposed upon them or in pursuit of newly perceived opportunities, whether or not consciously acknowledged, women may also seek autonomy, power and control.

What we have seen in feminist scholarship has been a steady movement from studies that emphasize the "state" of subordination to those that emphasize the "process." The essays in this volume reflect and advance that movement. Feminist scholars have recognized that structures do not determine everything else, and that individuals do enjoy some range of choice. In this volume we address the movement that takes place between structure, personal action, and choice—all of which are central to understanding the process of social change. In so doing, these essays show that change does not always affect men and women in the same ways, and that we must examine the complexity of women's situation in their own terms rather than as a lesser reflection of male patterns.

We have grouped the essays in three sections—structure, relationship and consciousness—not on the basis of scholarly disciplines but on the grounds of emphasis. As the reader will note, these groupings set up the wider comparative interplay that we hope our terminology encourages.

Structure: Collective Routes to Consciousness

The chapters by Bourque, Divine, and Ackelsberg explicitly demonstrate the significance of structure. For these authors structure includes the complex networks elaborated through family, school, occupation, and through participation in national political and economic life. All three authors link national patterns of political experimentation to women's altered understanding of their own lives. In so doing, the authors illustrate how macro-level changes can take on particular meaning in individual lives.

For Bourque, the study of upper-middle-class women in Peru is intimately tied to structural questions. Which women join women's groups and why? How are those choices related to the larger social structures in which they occur? Are shifts in the economy and in patterns of political participation related to such choices? What do the cultural backgrounds of individual women—their schools, religions, and family ties—contribute to their political assessments and to their responses to change? Bourque traces the contours of women's experience as they move toward political involvement. Her discussion suggests that the relation between the cultural and structural resources available to Peruvian women helped forge their basic responses to the changing political landscape in Peru.

Divine's study of Palestinian Arab women begins with the importance of structures, both family and religious, for understanding how a group of urban, upper-class women came to respond to the demands imposed in part by their nationalist struggle.

In discussing the significance of the threat to establish a Jewish National Homeland in Palestine, Divine shows how Palestinian men and women evaluated the dangers distinctively: men focused on the loss of political power and office, while women stressed the cultural sacrifices they were all expected to bear. Both sexes reacted differently to the opportunities created by the British mandatory rule, with its potential for expanding educational and occupational facilities. For women, the tensions between commitment to their tradition and to their threatened nation on the one hand, and their desire for more opportunities and broader experiences on the other, set the standards by which they constructed and judged their lives. The most persistent theme in Divine's analysis is the ability of these elite women to justify a new attitude toward work and family in terms of ancient traditions. Palestinian Arab women argued that their newly carved roles were not examples of breaks with the past, but were consistent with their customary responsibilities and their commitment to their own society.

This made social change, albeit for a small group, more acceptable and enduring. These women were effectively able to reinterpret their tradition to the point where it became a central aspect of what they called their own personal liberation.

The potential for religious structures to subordinate or oppress women is better appreciated than the capacity of religious traditions to mobilize women's energies toward change. Women who join movements to change their status often attack and reject the patriarchal values they find in their religion. A substantial number, however, also want to reinterpret inherited customs and religious practice, and to use these as sources of inspiration for new understandings or as anchors for a new consciousness. Religion, for some women, becomes an essential structure in the new order they imagine.

On the other hand, religious institutions can produce diametrically different reactions. In Bourque's examination of Peru, religious traditions inspire some women to visions of change. For one generation of Peruvian upper-middle-class women, Catholicism had the flexibility to support redefinitions of their roles without diminishing their attachment to their faith. These women redefined their behavior to be consistent with the tenets of the theology of liberation and simultaneously with their Catholic tradition. This religious redefinition propelled their involvement in a series of organizations directed at social change. For a younger generation of upper-middle-class Peruvian women, however, rejecting the Church's influence, particularly its views on women's sexuality, was a part of their growing political and feminist consciousness.

Likewise, the hold of religious tradition appears to have been minimal in the case of women anarchists in Spain, as Ackelsberg has discovered. In cases of the rejection of traditional religion—or a lack of concern with its hold—notions of social change were associated with more radical critiques of the social system and a more sweeping prescription for the reordering of society.

The papers by Bourque and Ackelsberg demonstrate how 13 differently similarly situated women view their own society, their place in that society, and the areas they attempt to restructure. Two important elements, age and political participation, intersect both analyses. Women evaluate their own situations quite differently depending on their age, the generation to which they belong, and the reservoir of political ideologies and categories available to them. For the Peruvian women, answers suitable during the 1950s and 1960s are rejected by those who came of age in the 1970s. Consciousness changes with respect to both the issues being addressed and the solutions being embraced. Moreover, political positions are not undertaken in suspended animation nor divorced entirely from the larger national configuration. This point is made vividly by Ackelsberg's study of Spanish anarchist women.

In the case of civil war Spain (1936–1939), men and women considered anarchism the way to personal and sexual liberation. They engaged in social experimentation that was often personally costly, but without parallel in terms of its potential for communal change. The questions for Ackelsberg are how women understood those experiments, and how they attempted to integrate aspects of communal change into their personal lives. Ackelsberg explains how women came to make sense of their anarchist experience— enjoying and believing in its benefits and short-run successes, but ultimately compelled to explain its collapse and failure. Ackelsberg's study gives us insight into the groups that were most open to change, most ready for it, and for whom it has had the most enduring effect, even in the midst of severe political repression. By focusing on their organizational experience with anarchism before the Civil

War, Ackelsberg sees the long-term impact of change as dependent upon the direct experience of political participation. Conversely, the relative ease with which some women became depoliticized derived from their earlier distance from the active political process. Moreover, Ackelsberg further suggests that a positive assessment of the anarchist experience can be passed along to the next generation. Her paper uncovers one linkage between women's openness to change and the permanent effect it has upon them and their societies.

Significantly the three papers avoid the assumption that all impetus to change is generated outside women themselves. Women are not viewed as simply reactive to forces largely outside their control. Without denying the importance of such macro-level change, the three authors suggest that women themselves become both the interpreters and constructors of change. That is, women have chosen in all three cases to work in groups that have political as well as personal objectives and meaning. Thus an explicit attempt to influence public policy emerges in terms of women's own understanding of the need for change.

While their issues are pointedly structural, these three authors suggest that relationships and consciousness are integral to understanding fully the process of change women experience, and the directions women might wish such change to take. Such issues are parallel to the concerns of identity and the reconstruction of the past undertaken explicitly by Foster, Gill, and Snoek.

Relationships: The Individual and Change

We have joined together the essays by Foster, Gill and Snoek. The women these authors have studied ordered both their perceptions of and confrontations with the world primarily in terms of their significant relationships. None of the essays claims a direct correspondence between the issues women see themselves facing and their particular primary relationships. Rather the essays highlight the dialectic that is engendered between events, the relationships in which women find themselves, and the ways in which women respond. Relationship serves as framework, metaphor, and symbol which, as these three authors suggest, often generates unresolved tensions between the processes of feeling, thinking, and acting. Nevertheless, women employ the word *relationship* to depict the several contexts in which they operate and, at the same time, to ascribe value to them.

In contrast to the urban Peruvian women discussed by Bourque, Foster's essay portrays a young Moroccan woman, Samira, who has a degree of political awareness and even an implicit ideology, but no apparent motivation to organize or engage actively in politics. Samira has chosen escape and the construction of a private world, which she has heavily invested with symbol and myth in order to cope with an environment that appears restrictive and dangerous.

Samira's narrative forces us to pay attention to the connections she draws, the causal sequences she establishes, and the patterned relationships she purposefully creates with men and women. The tension between men and women is made manifest through Samira's identification of her father and mother with two totally different and radically unequal cultures in Morocco—Islam and Judaism. Against the background of the Arab-Israeli dispute, the tension is certainly real, but it appears at least partially transformed into a metaphor of Samira's own complicated desires for autonomy. The close association she develops with men casts light on her ambivalence. Her strong judgments of her parents is assuredly her way of making statements about the world in general and about Muslim society in particular, where autonomy for women can be achieved only at the expense of full acceptance. The detail in Foster's essay helps us read Ackelsberg's study of Spanish anarchists with deeper sensitivity. We are reminded that participation, if empowering, is also enervating, often validating association with men and depreciating the development of close ties with women.

Gill's essay reminds us that to study women we must not only raise fundamental questions about their lives, we must also be prepared for unexpected answers. For Mary, living at the economic and social margins of the transformations in America during this century, her children constituted her primary commitment, and motherhood was the role through which she understood and structured her entire life. Or was it? One is led by Mary's own account to ask whether motherhood was her anchor in the world or the metaphor through which, in her old age, she explained, justified, and synthesized her own history.

Snoek writes of Mara, an American, middle-class, professional woman. While written from the perspective of a psychologist, it is a measure of the essay's richness that we can address it with questions essentially social in nature. Specifically, Snoek's study makes the important point that a sense of family disruption intensifies the desire for change in women. If, as he argues, this is true, then we can learn a great deal about the scope, structure, and directions of change from the psychology of bereavement. The argument makes good sense and accords with Divine's work on Palestinian women and with Warren's and Bourque's work on rural Peru. Moreover, Snoek's thoughtful elaboration of Mara's purposes urges us to consider the emotional dimensions of Palestinian Arab and Peruvian women, and the ways in which their activities are entangled with their own psyches.

All of the essays in this section assert the intense and comprehensive involvement women have with friends and family. The emotional energy women mobilize for their own

living cannot be understood apart from their family contexts as mothers, daughters, wives. As Snoek demonstrates
so adroitly, the response of women to their own problems
and the attempts they make to pursue their own goals are
constructed partly from their own familial histories and environments. Snoek brings the issue of family relationships
to mind rather sharply when he writes that "anger is often
the only emotion strong enough to motivate a decisive
break with our attachments to the past." Here there is the
contrast between Marx's notions of class consciousness and
Snoek's rendering of the process by which Mara's consciousness was raised. This contrast illuminates the distance between conventional views of class identification,
and political engagement as women, themselves, describe
it. To amplify our knowledge of political consciousness and
activity, we must recognize that women seem especially
concerned to establish some correspondence between their
private feelings and their public behavior.

Consciousness

When we turn to the last section, it is clear in the papers by
Freeman and by Warren and Bourque that consciousness is
embedded in familial relationships, friendship networks,
and broader political and economic developments. Both
papers draw attention to the continuous exchange between the political, social, and economic environments and
the particular elements of consciousness that persist in
the lives of men and women. The issue for understanding
social change is appreciating the circumstances and range
of choices that women can, in any instance, reasonably
perceive.

Freeman's study of a group of middle-class American
women, struggling to apply the messages of the current

women's movement to their own lives, gives us a sense of the highly personal struggle a public issue can provoke. By moving beyond the normal constraints of the psychologist's laboratory, with its severely controlled and artificial experimental setting, Freeman develops a methodology that corresponds with women's own accounting of their lives and experiences. Freeman's work stresses the conflict women feel when they attempt to assert their individual identity and offers an explanation for that tension. Women need and seek validation for themselves, for the choices they make, and the roles they craft. More often than not such validation is limited, especially where change is involved. If found, it must be invoked against a larger world valuing or condemning assertions of personal identity, new and old. Freeman underlines how issues of "personal individuation and development of an independent identity are moral dilemmas for women." Freeman also elucidates the extent to which women refuse to surrender their own desire for individuality and development; how difficult it is to accept those desires casually; and, of course, how costly they are to celebrate.

Freeman's analysis poses important questions to scholars who have attempted universal formulations of morality, without reference to time and place. Her evidence suggests that women's developmental patterns are much more closely tied to social context than has been previously assumed. Freeman's essay helps us see the contextual nature of women's definition of their responsibilities to others, and how women rewrite the significance of relationships and obligations in light of cultural constraints and opportunities.

In the final chapter, Warren and Bourque turn to a highland Peruvian setting to demonstrate the influence of the three elements of context on women's political behavior in community politics. Their approach refocuses our attention on gender and the politics of communication. Warren and Bourque argue that women may be forced to create alternative forms of expression when their access to the public arena and its discourse is blocked. This response to structural subordination at times deepens and at times diminishes women's consciousness of their restricted condition. This analysis delineates how community affairs are structured to mute or silence women's expression. The authors show the impact that different economic and political bases have on women's patterns of adaptation and their ability to challenge the structures of communication.

Warren and Bourque have taken on the central issue of how cultural patterns mask subordination and inhibit the formulation of alternative models of action. By examining the political and economic constraints that accompany the formulation of public discourse, their work helps us see the link between structure and consciousness. This essay also addresses the dimension of relationship, by examining the impact of female networks. The authors argue that, in addition to the important opportunities afforded by such networks, there are costs involved in their maintenance. Warren and Bourque's consideration of all three components of context help us appreciate the parameters of individual choice. At the same time, by identifying the political components of muting, they demonstrate for us the strategic considerations posed to women by their subordinate position.

As recreated in this section, the lives of all women depend upon the larger environment. Our perspective toward the study of women and social change is especially clear if we compare the life histories and moral dilemmas presented in the final two essays. Both of these raise the question: When can we say that change has occurred? The Freeman and Warren and Bourque studies, like the other essays in this volume, illustrate the dialectic between continuity and change, between the attachment to and the rejection of tradition, and the embracing and denouncing of the new.

Perhaps no segment of society has more to gain from liberation and change than women; yet their responses to change and to movements for their own liberation are, at times, highly ambivalent and unpredictable. Our studies indicate some of the reasons for this apparent anomaly. In each essay, the interplay between the elements of context (structure, relationship and consciousness) and an individual response to the various levels of the social system gives us a fuller and more complex guide to women's experience.

Conclusion

Rather than assimilate the varieties of women's lives into one general description, these essays argue that one can look at the *differences* in women's lives and see in them commonalities of a distinctive and dramatic order. To illustrate this point, let us take up again the issue of the past, an issue central to all of these essays. This issue also informs context, for structure and relationships are all influenced by, if not constructed from, the past. Thus consciousness, too, will be related to the past. For the past to serve as a meaningful bridge to the present, a connection must be forged; and for that connection to be established, the sense of past time, the flow of past events, must appear both relevant and comprehensible. Women must create their own distinctive bridges in order to recover and claim this legacy of the past. If this volume serves any one purpose, it is as a bridge, not as the first or the only entrance, but rather as a *mode* of entry into a world that has stood for too long with too little access.

Notes

1. Such ecological and compositional fallacies frequently lead to victim-blaming by attributing responses to individual dispositions, thus ignoring the contextual shaping of behavior.

2. Our presentation of these components is not intended to argue a temporal or hierarchical relation among them. Indeed, evidence suggests that consciousness or relationship can also animate the evolution of structures, which, in turn, provide their own possibilities for human activity.

3. Language, itself, may serve as a context into which overtly female interests and desires are placed. Feminist literary critics have produced pioneering readings of novels and poetry that have only recently enabled us to hear these female voices.

I

Women in Groups:
The Routes to Change

1

Urban Activists: Paths to Political Consciousness in Peru

by Susan C. Bourque

ricture several hundred women, ages ranging from early twenties to early sixties, assembled in an overcrowded, steamy hall in midsummer. A four-day program billed as a "Conversation" and sponsored by a leading feminist journal, *Woman and Society*, has brought together women from over twenty different organizations: representatives of women workers, women leaders from the marginal low income areas ringing the city, women from religious organizations, and the occasional individual who saw the announcement of the public meeting in the local newspaper. The speeches vary widely, from descriptions of the efforts of low-income women to organize women's groups in their communities (with the help of the local parish priest and against the resistance of some of their husbands), to calls for solidarity with the women of El Salvador, Nicaragua, and the women members of a revolutionary group, "Shining Path." The political message—particularly the mention of the last group which has been characterized by the government and local press as terroristic—makes some of the women in the audience squirm, while others enthusiastically applaud. The meeting, one of the largest ever held, has attracted the broad spectrum of women involved in feminist activities.

This scene occurred in 1981 in Lima, Peru, in a city and a society noted for conservatism and traditionalism. The presence of such a large group of women at a meeting called to discuss women's issues underscores one current of profound social change in modern Peruvian society: the growth and proliferation of women's organizations. [1] This growth, most marked in the past ten years, reflects Peruvian women's changing views as they respond to the important demographic, social, and political upheavals in their own society and to the changes set in motion through international feminist activity.

Peru in 1981 was an ethnically diverse nation of seventeen million people, primarily of Indian and Mestizo heritage. Divisions in Peruvian society are marked between modern and traditional economic sectors, geographic regions, and ethnic groups. Inequity is severe. One recent estimate put eighty percent of the population in the lower class. The upper-middle and middle class—while they have increased in the past twenty years—still represent a very small proportion of the total population. Peruvian political life in the twentieth century has consisted of alternating periods of competitive party politics and military rule. Political participation has been restricted throughout most of the modern period. Thus, the presence of such a large group of women represents an important departure from the current expectation of relatively limited levels of political concern and involvement.

The conference in Lima brought together the diverse factions of those who count themselves as feminists as well as those who eschew the label. They represented a spectrum of Peruvian women but not, however, the full range. Absent was any substantial representation of rural women, who still comprise forty percent of the total female population and slightly over half of the rural population. [2] Rural women are subject to some of the worst forms of subordination and exploitation. There were, at the conference, women from the urban squatter settlements, the home of many rural migrants to the city. By and large, however, those who attended would be classified as members of the middle and upper-middle class—exactly those women whom scholars have suggested would be the principal beneficiaries of the cultural ideal of *marianismo*.

Marianismo, often viewed as the female counterpart to male *machismo*, is credited with conferring upon Latin American women—especially those at the upper end of the class structure—a status equivalent to that of men. According to this theory of sexual complementarity, women achieve equivalent status through their domination of a separate sphere of influence in the home and through their recognition as the moral superiors of men. If this is an accurate description of either women's actual condition or women's analysis of their situation, then one might suggest that such women would be reluctant to join a feminist organization seeking change in women's status. Indeed, social scientists have argued that upper- and middle-class women would be particularly anxious to preserve the social and economic *status quo*, and would be unlikely to risk altering their relationships with men.[3] Speaking of the upper-middle class Peruvian woman, one author observes: "Having reached the respected and obeyed position of *reina y señora* (queen and married woman) in her family, it is doubtful that the Peruvian woman would strive to dispossess herself of the security and authority, no matter how little, this situation has allowed" (Schipske 1975, p. 431).

How, then, does one explain the participation of such women in a feminist meeting? What did their presence mean in terms of women's organizational activities in Peru? What does the growth of women's organizations in Peru tell us about the process of social change in that society and in others?

Historian Joyce Appleby has written that "it is through ideas that men and women grasped the meaning of modernization" (1978, p. 275). She goes on to point out that students of social change have done very little theorizing about what the *process* of imagining and anticipating new social arrangements is like for individuals and groups. How are we to understand the process by which individual women came to see the need to engage in an organization directed at the concerns of women? What "conceptual bridges" allow women to imagine a radically altered future?[4] (1978, p. 261).

One way of looking for these bridges and understanding how such a conference came about, as well as appreciating what it represents in the larger context of Peruvian politics, is to examine some of the individual life paths which led women to it. What do these paths tell us about the routes to feminist consciousness, about the changes in women's lives and in societies which lead to altered consciousness? What are the links between individual experience and societal change? How should we understand the emergence of women's organizations in the Peruvian political context?

What pressures in Peruvian national life fostered their creation, and what factors are likely to enhance or restrict the
impact of feminist organizations?

As noted above, the women at the Lima meeting were a
diverse group, reflecting the complexity of the women's
movement in Latin America. To demonstrate that complexity let us look at two groups of women attending the Lima
meeting and examine the routes each took to an imagined
future, which included greater equity for women. What life
experiences led women in each group to commit themselves to the struggle for the improvement of women's
status?

The two groups of women both come from upper-middle
and middle-class backgrounds. They are well to do members of society with university level educations. The two
groups are, however, separated in age by a generation (fifteen years). While living through much of the same social
and political context and exposed to cultural values and expectations associated with upper-middle-class urban Peru,
their experiences have been shaped at distinct points in the
life cycle. Their political responses, while bringing them to
the same meeting in 1981, have in some respects been
quite different.

One can trace the interplay between major political,
economic, and demographic shifts and the choices these
women have made in their lives. These are articulate women
with astute observations of politics; and one sees parallels
between changes in their consciousness, their choice of
associations and activities, and the broader patterns of
change in Peruvian national life.

These are not the elite women of the "jet set" feminists.
They would not be chosen to represent their government at
the Mexico or Copenhagen International Women's Conferences sponsored by the United Nations. In fact they view
such "round table ladies" as ineffective tokens, incapable of

dealing with the most serious problems of women. However, when the elite representatives return from the international conferences and contemplate action within their
own countries, these are the women to whom they turn.
The older group of women are now in their fifties. About
one third of the group has not married and several have divorced. They were all born into upper-middle-class Lima
society in the early 1930s and became politically involved in
the 1950s.[5] They were part of the first generation of Peruvian women to exercise the vote when General Manuel
Odría granted female suffrage in 1955. The younger group,
born in the late 1940s and early 1950s, became politically
involved during the years of the Velasco government (1968–
1974). While somewhat separated by age, both groups have
been affected by the significant change in Peru over the
past four decades.

The Peruvian Context

By any measure, Peru has undergone enormous transformations over the past forty years. The population has shifted
from sixty-five percent rural in 1941 to only forty percent
rural by 1981. Internal migration has been accompanied by
substantial social mobilization: the expansion of schools
and roads into the rural areas, the spread of mass communication, the elaboration of rural-urban linkages, and the
growth of urban areas through internal migration. These
patterns of social change combined to create a heightened
interest among politicians and political parties in the political recruitment of the peasantry and the recent urban
migrants.[6]

The concerns of politicians for these rural and urban
populations were similar to those expressed by various elements in the Catholic clergy, and the 1950s marked the be-

ginning of major shifts in clerical emphasis and concerns. The Chimbote Conference of 1953 signalled the recognition by Church hierarchy that they needed a new approach toward the people of Latin America if they were to compete successfully with the new ideologies of nationalism, communism, and protestantism challenging their traditional hold. The Church's response was to organize the laity into Catholic action groups for women, university students, peasants, workers, and youth. [7]

The large scale migration to Lima and the coast by highland peasants began in the 1950s. Over the course of the next thirty years, it transformed the city from the province of the wealthy to a city ringed by squatter settlements of migrants living in makeshift straw houses without benefit of electricity or running water. Wealthy Limenos decried the change and decamped to the suburbs when attempts to curb the flow of migration failed.

The response to these new political participants in both the city and in rural areas created a significant expansion of both political and non-political groups. The leading political parties, Apra and Acción Popular, as well as the parties of the left, competed to organize peasants and workers. Apra controlled the Confederation of Peruvian Workers, which commanded the loyalty of the majority of unionized workers until the mid-1960s. The Communists responded with their own confederation, as did the military when it came to power in 1968. These efforts were directed at coopting the leadership potential of new participants and directing their energies toward goals compatible with the interests of the sponsoring organization.

These changes in organizational opportunities have altered the shape of the political process. Citizens—male and female—have had new options for involvement in national life over the past forty years. Moreover, political leaders have faced the challenge of developing policies, programs, strategies and expertise that would allow them to continue to lead in the face of changed circumstances. The significance of women's organizations needs to be understood in light of this overall political process. Women's interests were seldom addressed directly in the new organizations, which focused on the concerns of peasants and workers. The church-sponsored peasant organizations, however, were a significant exception: peasant women were frequently included in training and leadership programs. This being the case, how did the older generation of upper-middle-class women find their way to political participation?

Sources of Individual Consciousness: Religion and Politics

The combination of events of the past forty years gave rise, within the older group of women, to a profound sense that they had a contribution to make to the development of Peru. Their responses combined a commitment to reform in Peruvian society with a belief in nationalism, Catholicism, and ultimately feminism as sources for the possible renewal of Peru. Their commitments led them from involvement with various Church reform groups to political parties and, finally, to women's organizations. Their efforts included an initial focus on the plight of the peasantry, which expanded to a broader political assessment of the structural impediments to change in national life. It ultimately led to efforts focused on the women of the Lima squatter settlements. Through their various organizational involvements, the Catholic church has maintained a position of critical importance in their lives and thinking, and has helped to inform their commitment to the construction of a more just social order in Peru.

The significance of Catholicism for this older group of women is directly related to the impact of attending elite Lima parochial schools. Apart from their extended families, Peruvian upper-middle-class women have formed most of their lifelong friendships and associations through their private Catholic schools. It is there that class position and responsibility are communicated in a forceful fashion by both lay and religious teachers. [8] The school experience laid the basis for lasting notions of proper conduct in these women's private lives and public associations. In addition, a formative influence on the self-conceptions of this group of women was their association with Matilde Perez Palacio, an outstanding lawyer, journalist, and national political activist, who taught them Peruvian history. Twice elected a deputy from Belaúnde's party, Acción Popular, she was widely expected to become the first female cabinet minister when Belaúnde returned to power in 1980. (Instead she was made the head of the national public assistance and child protection agency.)[9]

Perez Palacio's influence on the first generation of women was profound. She communicated to them the appropriateness of interest in political life and emphasized the contributions that women like themselves could make to the development of Peru. She also encouraged and exemplified an unusual level of egalitarianism in her relationships with her students, having them address her with the familiar *tu* form and allowing them to use her first name. Years later she still recognizes this group of former students, following their activities, and affirming their successes and contributions as important to the women of their nation.

The impact of Catholic school life, combined with the strong Catholic tradition of their families, resulted in a deep identification as Catholics and an important role for Catholicism in these women's lives. [10] This identification, however, has not been tied to a rigid doctrinal position. On the contrary, the women have been at the forefront of the Church's new commitment to the pursuit of social justice in Peru.

34 Most of the women went on to the Catholic University, pursuing such subjects as law, engineering, and the more traditional field of social work. More significant than their course work was their involvement in a Catholic youth group for university students. One aspect of the group's work was to build ties with students in other countries and with groups of young Catholic workers and peasants in Peru. Several of the women traveled to other Latin American countries to student conferences. There they heard about student activities in Uruguay and Chile and developed a conviction that there was much they could do within their own society to foster social change.

Meanwhile in Peru by the mid-1950s women had been granted the vote by General Odría in the hope that they would support his Conservative party. The nation returned to a period of competitive politics, beginning in 1956 and lasting until 1968 (with only one year of temporary military rule). These years saw the rise of Fernando Belaúnde Terry, the first large scale urban and rural land invasions, the establishment of squatter settlements around the cities, and guerrilla movements in highland Peru.

The women all started out politically as Belaúndistas. They saw in his Popular Action party a non-Marxist, nationalistic developmentalism, which matched their own notions of how social justice might be achieved within a Catholic, non-violent framework. When Belaúnde first appeared on the national scene, he appealed to this generation as the embodiment of the dashing, courageous, and energetic reformer that the nation desperately needed. He was a welcome alternative to the established parties and their aging, compromised leadership. By the early 1960s, he had been identified as one of the new breed of Latin American democrats, a key individual who John Kennedy hoped would be able to make the Alliance for Progress work by bringing about peaceful social change.

Belaúnde talked about the "Conquest of Peru by the Peruvians." This meant the opening up of the riches of the Amazon jungle through the construction of a network of highways and the integration of the coast and the highlands. This development formula was based on expanding resources and, thus, made it possible to imagine achieving social justice without conflict over redistribution. When Belaúnde came to power in 1963, he put into action a self-help program entitled Popular Cooperation to provide technical assistance from the central government for local development initiatives. The program was ideologically and socially based upon the surviving remnants of a Peruvian community tradition of cooperative public works. This tradition, credited to the Inca heritage, appealed to Peruvian, middle-class nationalistic sentiments as well. Belaúnde's party and ideology offered these women a political identification that combined their commitment to social justice, their nationalism and concern for the renewal of Peru with a plan of action that did not put their Catholic identification or class interests at risk.

Settling upon Belaúnde's solutions meant that the issue of redistribution could be largely sidestepped. Yet, however incomplete the women's political and economic analysis may have been, it marked the beginning of their notions of how a better Peru might be achieved. This starting point indicates the enormous ideological distance the women traveled in the course of their lives and how change, itself, was conceptualized distinctively at various points in their political consciousness.

At the same time that Belaúnde appeared to offer a resolution to the political problems of Peru, the Catholic church was undergoing a major reorientation. That reorientation led the Church to a new commitment to social justice for the poor majority of the Peruvian population and required new forms of social action directed toward the peasant population. [11]

The peasantry was viewed as the source of a number of the problems facing Peru. In the rural areas, their poverty was believed to make them easy marks for political agitators. Similarly, scarcity of land and lack of skills were deemed to be the major factors that pushed peasants into the overcrowded center city slums, and then into land invasions to establish squatter settlements. Elite groups began to seek ways to prevent the radicalization of the peasantry. The first responses were a variety of unsuccessful attempts to stem the flow of rural-urban migration by improving conditions in the rural areas. A second strategy attempted to recruit the most able peasants into organizations sponsored by a number of national groups, including the Catholic church, political parties, and labor unions. In these organizations, peasants were offered a wide variety of training and leadership courses, as well as technically based courses on agricultural production and cooperative organization.

The older generation of women found themselves involved in such a group—not surprisingly one sponsored by the Catholic church. In the early 1960s they took on jobs in the national office of the Institute for Rural Education handling administrative tasks, bookkeeping, and accounting. The women learned a great deal from this exposure and their commitment to social change was deepened. As the peasant base grew within the organization, however, the presence of the upper-middle-class women (and the sponsorship of a board of directors drawn from the upper class) seemed incongruous. Eventually it became a source of tension. The women withdrew from their work with the Institute, but not from their commitment to social change. [12]

Their departure from the Institute was followed by their

increased frustration with the Belaúnde government and its development strategy. Their high hopes for reform under his administration were replaced with disillusionment at the levels of corruption and disarray within the president's party. [13] The women recall their genuine embarrassment at the sight of Belaúnde's Acción Popular headquarters surrounded by the Lima police to prevent attacks upon one another by rival factions within the party. This event occurred just prior to the coup of 1968.

Given the disheartening experience with the Belaúnde regime, the women's support for the Velasco government is easier to understand. They initially looked upon the self-proclaimed Revolutionary Military government of Peru as a welcome and overdue change. They were enthusiastic about the new government's strong anti-imperialist position and were delighted by the speedy expropriation of the International Petroleum Company. They supported the sweeping agrarian reform when it was promulgated in 1969, and one member of the group went to work as a social worker in the effort. Their defense of the need for the reform put them at odds with members of their families, whose lands were being expropriated. One of the women would not accept her share of the family estate, because it was being divided into smaller units to preserve a larger share for the family and was thus undermining the reform. Another member of this group joined the military government's agency for social mobilization, SINAMOS, working first with peasant training programs and eventually specializing in work on women's programs. The women's support for the Velasco regime reflects the change in their political consciousness from an early belief that Belaúnde's developmentalism would be sufficient, to the recognition of the structural flaws in the Peruvian system which Velasco's programs sought to redress.

The rhetoric and political stance of the Velasco government (1968–1974) was important to these women for several reasons. The government maintained the position that it was neither capitalist nor communist; rather it argued for an independent path for Peru, a path that would end Peru's dependence on the United States. Moreover, the government carefully fostered the approval of and support from the Catholic church. While it did seek the deportation of several priests who criticized the government too openly, the first five years of the government also marked the flourishing of the most militant and radical elements in the Peruvian Church. This was a post-Medellín and pre-Puebla period in the Latin American Church which saw priests, sisters, and members of the hierarchy taking leading roles as outspoken supporters of social justice and social change. [14]

In Peru this period marked the development of a genuinely national church. Under the intellectual leadership of Gustavo Gutierrez and the Álvarez Calderón brothers, the Theology of Liberation gained considerable acceptance in Peru. The theology spoke most directly to the disparities in economic class and to the responsibility of Christians to oppose in society those structures that perpetuated inequality. The women read the new material, listened to Gutierrez, and found that his analysis resonated with their own understanding of Catholicism, its relationship to social change, and the pursuit of social justice. This is how Gutierrez describes the relationship:

> In order to be a Christian in our age, it is necessary to commit oneself in one way or another to the process of liberation, the emancipation of man.
>
> [Gutierrez, n.d.a.]

> What the Church must do is commit itself to the poor, to the disinherited of this country. This in one respect means disorganizing ourselves, to live as the poor of this world; it means breaking the ties that we have in this world to the established *DISORDER*.
>
> [Gutierrez, n.d.b.] [15]

Along with an appropriate theology, a movement called "Toward a Church of Solidarity" developed. This movement organized retreats and dialogues among men and women of various classes. In the context of these retreats, individuals who normally did not speak frankly and openly with one another could come to know something of how their social subordinates and superiors saw their lives and interaction. In these conversations, the upper-middle-class woman had a chance to hear how she was seen by a domestic servant and to hear the maid's evaluation of whether her employer's behavior constituted Christian attitudes and action towards others.

The women involved in the solidarity Church movement describe their experience as revelatory. In a number of areas of their lives, the women saw the need to change and revise their attitudes and behavior. Involvement in this movement underscored for the women the contrast between their lives and those of working class, domestic and unemployed women. It also underscored the fact they materially benefitted from the subordination of other women. That realization triggered in the upper-middle-class women an increased awareness of the importance of building cross-class alliances with other women. It also re-emphasized that aspect of the Theology of Liberation which argued that participation in social change was inherent in the definition of a Christian and Catholic life.

What was most influential, then, for this group of women was two parallel sets of changes—one in political life and another in the Catholic church. The women participated in and gave shape to both types of change as they moved from rather mild involvement in peasant training programs combined with support for Belaúnde's developmentalism, to a commitment to large scale social reordering under the ideology of the Velasco government. [16] Their support for the change-oriented aspects of the Velasco period reflected growing political consciousness, and dissatisfaction with the limited solutions of Belaúnde's policies. They had developed a much wider appreciation of the condition of other women's lives and an understanding of how their comfortable, middle-class existence was dependent on the subordination of others.

While the Velasco government only rarely talked about women's concerns (most specifically in article 23 of Plan Inca), the rhetoric of a fully participatory democracy which permeated his regime sparked a notion of inconsistency in the upper-middle-class women listening to it. The impact of this message manifested itself in a variety of ways, both during his government and in the years following its demise.

During the Velasco years, Peru played an important role in international forums, speaking for the interests of the non-aligned and third world countries, which sought a more independent and less economically subordinate position in relation to the developed nations. As such, it participated fully in many U.N. initiatives including the International Year of the Woman. In 1974, in preparation for the World Conference in Mexico City, the National Council of Peruvian Women was revitalized, and Peru sent substantial delegations to the U.N. women's meetings in Mexico City and Copenhagen. This participation brought Peruvian women's organizations into the mainstream of the international women's movement. The Velasco years also saw the appearance of a feminist critique of the existing Peruvian laws which discriminated against women; and fledgling attempts were made to expand women's participation in the military and the national police force. [17]

When the military set up the apparatus for a new constitution, the civilian delegates to the Constituent Assembly included equal rights for women in Title 1, article 2.2, of the 1979 Constitution. The achievement of that change was at least in part due to the efforts of women lawyers and professionals who negotiated with the lawmakers to assure the provision's inclusion. There are now several associa-

40

tions of these women who are rewriting the Civil Code to eliminate laws that discriminate against women, and to make the Code consistent with the guarantee of equal rights in the new constitution.

Despite these positive benefits, however, one must recall that the military government left power in a hasty retreat to the barracks in 1980. Discredited by corruption and the failure of its economic policies, the military watched Belaúnde return to power after his impressive victory in the 1980 elections (winning forty-five percent of the popular vote in a field of fifteen candidates). While the vote represented strong antimilitary feeling, it would be incorrect to suggest that Belaúnde's victory marked a wholesale rejection of the ideas which the Velasco government proposed or the social change it espoused. The existence of a feminist movement and the growth of women's organizations in Peru today are testimony to another inheritance from that epoch. Understanding what these groups seek to do, as well as the routes by which women came to identify with them, enriches the analysis of the course of Peruvian politics.

For the older generation of upper-middle-class women, the return of Belaúnde was a sad reminder of dashed hopes, and to date none has chosen re-involvement with his government. Rather, most have joined organizations working with poor women in the squatter settlements, promoting income-generating activities, organizing local women's groups, and providing legal counseling, literacy and nutrition training. The groups they joined were small, and often initially dependent upon precarious international financing. In some instances, the women explained that they had not taken explicitly feminist identifications for their groups because they wanted to avoid unnecessary resistance and misunderstandings based on negative reactions to a feminist label. They hoped to avoid the charge—frequently leveled at feminist organizations—that they were undermining the revolutionary potential of disadvantaged groups by pitting men and women against one another. They insisted in private, however, that their groups were feminist, that they themselves were feminists, and that the groups' activities focused on women. Avoiding the public *label* of feminist in this instance was a survival strategy, rather than a reflection of a difference in ideology.

While the hierarchy of the Catholic church appeared to be retreating to more conservative positions and backtracking on some of its more progressive stands on family planning (particularly after Puebla in 1978), the women still found allies among priests and sisters engaged in programs with rural women and the urban poor. Their notion of social change and social justice had not been weakened with changes in the Vatican. Thus the women's commitment to Catholicism remained intact, while their notions of how to affect social change and the focus of their activities were transformed over the years.

Feminist Organizations and the Parties of the Left

As noted at the outset, the women at the Lima Conference were a diverse group. There was substantial representation of groups considerably more to the left in their politics than the upper-middle-class women described above. Women with more leftist leanings belong to groups such as ALI-MUPER, Flora Tristán, Mujeres en Lucha, Perú-Mujer, and the Frente Socialista de Mujeres, among others.[18]

The younger women tended to belong to these organizations, reflecting important contrasts in the paths that led the generations to affiliate with feminist groups. While coming from the same class background as the older generation, they are fifteen years younger. More of them have been married than the older generation, and more have been divorced.

Their experience also varied with respect to Catholicism. Like the older generation, most of the younger women had attended Catholic girls schools and gone on to the University. But the teaching in the high schools remained unaffected by the Theology of Liberation that so influenced the older women. By the time the younger generation entered the University, it was the political parties and ideologies of the Left that captured their imaginations and loyalties. Many of the younger women criticize the Catholic church as an important source of women's oppression, decrying its stand against birth control and abortion, as well as its role in perpetuating a double standard of sexual behavior.

The political experience of the younger women begins with the Velasco government. Active feminism for many begins after 1978, during the post-Velasco era. The younger women began political involvement with the parties of the Left, and for many the struggle to accommodate feminism and leftist politics was difficult. Virginia Vargas, a member of Centro Flora Tristán, notes:

> One of the fundamental obstacles for the (feminist) organizations was how to fit feminism to the political positions of the left, given that these parties considered the problem of the woman irrelevant. [1982, p.9].

Ultimately this led women to create independent feminist organizations. But for some, the experience with political parties, while admittedly teaching them new political skills and tactics, had its drawbacks. As Vargas notes:

> The eagerness not to distance ourselves from the class struggle impeded us from rethinking, in our own terms, appropriate and creative forms of undertaking the women's issue, from seeing the forms that the oppression of women takes in our country and hiding, even from ourselves, the political and subversive character of the feminist movement. [1982. p.10].

Another difference between the older and younger generations of women was the greater interest and willingness of the younger women to confront issues arising from women's sexuality. To a far greater extent, they found the issues of birth control, abortion, sexual pleasure, and *machismo*, important elements in their understanding of women's situation and much higher on their agenda for change in Peruvian society. The older women, especially those who were single, were much more reluctant to deal with sexuality. The different saliency each group assigned to addressing sexuality may also be related to each group's ability to resolve Catholicism and feminism.

In a recent edition of the Lima magazine *La Revista*, three women from the younger generation recounted the path by which they arrived at a feminist identification and involvement. They recalled that they initially viewed feminism as something foreign, appropriate perhaps for the women in developed, capitalist countries, who were facing difficulties the Peruvian women did not. The Peruvians felt their first priority and the route to their liberation as human beings would come through their work with the popular sectors, in their struggle for socialism. Party activity kept them primarily involved with consciousness-raising among the proletariat, the peasants, and the dispossessed. At the same time, they found themselves relegated to minor maintenance tasks within the party, and they found the same pattern in their own homes with the party men they married. Eventually the women dropped out of active party involvement because it conflicted with their responsibilities as wives and mothers.

> We had children and serious doubts about how to raise them. Our relationships with our spouses were full of inequality and unsatisfactory. We were ignoring much of our own sexuality. . . . We were afraid to say outloud what we were thinking. We weren't independent women [that is,

even though in some cases we didn't use our husbands names we felt ourselves to be the wife of ——————]. [19]

In 1978, just before the Constituent Assembly, these women began to meet with a group of friends to discuss their concerns. The catalyst had been the failure of their compatriots in the leftist parties to accept legalized abortion as part of the Left's proposals for the new constitution. This led them to discussions of how women's sexuality is used by men to control and subordinate women. From such discussions emerged a new understanding of what feminism represented:

> We began to understand feminism as a form of expression which all women, organized or not, could use to fight against the oppression to which we have been subjected over the centuries. [20]

This group of women also came to believe that feminist concerns should not be subordinated to decisions based on the interests of political parties; since, in such cases, the women's issues would inevitably become secondary. That position separated them from members of leftist parties, both men and women, who felt it was most important to continue within the party rather than take a distinctly separate feminist position.[21]

Looking at these two groups of middle-class women attending the Lima Conference, one sees that the similarity in class background and the difference in generation highlight some important patterns. Presently both groups seek cross-class alliances with other women, both now eschew party politics, both have moved to an identification with less-privileged women and a commitment to social action to alleviate inequality. Both groups are leery of what they deem "lady bountiful" or "band-aid" responses to women's

45

issues; and both look to strategies that eliminate hierarchy and contribute in a meaningful way to the liberation of all women in Peru.

46   They identify the problems of peasant women as particularly difficult because of the cultural distance that must be traversed. Both groups view their relationship to domestic servants as troubling. Professional and public life would be impossible for them without servants, most of whom are women. Yet, the upper-middle-class women are concerned that by employing female domestic servants they may be perpetuating an image of women's servile role in their own homes and for their own children.

For the older group, the changes in the Catholic church have been an important part of their personal experience, and the Theology of Liberation gives meaning and structure to their involvement in social action. For the younger generation this has not been the case. While they do not necessarily take an antagonistic stance toward the church, they do associate it with their own sexual repression and as an important obstacle to women's ability to control their own bodies. This is an important factor in the younger group's feminism and a significant difference between the two groups.

Interpreting the Meaning of Social Change in Peruvian Women's Lives

Retrospectively, one finds similarities in the various routes these groups of women took to the 1981 feminist conference in Lima. Of comparative interest are at least four elements:

(1) A progressive movement, from early efforts to help other subordinated groups, to a recognition of their own subordinate position as women and to involvement in activities that reflect this changing analysis;

(2) Women's frustrated attempts to find an adequate route for change within the existing political parties and reform movements, first with Belaúnde and next with the military government and the parties of the left, which led finally to

47

(3) A movement toward a more radical analysis of structural issues combined with a decision to work with independent organizations created explicitly to help women and

(4) A continuing attempt to build cross-class alliances among women.

Much of this pattern holds, also, for what we know of the history of the United States' women's movement.[22] Its emergence from the Abolitionist movement in the nineteenth century, and from the Civil Rights movement in the twentieth century, parallels the Peruvian women's efforts to assist the peasants and the migrants to the urban squatter settlements. Similar, too, are the attempts to build alliances with the existing political reform movements, and the frustrations encountered when the women's agenda takes second place to party considerations or when women are relegated to housekeeping tasks and eliminated from policy-making positions. Similar, too, is the movement into smaller organizations focused more closely on women's issues, and the splintering among various women's groups with differing political analyses. Finally, there are these common elements in the paths leading both Peruvian and North American women into feminist organizations: the attempt to build cross-class and cross-race alliances; and the critical stance developed toward the structures, institutions, and values that perpetuate sexual and economic inequality.

Such patterns suggest several commonalities in the "conceptual bridges" that allow some women to conceive of radically altered social arrangements and to organize to work toward them. First, for some middle-class women in both the United States and Peru, injustice and subordination may have to be recognized initially in the lives of another group before it becomes apparent in their own. That is, they may need to confront the subordination of peasants in Peru or blacks in the United States before they are able to see and confront the structural nature of subordination in their own lives.

The reoccurrence of this pattern in widely different cultural and historical settings provokes another series of questions. Most notably, what is the relation between the class position of privileged women and their routes to involvement in women's organizations? As upper-middle-class women, they are the group toward which cultural ideologies—such as *marianismo*, the "cult of true womanhood," and the glories of middle-class suburban life—are directed. Not surprisingly, one finds considerable resistance to change among this group. Women who appear to be most favored by the prevailing idealization of female roles may find it necessary to begin the exploration of change in an arena somewhat removed from their personal situation. It may be easier for them to see the need for change among groups where the contradictions in the cultural ideals and social realities are most apparent. Identification with the disadvantaged might fire their sense of injustice or prompt social action. Certainly, and perhaps more importantly, they find the pursuit of justice for other groups less threatening than a direct challenge to their own middle-class roles.

Second, ideologies of social change are likely to be available from more than one source—the Church for some women, radical and leftist political parties for others. Moreover, women make very different assessments of such sources. The Catholic church evokes an especially complex response. As the source of the cultural ideal for female behavior—*marianismo*, derived from the veneration of the Virgin Mary—it provides some women with a justification and positive evaluation of their tradition's roles. Yet, for women who challenged subordinate status, the Church's Theology of Liberation provided an important framework for pursuing social change.

Finally, and perhaps most intriguing, inconsistencies be- tween the tenets of an ideology and the group's behavior toward women do not necessarily lead to rejection. In the case of political parties, such inconsistencies often led women to form their own independent groups. In the case of the Catholic church, some women could maintain a close religious identification, despite the Church's patriarchal organization. This suggests the degree to which ideologies have the potential to be reworked by individuals as they attempt to make sense of their societies and their lives.[23] It also demonstrates women's capacities to take existing ideologies, test them, extract the useful elements, and refashion the ideology to suit a new understanding of their situation or to meet the needs of an altered context. One might also note that the multiple sources of ideologies for change may limit the possibilities for women's ideological solidarity.

In closing, let us put this discussion of feminist organizations into proper perspective by locating these groups within the context of national political life. The pattern we have been describing does not suggest a transformation of Peruvian society, but rather the transformation of individual lives and individual subjectivities. The larger pattern of women's political participation is extremely limited and, despite some significant victories for women, the Peruvian political system in 1984 is not directed toward the ends or the concerns of feminists. Furthermore, as in the United States, feminist analysis has not been explicitly embraced by a substantial sector of the female population.

We should note, however, that Peruvian women hold a higher proportion of seats in the national Chamber of Deputies than do American women in the House of Representatives or British women in the House of Commons.

Moreover, the Peruvian equivalent of the Equal Rights Amendment became part of the new Peruvian Constitution of 1979, thanks to the organized efforts of upper-middle-class professional women and the cooperation of the overwhelmingly male Constituent Assembly.

50

The individuals we have been discussing may not be the vanguard of a revolutionary transformation; but their history and the personal changes that brought them into feminist organizations are essential to an understanding of the process of political change in Peru today. Not only have there been additional national meetings of feminist organizations, but in July 1983 Peru's feminist groups hosted the Second International Conference of Latin American feminists. The individual paths that led Peruvian women into these groups indicate the diverse and complex construction of the conceptual bridges to a radically altered future.

Notes

My thanks to Kay B. Warren, Donna Divine, and Stephen Foster for their insightful comments. Kay was especially helpful in working through the theoretical components of my argument. My thanks also to Jill K. Conway, whose penetrating questions about women's experience in the United States triggered a number of issues addressed in this paper.

1. The first such group in Peru was the Consejo Nacional de Mujeres (1981), organized as a result of Carrie Chapman Catt's visit to Peru in March 1923. Schipske (1975) comments on this group in some detail. See Vargas (1982) for the development of groups in the past ten years.

2. Instituto Nacional de Estadistica. For a fuller discussion of the problems of rural women, see Bourque and Warren (1981 a and b).

3. For a discussion of the concept of *marianismo*, see Stevens (1973). For predictions about how *marianismo* would affect the feminist movement in Latin America, see Jaquette (1976). Those familiar with nineteenth- and twentieth-century U.S. will see par-

allels in the recurring "cult of domesticity." In the nineteenth-century North American context such arguments emphasized women's responsibilities to raise democratic citizens.

Kay Warren and I have argued elsewhere (1981a) that this is an inadequate formulation of the relationships between the sexes. In many respects, the presence of such upper-middle-class women in feminist organizations suggests women's rejection of the balance presumed by a separate sphere. It is difficult to accept the viability of power derived from a separate sphere when the spheres are not actually separate. In the case of Peru, it is clear that women's sphere is dependent upon male control of political life and, consequently, significant areas of rule making and implementation. The likelihood of exercising *influence* from a separate sphere is well documented in the American case. Moreover, there are still lively and productive debates in the feminist scholarly community about tradeoffs between strategies for change emphasizing the acquisition of power and those emphasizing the use of influence.

4. Insight gained from Joyce Appleby's presentation for the Smith College Research Project on Women and Social Change, "If All the World were Riyadh: Another View of Women and Social Change in the West," 16 June 1981, was extremely helpful in the development of this paper.

5. This is of course a very limited group of experiences. Fortunately there is now some comparative data on middle- and upper-middle-class Peruvian women. See, for instance, Andradi and Portugal (1978); Barrig (1979); and Chaney (1980). Chaney's analysis of women's routes into formal political leadership is an important contribution to our understanding of women's paths into leadership in the established political system (1980, especially chaps. 5–7). Bryce (1981) offers a novelist's insight into the experience of this class of women. For a fascinating description of general characteristics and attitudes, see Burga and Cathelat (1981).

6. On internal migration, see Collier (1976). On social mobilization, see Bourque (1971); Larson and Bergman (1969); and Bourque and Warren (1980).

7. For changes in the Peruvian Catholic church, see Bourque (1971); Astiz (1973); and the reports of the Comisión Episcopal de Acción Social (1969 and 1973). For the overall pattern in the Latin American Catholic church, see Lernoux (1982).

8. For a powerful description of the Church's role in socializing upper-middle-class girls in private Catholic schools, see Barrig (1979).

9. See Bourque and Warren (1981b) for a discussion of the politics of this appointment. Lora (1981) reports that for the 1980 elections a group of women wanted to form a women's party and nominate Matilde Perez Palacio as their candidate for the Presidency of the Republic. She gently refused, explaining her loyalty to Belaúnde and Acción Popular.

10. The impact of Catholicism is obviously complex, and comparative data does not support a deterministic and unitary path between religious commitment and an involvement in social change. Obviously several generations of Latin American women have attended parochial schools, but that experience has not necessarily resulted in a predictable response to social change. Similarly, for this generation of women, most members of the same high school class did not choose the active organizational involvement of these women. The younger generation of upper-middle-class women reject the Church as the locus for their involvement in social change and turn instead to leftist political parties. Nevertheless, the older generation of women identify the Church, and their sense of themselves as Catholics and Christians, as significant elements in their personal understanding of the role they sought to play in social change.

11. This process is more fully described in Bourque (1971).

12. For some of the women there was a residue of disappointment and frustration that their efforts to "help" the peasant had been misunderstood and under appreciated. In some ways, their experience parallels that of white women in the Civil Rights movement in the American south in the 1960s as described by Evans (1979). Ultimately, the peasant's rejection led the Peruvian women to see the limits of social welfare schemes for alleviating poverty. In addition, this experience encouraged the women to seek forms of interaction that would avoid explicit forms of hierarchy in their subsequent organizational efforts.

13. For accounts of the failure of the Belaúnde regime, see the volume by Lowenthal (1975); and for another perspective, see Kuczynski (1977).

14. Medellin, Colombia and Puebla, Mexico, were the cities of the meeting of the Conference of Latin American Bishops, CELAM. At Medellin, in 1968, Pope Paul VI called for the Church's renewed commitment to social justice and an "option for the poor." Medellin is credited with the enormous expansion of the Church's role in the pursuit of structural change and the emergence of a

Theology of Liberation. Pope John Paul II attended the Puebla Conference in 1978 and, while reaffirming the Church's concern with the poor, argued strenuously that priests should refrain from political involvement.

15. Materials on the Theology of Liberation are now extensive. See especially Gutierrez (1973) and Cussianovich (1979). For the Latin American Church's account of the remarkable changes in their institution, see the reports of the *Comisión Episcopal de Acción Social* (1969 and 1973). (*Signos de Liberación* is available in English as *Between Hope and Honesty.*)

16. Characterizing the Peruvian "Experiment" and the ideology of the Velasco government has fascinated students of Latin American politics, and there is now a rich literature to consult. Among the best are Lowenthal (1975); Palmer (1980); and Stepan (1978). An insightful review and interpretation can be found in McClintock (1981).

17. Analysis of the discriminatory aspects of Peruvian law can be found in Rodriguez and Roca (1978). The military's efforts to recruit women into special units was most successful in the recruitment of policewomen. Zolezzi (1975) has described the military government's analysis of its program for the revaluation of women.

18. See issues 1 and 2 of *Mujer y Sociedad* (1980) which describe developments in Peru's feminist movement. For a discussion of the evolution of these groups and the differences among them see Vargas (1982). Another very useful comparative discussion of feminist groups in Peru, and a number of other Latin American countries, can be found in Flora (1982).

19. Lujan et al. (1981, p.23).

20. Ibid. (1981, p.24).

21. This is a fascinating structural echo of rural women's analysis of the difference between their development priorities, as women, and the communities' development priorities, as articulated in the male-dominated public sphere. Patterns of rural women's responses are found in Bourque and Warren (1981a).

22. For comparative material on the United States see DuBois (1978) for the nineteenth century and Evans (1979) for the twentieth. Eisenstein's (1981) provocative work also offers important contrasts in chapters 7 and 8. Chafe's study of American women (1977) is also useful for comparative material. We know far too little about the sources of consciousness in the case of nineteenth-century America, but the apparent parallels are likely sources for

future research. See, as well, Conway (1982) for a provocative and compelling discussion of the unresolved issues in the history of American women.

23. Another case of reworking Catholicism is perceptively analyzed in Warren (1978).

References

Andradi, Esther, and Ana Maria Portugal. 1978. *Ser Mujer el Peru.* Lima: Ediciones Mujer y Autonomia.

Appleby, Joyce. 1978. "Modernization Theory and the Formation of Modern Social Theories in England and America." *Comparative Studies in Society and History* 20, no.2: 259–285.

Astiz, Carlos. 1973. "The Catholic Church in Latin American Polities: Some General Considerations and a Case Study." In David H. Pollock and Arch Ritter, eds. *Latin American Prospects for the 1970's.* New York: Praeger.

Barrig, Maruja. 1979. *Cinturon de Castidad: La Mujer de Clase Media en el Perú.* Lima: Mosca Azul.

Bourque, Susan C. 1976. "Cholification and the Campesino." Latin American Studies Program Dissertation Series, no. 21. Ithaca: Cornell University.

Bourque, Susan C., and Kay B. Warren. 1980. "Multiple Arenas for State Expansion: Class, Ethnicity and Sex in Rural Peru." *Ethnic and Racial Studies* 3, no. 3: 264–280.

———. 1981a. "Rural Women and Development Planning in Peru." In Naomi Black and Ann Cottrell, eds. *Women and World Change: Equity Issues.* Beverly Hills: Sage Publications.

———. 1981b. *Women of the Andes.* Ann Arbor: University of Michigan Press.

Bryce Echenique, Alfredo. 1981. *Un Mundo Para Julius.* Lima: Mosca Azul.

Burga, Teresa, and Marie-France Cathelat. 1981. *Perfíl de la Mujer Peruana.* Lima: Fondo del Libro del Banco Industrial del Peru.

Chafe, William H. 1977. *Women and Equality: Changing Patterns in American Culture.* New York: Oxford University Press.

Chaney, Elsa M. 1980. *Supermadre: Women in Politics in Latin America.* Austin: University of Texas Press.

Collier, David. 1976. *Squatters and Oligarchs: Authoritarian Rule and Policy Change in Peru.* Baltimore: Johns Hopkins University Press.

Comisión Episcopal de Acción Social. 1969. *Signos de Renovación: Recopilación de Documentos Post-Conciliares de la Iglesia en América Latina.* Lima: Centro de Estudios y Publicaciones.

Comisión Episcopal de Acción Social. 1973. *Signos de Liberación: Testimonios de la Iglesia en América Latina, 1969–1973.* Lima: Centro de Estudios y Publicaciones.

Consejo Nacional de Mujeres del Perú. 1981. *Boletín Informativo* 1, no. 1. Lima.

Conway, Jill K. (with the assistance of Linda Kealey and Janet E. Schulte) 1982. *The Female Experience in 18th and 19th Century America: A Guide to the History of American Women,* vol. 1. New York: Garland.

Cussianovich, Alejandro. 1979. *Religious Life and the Poor: Liberation Theology Perspectives.* English trans. Maryknoll, N.Y.: Orbis Books.

DuBois, Ellen Carol. 1978. *Feminism and Suffrage: The Emergence of an Independent Women's Movement in America, 1848–1869.* Ithaca: Cornell University Press.

Eisenstein, Zillah. 1981. *The Radical Future of Liberal Feminism.* New York: Longman.

Evans, Sara. 1979. *Personal Politics: The Roots of Women's Liberation in the Civil Rights Movement and the New Left.* New York: Knopf.

Flora, Cornelia Butler. 1982. "Socialist Feminism in Latin America." Women in International Development Working Papers, no. 14. Ann Arbor: Michigan State University, November.

Gutierrez, Gustavo. n.d.a. *Hacía una Teologia del Desarrollo.* Lima: Centro de Informacion Catolica.

———. n.d.b. *La Iglesia Frente al Desarrollo.* Lima: Centro de Informacion Catolica.

———. 1973. *A Theology of Liberation.* English trans. Maryknoll, N.Y.: Orbis Books.

Jaquette, Jane S. 1976. "Female Political Participation in Latin America." In Lynne B. Iglitzin and Ruth Ross, eds. *Women in the World,* pp. 56–76. Santa Barbara: Clio Press.

Kuczynski, Pedro Pablo. 1977. *Peruvian Democracy under Economic Stress.* Princeton: Princeton University Press.

Larson, Magali Sarfatti, and Arlene Eisen Bergman. 1969. *Social*

55

Stratification in Peru. Berkeley: Institute of International Studies.

Lernoux, Penny. 1982. *Cry of the People*. New York: Penguin Books.

Lora, Victor. 1981. "Women and Politics in Peru." Paper presented at Yale University Council on Latin American Studies.

Lowenthal, Abraham, ed. 1975. *The Peruvian Experiment*. Princeton: Princeton University Press.

Lujan, Elba, Olga Mejía, and Armida Testino. 1981. "Feminismo un Testimonio." *La Revista* 1, no. 4: 22–25.

McClintock, Cynthia. 1981. *Peasant Cooperatives and Political Change in Peru*. Princeton: Princeton University Press.

Montes, Eva. 1980. "Avances del Movimiento Feminista en el Peru."*Mujer y Sociedad* 1, no. 2: 41–42.

Palmer, David Scott. 1980. *Peru: The Authoritarian Tradition*. New York: Praeger.

Peruvian Bishop's Commission for Social Action. 1970. *Between Honesty and Hope*. Maryknoll, N.Y.: Maryknoll Publications.

Rodriguez de Muñoz, Carmen, and y Elsa Roca de Salonen. 1978. *Compilación y Análisis de Leyes Sobre la Condición Jurídica y Social de la Mujer Peruana*. Lima: Universidad Nacional Mayor de San Marcos.

Schipske, Evelyn. 1975. "An Analysis of the Consejo Nacional de Mujeres del Perú." *Journal of Interamerican Studies and World Affairs* 17, no.4: 426–437.

Stepan, Alfred. 1978. *The State and Society: Peru in Comparative Perspective*. Princeton: Princeton University Press.

Stevens, Evelyn P. 1973. "Marianismo: The Other Face of Machismo in Latin America." In Ann Pescatello, ed. *Female and Male in Latin America*, pp. 89–101. Pittsburgh: University of Pittsburgh Press.

Vargas, Virginia. 1982. "El Movimiento Feminista en el Perú: Balancia y Perspectivas." Paper delivered at annual meeting of the Latin American Studies Association, Washington, D.C., 6 March.

Warren, Kay B. 1978. *The Symbolism of Subordination*. Texas: University of Texas Press.

Zolezzi Chocano, Mario. 1975. "La Revaloración de la Mujer en el Perú: Analisis y Perspectivas." *Convergence* 8, no.1: 41–48.

2

Palestinian Arab Women and Their Reveries of Emancipation

by Donna Robinson Divine

In a luminous passage, the Palestinian Arab poet Fadwa Tuqan recalls the death of her father: "In 1948, my father died and Palestine was lost. . . . These events enabled me to write the nationalist poetry my father had always wished that I would write." (Tuqan 1978-1979). The sequence of events that Fadwa Tuqan draws together yields a perspective shared widely among urban, upper-class women during British rule in Palestine, 1918–1948, because it taps the truth of an experience common to them all. That experience and the historical sources critical to its development are my concerns here.

Embedded in the intense developments in Palestine during the century before the end of the British Mandate was a series of political, economic, and cultural changes. These changes interacted in such a way as to produce a gradual weakening of the traditional family structure. Such changes—which might also be described as a process of slow differentiation with geographical, social, and gender dimensions—placed urban, upper-class women in a new context which deeply engaged their attention. While the consequences hardly appeared transforming, the lives of these women were so altered in the final decades of the Ottoman Empire that the ordinary world of their daily experiences was never again quite the same. One concrete example should suffice.

At the end of World War I, a number of organizations founded and managed by women emerged and, in general, marked a new stage for the whole society. These organizations particularly illustrated how fundamentally affected the women were by the three principal historical forces to which Palestinian society was subject: political centralization and the establishment of formal institutions, socioeconomic adjustment to the expansion of the population, and the improvement in educational opportunity.

A world once ordered exclusively by the personalism of the urban patriarch or warrior village *shaykh*, or local religious leader, disappeared forever; and a society of relatively autonomous families gave way to quite different sets of political, administrative, and economic dependencies. These changes were followed by a substantial increase in the non-Arab population, supported and encouraged by the British Mandate's sponsorship of a Jewish National Home in Palestine, thus adding considerably to the strangeness, abruptness, and consciousness of the new age. An expanding marketplace, coupled with a shrinking agricultural base, drastically shifted not only the productive forces but, more importantly, their accessibility. This made the issue of controlling and preserving the land central for both men and women.

Finally, the linchpin of the Palestine Arab community—culture—was challenged from without, as European and Jewish schools expanded and ultimately threatened the community through the impact of significantly different educational experiences. Enormously important scholarly efforts have been made to map the ideologies and outlooks of the men who lived and charted this history.[1] But never before has it been thought interesting or important enough to conduct a sustained and detailed examination of the women of any class, implicitly denying to them any historical provenance. As a result, two sharply contrasting paradigms of the Ottoman Empire's nineteenth century emerge. By placing them in opposition, we can examine closely our knowledge of Palestinian Arab women and, more interestingly, interrogate the assumptions about it.

The first paradigm denotes economic and political transformations. The many travellers to Palestine during the late nineteenth and early twentieth centuries wrote of a society situated on the threshold of substantial changes: an expanding network of transportation, an improved system of communication, an enhanced economy, and a more effective government (Ben-Arieh, 1977; and Pollack 1962). The second paradigm creates the impression of social continuity, even rigidity; for many of these same observers of Palestinian society record that little had changed for women in this period. Their lives were enclosed and restricted by a religious tradition whose discrimination of women appeared timeless and problematic in the changed circumstances (Bartlett 1855; Ewing 1930; Finn 1878; Martineau 1850; and Vester 1950).

60

I have juxtaposed the sense of rapid change and the equally strong notions of arrested development in order to highlight how jarringly at odds the situation of Palestinian women really was with the received wisdom (Baer 1964; and Granquist 1975). If we abandon, or at least suspend, belief that the overwhelming changes that took place in late nineteenth- and early twentieth-century Palestine did not, in a fundamental way, affect the lives of women, then we must ask how Palestinian Arab women experienced the transformations that convulsed their society. I put the question in this way because, in spite of its apparent relevance for any analysis of social change in Palestine, the question has neither been raised nor addressed (Appleby 1981).

The women whose lives are described here were part of the collective experience of Palestine during a century of development. They were all daughters of comfortable families, born and raised in cities, with little likelihood or need to enter an occupation. Their fathers, brothers, and sometimes husbands were politically active, and their homes became arenas for political discussions and political activities. It is generally accepted that these upper-class urban women were, literally, the most secluded of all the female Palestinian population, because economic necessity did not force them out of their houses and into the market or the fields. These same women, however, divided their time during the years of the British Mandate between social, educational, and health care work and political activities (Antonius 1980; and Israel Archives, *Record Group 3939*).

It is hard to imagine a context in which these transformations came about more subtly than they did in Palestine from the mid-nineteenth century to the outbreak of the Second World War. Within the family, the extended kin relationships appeared strong, so status for men and women was still calibrated in terms of lineage (Shimoni 1947). At the level of personal appearance, urban Palestinian women were among the last of the upper-class, educated Arab women to discard their veils and to move out of formal seclusion. At the organizational level, the women's groups formed in Palestine did not achieve the same prominence as their Egyptian counterparts, nor were there the same dramatic and public assertions of emancipation (*Arab Women's Congress* 1938; and Mogannam 1936).The history of upper-class Palestinian Arab women cannot be mapped as a simple progression in visibility, a continuum beginning in seclusion and ending in formal emancipation; but neither can it be interpreted as captive to a set of traditions so inflexible as to foreclose any and all change.

A shared phenomenon for these particular Palestinian women was their social and political work, while a shared experience was the consciousness of themselves as individuals dissociated from their family existences. Individual self-awareness became a central preoccupation for women, even as it was produced dialectically from within the medium of traditional social relations. The family was, of course, a necessary component of these social relations, but it was not the only set of relations that women experienced. In this period in Palestine, the understanding that women generated of their own lives was elaborated through the representations they began to make of the cities in which they lived and the polities to which they belonged.[2] It had not always been this way, nor could it have been, had not important political, economic, and cultural changes occurred. While social scientists might see, in the political and economic developments unleashed in nineteenth-century Palestine, pressures for social and individual change, few would see such circumstances as creating new possibilities for both men and women (Shapiro 1981).

In the nineteenth century, the Ottoman rulers of Palestine embarked on a development program which included major efforts to improve the Empire's military power, transportation networks, communication linkages, and provincial administration (Shaw and Shaw 1977). The most imaginative proposal may have been the railroad construction, popularized by the somewhat distorting goal of the Berlin-to-Baghdad railroad—distorting because one of its terminals attaches the wrong meaning to the enterprise. It suggests that these technical changes were not only externally inspired but also externally controlled. Not so. The railroad enterprise was the work of an Ottoman political establishment, stimulated by the need to extract more wealth from the imperial provinces in order to improve political control. If the railroads did not succeed in ultimately centralizing the Empire, they did tighten it and intensify contact between its parts (Khalidi 1980; and Ochsenwald 1980). From the Palestinian perspective, more Palestinians travelled to Constantinople and to other cities in the Arab provinces (Little and Türgay 1979).

There were strong reasons for the Ottoman Sultan and his entourage to concentrate on broadening the links between the parts of the Empire. Failure to do so was generally believed to be the formula for imperial disaster and disintegration. A sense of imperial decline had begun more than a century earlier in the eighteenth century, and its imminence was read into every ethnic and national uprising, and each outbreak of religiously-motivated violence during the nineteenth century. Hence the measures devised to cope with these problems became bolder and bolder.

While the most persistent investments were military, the most sophisticated of the reforms were administrative. A benchmark for these efforts, the famous Rescript of Gulhane of 1839, began to make available by the end of the nineteenth century, bureaucrats and provincial governors who were more educated and knowledgeable about government and economics (Szyliowicz 1975). As a result, Palestine was more efficiently and effectively administered. A greater awareness emerged of the needs of the farming peasantry, of the health level of the population, and of urban issues such as sewage disposal and water supplies. Quarantines were systematically put into effect to minimize the outbreak of diseases and plagues; taxes were often adjusted downward in the aftermath of droughts and substantially reduced harvests (Gerber 1978). Such instruments for transforming the society implied even greater social and political transformations, and the behavior of the population suggests a consciousness of this possibility.

The fact that these changes did not ultimately preserve the Empire does not justify assuming constant and continuous imperial decline. In the nineteenth century, the Ottoman Empire considerably improved its power to control local administration. The central problem, that of retaining the loyalty of the local notables, the *ayan*, was resolved by the steady multiplication of administrative tasks entrusted to them and by increasing government pressure for the satisfactory performance of these tasks (Findley 1980). One should not, of course, overestimate the local effectiveness of central authority. Policy still had to pass through a filter of local interests—among which was family—before implementation. And the relationship between central government and unpaid local officers at all levels involved a constant balancing of local and imperial powers. Yet there can be no mistaking the general trend toward augmented governmental authority and administrative activity begun in the Ottoman Empire and later expanded during the British Mandate (Wasserstein 1978). When imperial or national institutions existed as forums for initiating policy and resolving conflicts, the effectiveness of family groupings, which once monopolized these functions, had to be attenuated (Firestone 1975). In fact, these reforms disrupted the very process through which political hegemony in the Ottoman Empire had formally been secured. In earlier generations, political power emerged from the continuous bargaining and fighting among the several elements essential to individual and communal survival: bedouin, fellahin, and urban notables. Within this complex web of relationships, marriage was an instrument used to enhance communication, broaden the material base of alliances, and intensify trust. The wives of urban notables were frequently from villages and transmitted access to vital resources otherwise inaccessible to city dwellers. While marriage ties did not automatically bind allies forever, they did contribute to their longevity (Bailey 1980).

The consolidation of political authority, with its institutional evolution, made the achievement of power less a matter of building bridges and controlling relationships—among bedouin, village shaykh, and urban notables—than of commanding skill and influence. Not that the two criteria were totally distinguishable, nor had they been totally irrelevant in former times. It is instructive, however, to examine how they began to be applied self-consciously by the Ottoman rulers. In the pre-Reform period, many of the local, administrative urban appointments were effectively made through a kaleidoscopic consensus of local interest, only later to be confirmed by the central imperial authorities. The imperial confirmation presumably resulted partly from years of gift giving, thereby assuring Ottoman officials acknowledged local status (Abu-Manneh 1979).

The political transformations of the Reform period shifted the locus of power away from villages, and more firmly into cities; away from local power bases which cut across rural/urban sectors, toward more exclusively urban and, more importantly, Arab/Turkish alliances. Given military improvements and changes in military technology unavailable to bedouin or fellahin, Turkish army units could more effectively dispose of threatening rebellions or attacks on commerce and travel. Moreover, the improved administration rendered the purely political a more important point of departure from which to dominate the entire society. Precisely because marriage often grew out of the desire for political power, marriage arrangements changed with the emergence of a new political context. Those women brought from villages no longer commanded an important presence, since the village resources to which they had access were no longer vital ingredients in the structure of political domination.

As a new political order developed so did a new order of social relationships, whereby wives of urban political leaders were expected to give aid and support to their husbands' political careers. They managed large households, and sometimes more, providing care for their children and spacious facilities for male political assemblies and male receptions (Cole 1981; and Kark and Landman 1981). As improved transportation increased, marriages were more frequently arranged between urban notable families from various parts of the Empire. This intensified intercity contacts among notables, and made politically conscious people more aware of the importance of empirewide connections. Women, however, still travelled less frequently than men, so such intercity marriages created the need for establishing broader female ties. Because the female relatives acquired through marriage were often infused with underlying tensions, women began to seek friends and build support networks outside of their own families (Tuqan 1978–1979).

Economic forces fostered similar processes of change for Palestinian Arab women. The demographic expansion seems to have resulted partly from the decline in mortality rates brought about by improved methods of health care, including the previously noted precautions taken to minimize the spread of disease (Gerber 1978). In addition, the increased military capacity of the Ottoman Imperial forces afforded greater security in the Palestinian countryside, thereby attracting larger number of fellahin to farm and to settle the land. One notable consequence of the general increase in population was the slow but steady pressure of a prolific population upon inelastic resources. The most important of these was land. That pressure led to the gradual redistribution of the population. For the landed upper classes, the surplus population was absorbed in commerce, education, and administration (Schölch 1981). The shifts in employment were made possible by the increase in trade between the Ottoman Empire and Europe, and by the institutional developments of the Imperial Reform period and of the British Mandate. These changes represented substantial progress toward the integration of the predominantly Muslim parts of the Ottoman Empire and eventually of a Palestinian community. Both were achieved at the expense of local and family integration and autonomy. Moreover, the increased involvement of Palestine in an international and expanded imperial commerce created, ironically, both the material base for an enriched and highly integrated family structure and the disposition to create support and ties external to the family network (Abu-Manneh 1979).

The overall impact of economic changes also disrupted the old social order for upper-class urban women. The increased agricultural dependence on European markets, from the middle of the nineteenth century, generated more surplus value, but it put that wealth more tightly in the hands of absentee landowners, middlemen, and tax collectors (Schölch 1981). A corollary of this trend evolved into the practice of linking the families of landowners with those of merchants, and the families of administrators and scholars with those of commercial agents. In a society where the prestige rankings were so finely tuned as to distinguish families based not so much on the amount of their wealth as on its source, these newly emerging marriage practices were not without their own stresses. Such marriages frequently may have insured the family's economic viability; but paradoxically, from the women's perspective, they would bring it to the point of social collapse.

With respect to culture, education itself accentuated the differences among members of the same family. The gradual improvement in the quality of education was of considerable significance; yet the impact was not equally strong for all family members, nor was it the same for all Palestinian religious groups (*Arabic and Islamic Garland* 1977). Christians were more willing than Muslims to attend the schools established as part of European religious missions and thus were more directly exposed to Western culture. Muslim women were often educated at home by tutors and, if sent to school, attended for much less time than their brothers or male cousins or female Christian friends. Within the same family, different educational levels and orientations existed; and, inevitably, different values were engendered through these radically different educational experiences (Abu-Ghazaleh 1973).

For Muslim women, especially, the education was largely in Arabic. Their textual foothold on Western culture was necessarily weaker than that of men, who were more likely to have studied a foreign language and to have received advanced training in European schools. The focus of women was almost exclusively on their own religious or political histories. Sensing the changes in their own family relationships and ties, women began to identify more personally and more fully with the controversies and disagreements embedded in Muslim history. Interestingly, whereas Muslim men could describe their own history in Western terms, Muslim women had to use Arabic terms and often Muslim notions to represent their understanding of their collective past and religious heritage.

For Palestinian Arab men, at least part of the incentive for change came from outside, from non-Muslim sources, whereas the movement described by women came almost entirely from within their own tradition. Men and women came to hear, learn, memorize, and recite the same poetic lines of Shauqi:

> You [Cromer and England] threatened us with perpetual slavery and continuing abasement and a state which permitted no change. Did you think that God was less than you in power, incapable of change and alteration? God rules kings, and states that vie with him in power do not prevail.
>
> [Khouri 1971, p. 68]

They seem, however, to have experienced them very differently. When Ibrahim Tuqan sounds the tocsin for the Palestinians, it is to revolt against corruption and against selfish, untrustworthy politicians. When his sister, Fadwa, testifies to the evils besetting her society, she is as maddened, not uncharacteristically, by her father and the traditional family structure as by any of the more general social and political problems Palestinians encountered. This difference between men and women could only impose further strain on the family structure and make the traditional demands on women more difficult to meet.

The thesis here is not the passing of the traditional Palestinian Arab family. Many features of the traditional family structure persisted throughout the British Mandate. The continuities of the Middle East family are striking, but no less impressive are the discontinuities. It is with these that I am principally concerned. Simply, the distinctions of education and the changes in polities and economies, from the middle of the nineteenth century, introduced new forms of strain on the family. Women were forced to rethink their positions and inevitably to dissociate tradition from remaining forever in their fathers' or husbands' households. The conflict and strain of this process culminated in a struggle by women to create a social world in their own image, which they believed was legitimized by their new under-standing of tradition.

One of the most interesting lives to study in this connec-tion, is that of Fadwa Tuqan. Her life illustrates how the process of social change may be animated almost entirely from within the tradition. Aside from some brief visits to Jé-rusalem, she grew up in Nablus and spent much of her time in her father's house. According to her own recollec-tion, women in Nablus stopped wearing the veil only in 1948, so the city itself stood squarely in the midst of a powerful Muslim tradition and presence. Fadwa Tuqan at-tended school for a short time, but left at the age of eleven or twelve because she was thought to have engaged in shameful conduct—accepting a flower from a sixteen-year-old boy. So fearful was her family of the possibility of public dishonor, that her mother and father forced her to withdraw from school and forbade her to leave the house without an escort. In her youth, she never learned a foreign language and had to rely either on private tutoring, especially from her brother, Ibrahim, or on self-education through the po-litical poetry she, herself, read in Arabic.

It is this provinciality that makes her life intriguing and important for the study of social change. Women like Fadwa Tuqan had very little exposure to the philosophical and po-litical literature of Europe. It was largely the resources of the Arab literature available to them that served as a reser-voir of serviceable images and metaphors to explain their feelings about their societies, families, and selves. Driven by a sense of desperation as strong as that of the Palestinian men who urged social and political change, yet provided with fewer cultural outlets, women were forced to develop more internally and authentically Arab and Palestinian solutions.

While the transformations of family and society weighed heavily upon both Palestinian Arab men and women growing up during this period, the weight was distributed differently between the sexes. The difference becomes manifest in the vocabulary that men and women use to evaluate British rule in Palestine. British rule presented dangers and created opportunities. The most immediate danger, of course, derived from the British sponsorship of a Jewish National Homeland. Palestinian political leaders directed their responses to the ultimate disposition of sovereignty in the land, to the distribution of offices of state, and to the principles implicit in the form British rule was to take. The concern of Palestinian men appeared overwhelmingly political, focused on the prospects of bringing to an end the development of Jewish settlement and promoting in its stead a Palestinian Arab state. For Palestinian Arab men, prospects for personal fulfillment were seen to depend on progress in enlarging Arab political power and the prospects for Arab statehood in Palestine. Khalil Sakakini resigned his post as headmaster of the teachers training college and left the country when Herbert Samuel, a Jew, became Britain's first High Commissioner in Palestine (Tsimhoni 1978, p. 80).

The British Mandate also promised opportunities for the Palestinian political elite. The notion that formal political power constituted the only means of determining the basic conditions of social life was an idea that had been accepted by Arabs and Turks during the last several decades of the Ottoman Empire. The British reputation for structuring an efficient, powerful, and popularly supported government then raised the possibility of political benefits, the prospects of which seemed only to intensify the political ambitions and anxieties of Palestinian Arab men (*Palestine, A Study of Jewish, Arab and British Policies* 1947).

For Palestinian Arab women, the dangers of British rule were calibrated differently; and the opportunities were not perceived, strictly speaking, in political terms. While the responses of these women had ultimate and profound political consequences for Palestinian society, their preoccupation was not to demand, acquire, or control political offices of state.

Occasionally, circumstances forced Palestinian Arab women to make political pronouncements and even to assert their political positions through protest and public demonstration. Mrs. Matiel E. T. Mogannam, first secretary of the Executive Committee of the Arab Women's Congress in Palestine, correctly located the origins of this committee's political struggle in the "distressing circumstances as those in which Palestine was found in 1929." But she incorrectly suggested that these circumstances "resulted in the greatest change in the life of the Arab women in Palestine and in the concentration of their forces" (Mogannam 1936, p. 69).

Women first understood the dangers of a Jewish National Homeland as cultural, as a loss of uniqueness and identity. For that reason, many women persisted in wearing the veil as an assertion of their communal integrity, rather than as a fulfillment of traditional or religious obligation. Moreover, for women, the British presence and its creation of a socio-cultural administration meant the possibility of work. This is not to say that the issue of sovereignty was unimportant for women or that employment opportunities did not concern men; rather, that the weighing of communal and national priorities depended to an extent on gender. The language used to explain their activities offers some indication of how deeply divided Palestinian Arab men and women were on these issues.

The imagery of military defeat and political subjugation courses through the poetry of Ibrahim Tuqan:

> People, your enemy will not soften or have mercy. People, only exile [literally, evacuation] lies before you. So start packing!
>
> [Jayyusi 1977, p. 287]

In contrast, the continuity of the Palestinian nation and of its human triumphs, even in the midst of political defeats, is evoked in these lines of Fadwa Tuqan:

> I had been swept by the daze of defeat. Hamza said, This land, my sister, has a fertile heart. It throbs, doesn't wither, endures. For the secret of hills and wombs is one. . . .
>
> [Boullata 1978, p. 150]

The predicates of Palestinian existence embraced the notion of political sovereignty; but its importance, rather the consequences of its absence, did not form the basis of a universal consensus for all Palestinians. To reflect properly the tonalities in which Palestinians, themselves, understood their own history and society, it is necessary to recognize that the concepts and norms they employed were shaped and constrained not only by social class, religion, or residence but also, and not insignificantly, by gender.

Fadwa Tuqan describes her childhood as torn between her individual desire for education, travel, and contact with the world and the sense of responsibility to her family as defined by her father. In his own way her father, while recognizing the home and housework as the proper locus for women, had encouraged his daughter's efforts for self-fulfillment by providing Fadwa with an education, either at school or in later years, at home. Fadwa's father recognized and sought to nourish his daughter's literary talents. Taking his own nationalist political activities seriously, he called on her to put her talents at the service of her people by writing nationalist poetry. At the same time, he insisted that she continue to dedicate her daily activities to home and family. That established the parameters of her crisis: without education and experience it became impossible to serve the nation properly; with education and experience, it became impossible to remain at home secluded from what was presented as her political duty.

Fadwa Tuqan's life may not have been typical of this class of women, but her encounter with a particular set of political, economic, and cultural circumstances was. The real and imagined worlds of Palestinian upper-class women were often vastly different in detail. While Fadwa Tuqan described her father as imposing on her a traditional and suffocating dependency, Inbara el-Khalidi spoke lovingly of hers as the source of her determination to be an independent woman. But economic, political, and cultural forces made the worlds of all of these women appear disordered, if not turbulent, resulting in a common determination to understand their environment more fully and to control it more effectively. The women who first dreamed of freedom as the principal effect of these efforts summoned to their sides other women who shared their social circumstances and their historical experiences.

The term social class does not fully describe the collective portrait of these Palestinian Arab women for it fails to capture their individual diversity. There are, however, significant characteristics that they shared and that bear, simultaneously, on social status and emotional development. First, these women are younger female siblings, with older sisters who have married and followed the traditional and expected course. Perhaps the unrelenting pressure for suitable marriage and expansion of family networks had been thrust upon the older girls, thereby relieving the younger sisters of the absolute conviction that only marriage could render their lives meaningful.

Second, their preoccupation with their own futures and their own independent activities seems to spring from their education, broadly conceived. Their reading of contemporary Arabic poetry inspires them to more serious consideration of their own lives and their own society. Through this poetry they begin to conjure up an image of society and to imagine their place in it. Through literature, they have glimpses of people from whom they are kept apart by force of the authorized and unchanged tradition. Education is absolutely central to the lives of these women and forces them to re-examine their positions in their families and in their societies. The poetry is empowering, giving them a sense of being able to create their own futures. They recognize that they have a limited hold on their present and begin to imagine a future where the power over their lives would be intractable and absolute.

Reflection upon the intensity these women brought to bear on even their limited education, shows education as granting women access to their own inner emotions and desires. From Marxism, Fadwa Tuqan could meditate on the word "consciousness" until it fostered a new and different meaning. For her, consciousness became a word descriptive of a sense of self, of personal desires, and of the structure of life. Nationalist ideologies and slogans served similar purposes for other women, presenting to them terms that they could make highly personal and subjective.

Third, the centrality of education, paradoxically, makes clear how dependent they are on the good will and support of others who have inserted themselves into their lives. Inbara el-Khalidi writes of the women teachers who inspired her and of the encouragement she received from her father in her educational pursuit. Fadwa Tuqan values her friends at school and her brother's tutorials as indispensable to her awakening. Educators and schoolmates animated lives that would otherwise have been quite static and undistinguished. An·awareness of a collectivity outside of their family, to which they belonged in accord with the instruction of parents and teachers, enabled these women to carve out a new map of opportunities for themselves. Duty toward family could be fulfilled by discharging responsibility to society.

And fourth, in this focus beyond family, marriage may or

may not have taken place, but it became a much less crucial factor determining the sequence of events and direction of these women's lives. They began to make their own decisions and to assert their right to do so. As they worked to open up new options for themselves, they were aware of a fundamental break in outlook from that of their parents. This awareness, however, mandated its own emotional costs. Quite often the energy, resolution, and determination of these particular women alienated them from other upper-class women—typically from mothers and aunts. Most upper-class women still appeared, literally and figuratively, unchanging. And for all the exuberance of these active women, they also recognized that the expanded opportunities they sought, given their own social circumstances, entailed palpable sacrifices. Many agonized over the ruptured relationships with aunts and mothers. Those who chose not to marry, asserting that marriage might foreclose all possibilities of personal freedom, tempered that assertion with the sense of impoverishment, stirred by the deprivations such singleness would likely spawn.

In periods of rapid change, tensions and disputes between generations are likely to develop, but the strains and resulting ambivalence Fadwa Tuqan felt toward her parents created a sentiment strongly expressed and shared primarily by women. Although Inbara el-Khalidi celebrated and praised her father's contributions to her education and intellectual growth, it is also clear that her sense of the world and of herself began with a departure from the life her parents lived and wanted, strictly speaking, to transmit. The life Inbara constructed for herself had literally no precedent either in her parents' generation or in the culture that generation endorsed. Conversely, the Palestinian Arab leader, Ahmad Shuqayri, who was actually mistreated by his father and stepmother, did not choose to locate his turbulent and unhappy early years as conflicts inherent in his family. Ibrahim Tuqan celebrated his family, particularly his father, as sustaining his nationalist politics and patriotic ideals. The social problems Ahmad Shuqayri and Ibrahim Tuqan experience are recorded as inseparable from the political struggles of the Palestinian Arabs and their, as yet unfulfilled, goal of sovereignty. This difference is not idiosyncratic; it would appear that women felt and understood the complex changes absorbing the Palestinian family in a more intensified and personal way than men.

While the changes in the family entailed a substantially new course for women, they also encouraged them not to proclaim themselves as new women molding a new society. The women were able to create careers for themselves while implying that those careers formed an inseparable bond with their ancient traditions. In the midst of the widely felt incoherence of social life, with Palestinian Arabs being tossed about by rapid changes over which they had no control, these "working" women discovered a mechanism—their work—through which that change could be contained.

Sharing a desire for work and an impulse for preserving tradition, hundreds of Palestinian Arab women turned their commitment to their newly discovered people into a series of organizations, whose stated purposes were to help educate or improve the lives of the Palestinian peasantry. The remarkable fact of these organizations, which in many ways were primarily philanthropic, is that the officers often received a salary. If not a salary, they received perquisites of office: a place to work, a car, a telephone. (*Record Group 3939*). The philanthropic nature of these organizations might have been understood as nothing more than the clubwomen phenomenon of nineteenth-century America (Blair 1980); but the peculiar efforts of Palestinian Arab women to insist that membership amount to real work gave these organizations their distinctive characteristic.

If the fact of public work constituted for these women a

dramatic departure from tradition, the location of their work often represented a strong commitment to the very center of their heritage. The common workplace for the women was the village, the place where the boundaries of the tradition seemed strongest and the collective symbols of their tradition still intact (*Record Group* 3939). The focus on the village was important not only for its acknowledgement of tradition, but also for its mediation of the generational and parental conflict. The decision not to focus their work in the cities in which they lived suggests efforts to avoid ruptures with their families. In another way, it signaled that they held their tradition to be both expandable and inviolate. This separation of workplace and home was made possible not only by the introduction of modern transportation like the automobile but, more importantly, by the topography of Palestine, with relatively short distances between major cities and satellite villages.

It is important to stress, once again, how autonomous and self-contained the inspiration for this work was. The organizations, begun before the outbreak of World War I, continued to increase in number in cities, small and large, throughout the British Mandate period. Many of these organizations received funding from the Ottoman or British authorities. The overwhelming absorption of these women was social and not political; and this was the great difference between the women's and men's organizations in Palestine, particularly during the British Mandate. The women were no less touched by the politics and economics of their societies, especially with respect to the British Mandate and its sponsorship of a Jewish National Home in Palestine. But their work was less absorbed by political considerations, narrowly conceived; and their participation in political demonstrations appeared orchestrated by men, who were the acknowledged political leaders of Palestinian society. To understand the activities of these Palestinian Arab women simply from the political perspective is to trivialize and distort them. What sustained their organizations and their newly fashioned lives were their daily, albeit less dramatic, social enterprises.

Evidence for this is everywhere at hand: the health clinics, the elementary schools, the vocational institutions, the homes for orphans, the disbursements to the widows and peasant families impoverished by prolonged war and violence or by economic upheaval. Some organizations were more successful than others: some had very short institutional lives, while others still survive. But the fact that women seemed determined to re-establish institutions in the aftermath of failure indicates how committed they were to this work and how much formal institutions counted for them (*Record Group 3939*). The uniqueness of these institutions is striking given the general weakness of male-dominated political institutions in mandated Palestine.

Palestinian Arab women were able to use their traditions as a basis for their own liberation. Even religious pilgrimages served as sources of inspiration for freedom. Several pilgrimages achieved almost national prominence: the Nebi Musa for the peoples of Jerusalem, Hebron, and Nablus; the Rubin for Palestinian Arabs of Jaffa; and the Nebi Saleh for the men and women in Ramleh. While only men could participate in the ritualized and formal activities, the parades and the marches, these holidays were as important for women as they were for men. For men, they became occasions for political protest; for women they were symbols of freedom, of travel, of congregation. And they were ultimately translated into an awareness of the restrictions governing their lives (Canaan 1927; and Tamari 1979).

The social organizations created by women and the activities they sponsored helped certain Palestinian women transcend their common predicament, for they recognized that their lives were encased by tradition and family obligation.

They saw themselves distanced from social and political realities. And they perceived engagement, alone, as the solution, the sole means of releasing the personal resources required for the national tasks they were instructed to undertake.

The history of Palestinian Arab women reveals how the crisis of religion and values, which convulsed traditional Palestinian society, resulted not only from contact with the West, but also from an irremedial pressure from within the society. For that reason, Palestinian women's emancipation took the form of a determination to create new roles, while maintaining a programatic allegiance to the collective life of the traditional culture they sought to change. Palestinian Arab women were, of course, not alone in this allegiance to tradition; but Palestinian Arab women had to build their new social contributions by pressing traditional notions into new contexts. Their education and experience provided them no other choice.

Their desire for emancipation may be called a reverie, because it was an act of imagination that conjured these new roles. This emancipation is characterized by the authorization of a new mobility, a new set of activities, in the name of a newly understood nation that could substitute for the family. The articulation of this new source of legitimacy, however, could only have developed when the strains in the family structure had reached a point where it was impossible to maintain faith in its inviolability. The break for women came not as a seduction from without, but rather as a conversion, an imaginative leap from family to nation. Interestingly and conversely, the break with tradition for men, who were much more directly exposed to Western culture and politics, often appeared as a rejection of the old and as an effort to import ideas, values, and institutions. For men, becoming modern entailed control of politics and of public institutions. For Palestinian Arab women, the discovery of a space where social institutions could grow and predominate became one of the points at which they changed, if not wholly became modern.[3]

Notes

This article is part of a larger work on the social history of Palestinian Arabs from 1839–1948, supported by grants from the Andrew W. Mellon Foundation, National Endowment for the Humanities, and the Social Science Research Council. The analysis was aided in countless ways by the close reading of several colleagues in the Smith College Research Project on Women and Social Change. I want to thank Martha Ackelsberg, Kathryn Pyne Addelson, Susan C. Bourque, and Susan Van Dyne for their valuable suggestions. I must also acknowledge the extraordinary assistance of the Jean Picker Fellowship program at Smith. Through the generosity of that program, I am turning this study into a book of much larger scope.

1. Lesch (1979); Migdal (1980); Porath (1974).

2. Unless otherwise cited, the material for this essay comes from the following autobiographical sources: al-Shuqayri (1969); el-Khalidi (1975); and Tuqan (1978–1979). Interviews with Zlikha Shihabeh, Damiya and Halah Al-Sakakini, and the personal records and letters of men and women from the urban middle- and upper-classes are preserved at the Israel State Archives.

3. A similar point is made by Goldberg (1982).

References

Abu-Ghazaleh, Adnan. 1973. *Arab Culture Nationalism in Palestine*. Beirut: Institute for Palestine Studies.

Abu-Manneh, Butrus. 1979. "Or Hadash Al-Aliyat Shel Mishpaha Husaini Be-Yerushalayim Be-Mea ha-Shmoneh-'Esrai" [New Light on the Rise of the Husaini Family of Jerusalem in the Eighteenth Century]. *Be-Rashit ha-Tekufa ha-Ottomanit* [In the Early Ottoman Period]. Jerusalem: Yad Izhak Ben-Zvi.

———. 1979. "The Rise of the Sanjak of Jerusalem in the Late Nineteenth Century." In Gabriel Ben Dor, ed. *The Palestinians and the Middle East Conflict*. Ramat Gan: Turtledove.

al-Sakakini, Damiya. Interview.

al-Sakakini, Halah. Interview.

al-Shuqayri, Ahmad. 1969. "Arba'un 'Aman Fi-l-Hayyat al-Arabiyya wa-l-Dawliyya" (memoir).

Antonius, Soraya. 1980. "Prisoners for Palestine: A List of Women Political Prisoners." *Journal of Palestine Studies* 9, no. 35: 29–80.

Appleby, Joyce. 1981. "Social Science and Human Nature." *Democracy* 1, no. 1: 116–126.

Arabic and Islamic Garland: Historical, Educational and Literary Papers Presented to Abdul-Latif Tibawi. 1977. London: Islamic Cultural Centre.

Baer, Gabriel. 1964. *Population and Society in the Arab East*. London: Routledge and Kegan Paul.

Bailey, Clinton. 1980. "The Negev in the Nineteenth Century: Reconstructing History from Bedouin Oral Traditions." *Asian and African Studies* 14, no. 1: 35–80.

Bartlett, W. H. 1855. *Jerusalem Revisted*. London: Arthur Hall, Virtue.

Ben Arieh, Yehoshua. 1977. *Ir Be-Rayi ha-Tekufah* [A City Reflected in its Times]. Jerusalem: Yad Izhak Ben-Zvi.

———. 1979. *The Rediscovery of the Holy Land in the Nineteenth Century*. Jerusalem: The Magnes Press.

Blair, Karen. 1980. *The Clubwoman as Feminist*. New York: Holmes and Meier.

Boullata, Kamal, ed. 1978. *Women of the Fertile Crescent*. Washington, D.C.: Three Continents Press.

Canaan, Tawfik. 1927. *Mohammedan Saints and Sanctuaries in Palestine*. London: Luzac.

Cole, Juan Ricardo. 1981. "Feminism, Class, and Islam in Turn-of-the-Century Egypt." *International Journal of Middle East Studies* 13, no. 4: 387–407.

el-Khalidi, Inbara Salam. 1975. *Joula Fi Al-Dhikriya Bein Lubnan Wa-Filastin* (memoir). Beirut: n. pub.

Ewing, W. 1930. *Paterson of Hebron*. London: James Clarke.

Findley, Carter V. 1980. *Bureaucratic Reform in the Ottoman Empire*. Princeton: Princeton University Press.

Finn, James. 1878. *Stirring Times*. London: Kegan Paul.

Firestone, Ya'akov. 1975. "Production and Trade in an Islamic

Context, Sharika Contracts in the Transitional Economy of Northern Samaria." *International Journal of Middle East Studies* 6, nos. 2, 3: 185–209 and 308–324.

Granquist, Hilma. 1975. *Marriage Conditions in a Palestinian Village*. New York: AMS Press.

Gerber, Haim. 1978. "The Ottoman Administration of the Sanjaq of Jerusalem, 1890–1908." *Asian and African Studies* 33–76.

Goldberg, Hillel. 1982. "An Early Psychologist of the Unconscious." *Journal of the History of Ideas* 43, no. 2: 269–284.

Jayyusi, Salma Khada. 1977. *Trends and Movements in Modern Arabic Poetry*, vol. 1. Leiden: E. J. Brill.

Kark, Ruth, and Shimon Landman. 1981. "La-Yitzia ha-Muslimit Mehutz Le-Homot Yerushalayim Be-Shlei ha-Tekufa ha-Ottomanit" [Muslim Neighborhoods Outside the Jerusalem City Walls During the Late Ottoman Period]. *Perakim Be-Toldot Yerushalayim Be-Z'man Hehadash* [Jerusalem in the Modern Period]. Jerusalem: Yad Izhak Ben-Zvi and the Ministry of Defense.

Khalidi, Rashid. 1980. *British Policy Towards Syria and Palestine, 1906–14*. London: Ithaca Press.

Khouri, Mounah A. 1971. *Poetry and the Making of Modern Egypt*. Leiden: E. J. Brill.

Kupferschmidt, Uri. 1978. "Attempts to Reform the Supreme Muslim Council." In Gabriel Ben-Dor, ed. *The Palestinians and the Middle East Conflict*. Ramat Gan: Turtledove.

Lesch, Ann Mosley. 1979. *Arab Politics in Palestine, 1917–1939*. Ithaca: Cornell University Press.

Little, Donald P., and A. Üner Türgay. 1979. "Documents from the Ottoman Period in the Khalidi Library in Jerusalem." *Die Welt des Islams*, 20: 44–72.

Martineau, Harriet. 1850. *Eastern Life*. London: Edward Moxon.

Migdal, Joel S. 1980. *Palestinian Society and Politics*. Princeton: Princeton University Press.

Mogannam, Matiel E. T. 1936. *The Arab Woman*. London: Herbert Joseph.

Ochsenwald, William. 1980. *The Hijaz Railroad*. Charlottesville: University Press of Virginia.

Peri, Oded. 1981. "Tmurot Politiot ve-ha-Shlachuteihen Ke-Gormin be-Yesod Awqaf be-Yerushalayim Shel Sof-ha Mea ha-Shmoneh 'Esrai" [Political Changes and Their Effects on the Establishment of Awqaf in Late Eighteenth Century Jerusalem]. *Cathedra* 21: 73–88.

Pollack. F. W. 1962. *The Turkish Post in the Holy Land*. Tel Aviv: The Holy Land Philatelist.

Porath, Yehoshua. 1974. *The Emergence of a Palestinian-Arab National Movement, 1918–1929*. London: Frank Cass.

Schölch, Alexander. 1981. "The Economic Development of Palestine, 1856–1882." *Journal of Palestine Studies* 10, no. 39: 35–58.

Shapiro, Judith. 1981. "Anthropology and the Study of Gender." *Soundings* 64, no. 4: 446–465.

Shaw, Stanford J., and Ezel Kural Shaw. 1977. *History of the Ottoman Empire and Modern Turkey*, vol. 3. Cambridge, Mass.: Cambridge University Press.

Shihabeh, Zlikha. Interview.

Shimoni, Ya'acov. 1947. *Aravei Eretz Israel [The Arabs of Israel]*. Tel Aviv: Am Oved.

Szyliowicz, Joseph S. 1975. "Changes in the Recruitment Patterns and Career Lines of Ottoman Provincial Administrators During the Nineteenth Century." In Moshe Ma'oz, ed. *Studies on Palestine During the Ottoman Period*. Jerusalem: Magnes.

Tamari, Shmuel. 1979. "Maqam Nebi Musa Shel Yad Yericho" [The Holy Place of the Prophet Moses Near Jericho]. *Cathedra* 11: 153–180.

Tsimhoni, Daphne. 1978. "The Arab Christians and Palestine Arab National Movement during the Formative Stage." In Gabriel Ben-Dor, ed. *The Palestinians and the Middle East Conflict*. Ramat Gan: Turtledove.

Tuqan, Fadwa. 1978–1979. "Memoirs."

Vester, Bertha Spafford. 1950. *Our Jerusalem*. Garden City, N.Y.: Doubleday.

Wasserstein, Bernard. 1978. *The British in Palestine: The Mandatory Government and the Arab-Jewish Conflict, 1917–1929*. London: Royal Historical Society.

3

Revolution and Community: Mobilization, De-politicization and Perceptions of Change in Civil War Spain

Martha A. Ackelsberg

The generals' rebellion against the Popular Front government, which began the Spanish Civil War on 18 July 1936, set off in response a massive and broad-based revolution. In the days and weeks that followed, virtually all effective power was local. In the major Republican cities, working people took to the streets to oppose the rebellious army, and union organizations undertook the task of establishing "public order." Militias replaced the army; popular tribunals replaced courts; labor unions organized to provide food and supplies to both combatant and non-combatant populations. Even more significant, perhaps, were the substantial changes in the structures of daily life, which took shape during those first few months. In industrial and agricultural areas of Catalonia, in rural Aragon, and in parts of Castilla and the Levante, anarchist and socialist collectivization transformed social and economic life for an estimated seven to eight million people who worked in collectives, marketed through cooperatives, and restructured long-standing patterns of interpersonal relationships.

Participation in these events fundamentally changed the lives and consciousness of many. For the first time, large numbers of working people felt in control of their world, participants in a process that was transforming it totally:

> . . . great things were done in Spain . . . when you saw the *compañeros* of the unions, who were able to organize what they organized, that was an experience that no one has had. You have to live it in order to understand it. I saw those *campañeros* who created the collectives, who organized the socialization, *compañeros* with responsibilities, who took charge of things without any pay or compensation whatever, only so that the *pueblo* would have what it needed. . . .
>
> [Carpena 1981]

For some, the impact was so dramatic, they barely had words to express it:

> . . . the times that we lived during the war, six months were like three years in another context. . . . So that, for me, the three years of war, all that I lived through, were like . . . ten years of my life. . . . When I was fourteen and fifteen I had experiences that would stay with me all my life, engraved in my mind, such a flowering of ideas-made-reality that happened during this period. Even if I had died, I wouldn't have wanted not to have had that experience.
>
> [Carpena 1981]

Yet, for others, the revolution seemed distant, if not irrelevant. Asked how life changed during the period of the war
and revolution, for example, a number of people replied,
simply, "queues."

How is it possible to understand the nature of these
differences? How did the tremendous exhilaration felt by
some participants go completely unnoticed by others? This
paper explores the factors that contributed to the consciousness of change among working people in Spain, and exam-
ines the contexts that seem to have encouraged or inhibited
that development. More specifically, I suggest that those
who took active roles in effecting change were more deeply
and lastingly affected by it than those who did not; and that
connection with a community of people is crucial, both as a
context for coming to a changed consciousness and as a
source of continuing support for, and validation of, those
changes. Beyond that, within the revolutionary context,
women had different concerns and evaluated their experience according to criteria different than those of men.
Ultimately, people experience social change through the
communities in which they live. Only by looking at those
communities and the changes within them is it possible to
come to a full understanding of the dimensions of revolutionary change in the lives of both women and men.

In order to understand the extent and depth of such
changes, it is necessary to have some idea of what life was
like for working-class women and men in Spain before collectivization. Generalizations are difficult, as Spain was by
no means unified—politically, economically, or culturally.

Politically, regional and ideological differences were
marked. One commentator writes of "the several Spains"
(la Souchère 1964, chaps. 2, 7, and 8): a variety of semi-
independent regions, each with its customs, and, often, its

language, and many characterized by the presence of strong autonomist sentiments; and the central provinces, dominated by an increasingly unwieldy government bureaucracy and large landholders whose orientation was to a strong central government in Madrid. Regionalist, anarchist, and socialist movements were growing in one or another of these areas (the main regions of anarchist strength were Catalonia and Andalusia); and all were opposed by centralist elites, the Catholic church, and the over-officered army.

Economic divisions paralleled (or underlay) many of these political cleavages. As a country, Spain was characterized by extremely uneven economic development: industrial Catalonia seemed almost a different country from rural Galicia; the small-holding farming areas of Aragon were worlds apart from the huge absentee-owned tracts that dominated Andalusia. While union strength centered for the anarchists in industrial Catalonia and in the Levant, and for the socialists in Madrid and Asturias, employers' organizations were strong everywhere, and generally could count on the support of the government (including the use of military force) to control strikes.

Most industrial workplaces operated on a relatively small scale—factories employing one hundred workers were considered large. Employer "paternalism" was always backed by the threat (or actual use) of force. In most workplaces—whether industrial or agricultural—workers had little, if any, control over the conditions of their work, salaries, or hours. In rural areas, those who owned no land, or owned plots insufficient to support themselves and their families (a situation common in Catalonia and some areas of Aragon), labored for wages on land owned by others. Agricultural workers put in long hours at very low pay, and many lived their entire lives in debt.

The situation of women in general, except for the small

numbers of professional women, was one of almost total economic dependence on men. (Kaplan 1977; and Nelken n.d., pp. 30–31, 57, 75–76, and 86–87). Few women were employed outside the home: those who were tended to be unmarried and to work as domestics, or in textile factories, or as "out-workers" in their own homes for extremely low wages. Few of these women were organized into unions.

Socially and culturally as well, Spain's population often seemed more divided than united. The dimensions of division were many; important among these was that between men and women. In all but the most advanced industrial areas—and, to a considerable extent, even there—men and women lived almost totally separate lives. Women's activities were largely circumscribed within the larger domestic arena: caring for children and household and, in rural areas, tending the family garden plot. Most women's social circles consisted almost entirely of other women: family members, neighbors, fellow workers, or those they met at the marketplace. Men, conversely, tended to operate in a largely male world, whether in the factory, in union meetings, or relaxing in local bars.

Illiteracy compounded these sexual divisions. Most working-class families could ill afford to send any of their children to schools (public education not being available in Spain until the mid-1930s); and those lucky few who did receive an education tended to be boys. Lack of literacy and of any programs of health education added to the difficulties women experienced in controlling conception or caring for children.[1]

The Catholic church tended further to divide people. In some areas of Catalonia and Andalusia, the Church had already begun to lose influence among working-class people, particularly males, during the mid- to late-nineteenth century, when it clearly identified with large landholders or big business against newly-organizing, working-class organizations. In Barcelona, for example, pent-up frustrations and anger on the part of working-class people against the Church was expressed in the looting of some churches during the anti-government riots and demonstrations in 1909, which came to be known as the "Tragic Week."[2]

The Spanish anarcho-syndicalist movement, which had been developing for approximately seventy years by the time of the outbreak of the Civil War, responded directly to many of these problems and tensions. It was a working-class movement committed to the establishment of a self-managed, non-hierarchical society through the practice of direct action. Anarcho-syndicalists, who gathered into a number of organizations the largest of which was the Confederacion Nacional del Trabajo (National Confederation of Labor)[3] opposed what they termed vanguardism and elitism; and they insisted on the importance of education, "preparation," and participation in bringing about revolutionary transformation (Ackelsberg 1981, 1984, and 1985; Bookchin 1979; Brademas, 1974; and Peirats, 1971). In the years immediately preceding the Civil War, the movement gave rise to a complex network of storefront schools and cultural centers, union organizations, and apprenticeship programs designed to put those commitments into practice.

Years of such organizing found Spanish workers remarkably well prepared to confront the chaos brought about by war and revolution. Almost as soon as the generals' rebellion was defeated in Catalonia, members of union organizations and others committed to change created municipal and regional "revolutionary committees." These were usually composed of representatives of union and political organizations. In many communities—large cities as well as agricultural villages—these committees declared the municipalization of property, and tenants ceased paying rents to private landlords. In rural areas, village "government" often came to consist of general assemblies of the residents. (On the revolution see Bolloten 1980; Chomsky 1969; Confederación Regional 1970 and 1971; Dolgoff 1976; Fraser 1979; Leval 1975; Mintz 1970; Pérez-Baró 1970; *Realizaciones . . . Monzón* 1977; and Simoni and Simoni 1977.)

These changes in the "political" arena were more than matched by changes in the forms of production and distribution. In industrial Barcelona and its surrounding areas, for example, union organizations collectivized virtually all production, from barbershops to textile factories, electric power generation to bakeries, logging to furniture retailing. Factory committees formed to direct production and coordinate with other units within the same industry. Union organizations created coordinating bodies across industries and regions, which took charge of both the production and distribution of manufactured goods. In some of these industries—wood, hairdressing, and bread baking, for example—reorganization meant not only a change in management, but closing down small, ill-equipped shops; building new and larger workplaces; and developing more efficient production techniques. (*Boletín del Sindicato* 1936–1937; Borrás 1981 and memoirs; Costa 1979; Dolgoff 1976; Fraser 1979; Hoy 1936–1937; Leval 1975; Pérez-Baró 1970 and 1979; and Pons Prades 1974 and 1981).

Reorganization of the textile industry, in particular, had specific impacts on women. While considerable numbers of women had worked in textiles in the pre-War period, the majority of them were employed as outworkers and paid at piece rates. (Balcells 1972; Carmen 1979; Costa 1979; and Kaplan 1977). One of the most immediate consequences of the collectivization of the textile industry in the Barcelona area was the abolition of piece rates and outwork by the union administration. The CNT began seriously to unionize women and to bring them into the factories to work for a daily wage.[4] In addition to these changes in the textile industry, many women entered the ranks of paid laborers in the new war industries, particularly as chemical and metal workers, or in public transport.

General assemblies of workers in these collectivized industries decided policy, although elected committees managed affairs on a day-to-day basis. Among other changes, they reduced wage differentials considerably, both between men and women and between technical and manual workers. (Costa 1979 and 1981; Pérez-Baró 1979; and Pons Prades 1981).[5]

In rural areas, changes were even more pronounced. In many communities, anarchist organizations took complete control of both "governance" and production, creating municipal collectives of which all who worked the land in the community could become members. In slightly larger villages, workers expropriated and collectivized the lands of large holders, allowing those who had previously owned the land to continue working it, but assuring that all who had been sharecroppers or day-laborers became full members of the collective. Many of these collectives distributed produce from their farms through community storehouses; some used rationing; and all devised some means of making wages more equal. (Certificats de Treball; Colectividad Campesina 1936; Mintz 1970; and Simoni and Simoni 1977).[6] Production on collectives tended to be organized by work-groups, each of which was composed of eight to ten men (in most collectives, women worked in the fields only during harvest season). Often collectivists pooled their farm animals, and many collectives built new barns and/or storage areas. (Breitbart 1978; Catlla 1976; Dolgoff 1976; and Leval 1975).

In both rural and urban areas, the most significant economic change was in the direction and structure of work. As one respondent described the situation, "The director is now the working class, organized into unions" (Costa 1979; see also Tauber 1977). The significance of this difference cannot be overemphasized. For many, it was the essence of the revolution. Rather than working either as isolated work- ers, or even as members of a union whose primary role was to protect the interests of its members against those of the owners, workers now worked collectively, at wages and hours set, at least officially, by themselves or their direct representatives. This difference was most notable in the countryside where, in the words of one participant, it had a "contagious effect" (Carrasquer 1981).

93

For many women the essence of the revolution involved changes affecting the structures and practices of family life. In most collectivized areas, for example—particularly in Catalonia, where the influence of the Church within the working class had weakened even in the pre-War period— religious marriage was virtually abandoned (whether be- cause of the absence of priests or because of popular rejec- tion of the sacraments is not always clear). In addition, while most people in rural areas had practiced some, how- ever rudimentary, form of birth control, the practice became more widespread. Birth control information was much more readily available, in many cases provided by *ateneos libertarios* (storefront cultural centers and free schools that sprang up in many rural towns and in every working-class *barrio* of Barcelona and neighboring cities in the early years of the Republic), by CNT unions, or by centers spon- sored by the anarchist women's organization Mujeres Li- bres.[7] In general, young men and young women were able to associate more freely; and in many rural areas women were able, for the first time, to choose their own *novios* (boyfriends) (Matilde 1979; and Simoni and Simoni 1977, p. 247). In Barcelona, as well as in some rural areas, CNT- affiliated groups and Mujeres Libres organized daycare centers, maternal and child health centers, and other educational programs. (Ackelsberg 1985; Federación Nacional 1937; and Nash 1975). Abortion was legalized in Catalonia and, for the first time, it became more widely available to working-class women.[8]

Despite these changes, it should be noted that nuclear families remained the normal units of social organization. The much-discussed doctrine of "free love" meant simply, living together without civil or religious marriage. There was, apparently, considerable pressure to maintain relationships over time, although separations did occur.[9] Women continued to bear primary responsibility for child-rearing and for domestic tasks, including, in rural areas, tending the household garden plot. They worked for wages only under relatively unusual conditions, such as the absence of a male to support the family.[10]

Of course, revolutionary change did not affect everyone equally. In some areas the social and economic transformation was more thorough-going than in others; and some groups of people, generally anarchist militants, were much more involved than others in bringing about what changes there were. Nevertheless, the most striking thing about participants' recollections of these events is the extent to which their sense of themselves as members of a community—especially one in which they were *active participants* in creating transformative change—provides a crucial context and interpretive framework for their understanding of these events.

Participation, Community, and the Structuring of Behavior and Meaning

Changed consciousness is surely one essential component of revolutionary change, and numerous recent studies of movements for social change have pointed to the importance of taking part in creating change for the development of a new consciousness. [11]

The anarchists' insistence on a strategy of direct action, self-organization, and decentralization itself both reflected and emphasized their claims about the importance of active participation in revolutionary activity. In fact, anarchists traditionally differed from Marxists (and, particularly, from self-defined "Marxist-Leninists") precisely on the importance of direct action and worker self-organization. (Bakunin 1970; Guerin 1970; and Kropotkin 1913 and 1970). The Spanish anarcho-syndicalists, in particular, manifested an awareness of, and a concern with, this issue in their extensive programs of "preparation." The network of free schools, unions, and journals developed in the years before 1936 provided both a practical and a theoretical framework within which people could act. In addition, participation in this network became the basis for people's analyzing and understanding their own experience.

The degree of actual participation, however, whether in the process of collectivization or in controlling the daily work process, varied considerably. In some areas only a small group of militants exerted leadership and took responsibility for collectivizing farming, while in others the move to expropriate owners or socialize production was much more broad-based. The more extensive the participation on the part of individual workers, the more deeply affected they were by the revolution.

Thus, while those who held supervisory positions in collectivized factories were active in effecting whatever changes were made, and did experience a new sense of themselves and their competence, many "line workers" reported that their workplaces changed very little. Some claimed that what collectivization meant was that the CNT simply replaced the former owner as director of the factory (see, for example, Pons Prades 1974). This perspective was, no doubt, most common among those workers in factories that continued to be managed by their former owners, albeit under the direction of the CNT. Yet, one such worker reported that when those workers did participate and take power over their own situation, both the workplace and their self-concepts changed dramatically:

> We took over. We were told [by an elected worker committee] how much we had to produce, but *we* organized the production and decided who would do what. . . . It worked well. No one needed supervision, since we knew what we were doing. We had a meeting every week or two, whenever problems came up . . . and we'd tell the *delegado* what he was supposed to do when he went to meetings of the union: And the amazing thing was that, with that much shorter week, we produced almost as much as we did before. Because we were less tired, and we were in charge. . . .
>
> [Cassanes 1981]

Conversely, a lack of active involvement in the collectivization process appears to have had particularly detrimental consequences for workers' morale. For example, virtually all who were interviewed agreed that production in the textile industry fell dramatically with the onset of collectivization, and that people did not work as hard as they had before. Part of the drop was due no doubt, to the ending of punitive factory discipline and, consequently, to a lower rate of worker exploitation. Supervisory personnel (themselves anarcho-syndicalists) tended to attribute it to a "falta de formación"—a lack of proper revolutionary commitment—on the part of workers. Yet, this phenomenon also suggests that, although the formal conditions of work had changed, the situation for the workers was far from "revolutionary" since *their own* roles had changed very little.

The patterns were similar in rural collectives, and the role of the anarcho-syndicalist movement, itself, was even more obvious. It served not only as a facilitator for shared experience, but also as a creator of shared meanings and interpretations. It was, in fact, precisely the communal nature and context of the Spanish movement that made it so powerful in the lives of those who participated in it. And the "community" that the movement envisioned was, in theory at least, a fully participatory one.

The impact of the communal-participatory focus of the movement—and of its interaction with local conditions— can be seen clearly in a comparison of the experience of collectivization in two rather different areas. Aragon was a region in which the CNT had done extensive organizing in the early years of the Republic, beginning in 1931. They had developed a network of *ateneos* (storefront schools or cultural centers) and other institutions for the spread of anarchist ideas. Much of the land there was held in small plots. Almost all laborers had some land of their own, although many did not have enough to support themselves and their families, and worked as hired labor on the farms of other, larger landholders. The process of collectivization in such an area could be, and apparently was, participatory to a significant degree. Small holders pooled land and farm animals, if they owned any, and reaped the benefits of cooperative production. [12]

In Lerida, by contrast, where collectivization apparently had much *less* impact on the workers, the context—both of landholding and of movement activity—was considerably different. So too was the level of actual participation. The CNT had never been particularly powerful in Lerida, which was a stronghold of the Trotskyist POUM (the Worker's Party of Marxist Unification). Many—if not most—of the workers on the collective were people who did not, themselves, own any land at all, but who had worked previously as hired laborers on the farms of others. Much of the land was acquired through processes of expropriation in which very few of the collectivists actually took part. Although the

formal structure of their work changed, many did not feel
that their own actions had much to do with those changes.
In such a context, it is not surprising that they report having been little moved by collectivization.

In short, the background of successful CNT activity in
Aragon provided workers there both with an organizational
stimulus to their participation and with a communal context within which to give meaning to that participation. The
relative absence of CNT activity in Lerida before the war
left most rural workers there unprepared, either to participate actively in revolutionary activities, or (even if they did)
to perceive changes in the management of their work-lives
as reflective of any more significant social transformation. [13]
However important participation was in the lives of men,
it appears to have been even more significant for women.
Despite the fact that the mainstream of the anarcho-
syndicalist movement did not address with equal force those
issues of primary concern to women—literacy, child care,
preparation for factory work, health care (Kaplan 1971; and
Nash 1976 and 1981)—significant numbers of women were
directly involved in revolutionary activities. These included
the CNT and Juventudes, organizations such as Mujeres Libres, rationalist schools, and maternal and child health centers. For them, participation in the movement in general,
and in revolutionary activities in particular, had a dramatic
impact on their lives and consciousness. In the words of one
woman:

> It was an incredible life, the life of a young activist. A life
> dedicated to struggling, learning, renewing society. It was
> characterized, almost, by a kind of effervescence, constant
> activity. . . . I was always involved in strikes and things, any-
> where in my *barrio*, even if they were in a different branch
> of the industry. . . . It was a very busy life, working eight
> hours [or sometimes ten, if we got overtime], going every-

where on foot to save money to have for the organization . . .
and, of course, the *ateneos* and the union. After work, I'd go
to meetings. And after those meetings, there would be others, to plan the next one, or some action. . . .

[Estorach 1982]

Her response, and the responses of other women, clearly reflect the significance of the social/communal aspect of participation in experiencing revolutionary change.

But what of those who lived in collectivized rural areas or
worked in collectivized industries, but did not join actively
in the revolutionary movement? How did they experience
those changes? What impact did those changes have on
women, in particular, and on the relationships of women
to men?

Neither revolutionary activity nor its consequences involved or affected men and women equally. At least among
those with whom I spoke, men tended to report a more significant sense of change than did similarly situated women.
More importantly, women's discussions of change or lack of
change often focused on different factors than men's.

The major achievements of the revolution at the workplace—collectivization of industries, salary equalization,
improved working conditions, new forms of incentives and
sanctions—affected men much more than women, not
least because many more men than women were employed.
In addition, few of those changes at the workplace affected
the specific conditions of women's work or, more significantly, their subordination *as women* within the workplace.
There were, of course, exceptions—for example, those
women whose sewing was "industrialized" through the
efforts of the CNT in Barcelona, and those women who
joined the industrial workforce for the first time in war industries. But even those who engaged in paid factory labor
remained economically subordinated to men in an overall

sense. More significantly, they continued to live significant portions of their lives in other contexts, such as home and family, which were much less affected by change, especially in urban areas.

Nevertheless, there were changes in daily life that undermined or challenged aspects of the subordination of women manifest in social or domestic relations. And, while men focused primarily on changes in the nature of *economic* relationships in their discussions of change, women referred most frequently to changes in domestic, interpersonal, and sexual arenas. Women's focus on these issues clearly reflects the ways in which the context of their lives differed from men's, and the resulting implications of those differences both for women's participation in revolutionary activity and for transformations in consciousness.

Most of the changes that mattered to women—many of whom had never played a significant role in the paid labor force—were changes in the patterns and possibilities of social life, increased freedom of movement, greater access to birth control and information about sexuality in general. What these women thought most significant was change in the social context in which they lived their lives. Even though their economic roles may not have changed very much, many women began for the first time to be treated, and to experience themselves, as full persons. Interestingly, men almost never referred to changes in the domestic arena. For them, the crucial hours of the day were spent at the workplace, and their reports of those years clearly reflect such a focus.

Collectivization and the changes attendant upon it provided a context for the potential development of a new consciousness of self and one's place in community. This is an essential aspect of revolutionary social change. This new consciousness was probably less developed among women

than among men for two reasons: the relative lack of attention paid by the movement to issues of concern to women;
and, the fact that much of the activity focused on arenas of
social life in which women were not as deeply involved as
men. It would appear, then, that women responded differently than men to the experience of revolutionary change
both because it *affected* them differently and because they
evaluated it according to different criteria.

Another line among which male and female responses
differed was in the salience of the *community* of anarchist
militants. In their discussions with me, male respondents,
even the most committed activists, devoted relatively little
attention to the movement's impact on their *personal* lives.
They clearly respected their *compañeros*, and counted on
them to act together; but they tended not to talk extensively
about the support or sense of community they themselves
experienced by participating in the movement.

Women activists, on the other hand, unfailingly mentioned the significance of the movement's community to
their lives and work. While this contrast in emphasis might
simply be the difference in the particular people interviewed,
it is equally likely that the communal aspect of movement
activity, while significant for both men and women, was especially so for the latter. Coming from situations in which
they had relatively no freedom of movement and few, if any,
opportunities to act independently of men, young women
who became involved in the organizations of the anarchist
movement found comradeship, freedom, and respect among
male and female peers. Participation in movement activities
may well have made a much greater difference in the lives of
women than in those of men precisely because of the subordination of women in Spanish society. In that context, it is
not surprising that so many women with whom I talked
focused on the role and significance of the movement in
their lives; or that the collective anarchist visions they devel-

oped there provided an interpretive framework within which they evaluated their experience.[14]

This examination of both women's and men's responses to collectivization points up a number of important factors in understanding social change. First, if the impact of social change on women is to be fully evaluated, it is important to look not only at changes in women's participation in the paid labor force, but also at the ways in which new forms of social and economic organization affect the particular circumstances of their daily lives. What seems to matter—particularly in terms of changing consciousness—are those transformations that affect the conditions of people's day-to-day lives over which they feel some degree of control and which, in some way, empower them in the context of their own lives. That perspective is as essential, if not more so, for understanding the impact of social change on women, whose primary concerns were caring for home and family, as it was for understanding the impact of those changes on male wage laborers.

Finally, an examination of women's responses seems to underscore even more directly the importance of participation. Perhaps, precisely *because* of their especially exploited status, women who *did* become actively involved in bringing about change felt those changes deeply. On the contrary, those who did not participate actively may well have experienced even revolutionary activities as simply one further manifestation of their relative marginality.

Community Over Time: Politicalization and Repression

Many of the differences in people's responses to the events they experienced had to do with the quality of the revolutionary experience itself and with their own levels of participation in it. Post-facto reports of those experiences are, of course, filtered through the lens of their succeeding life histories. The revolution in Spain took place during a brutal civil war. The war was followed by forty years of Franco's dictatorship. Surely the experiences of those intervening years had a significant impact on memories and perceptions.

It is clear that continuing association either with an organization of the anarchist movement or with some other organization committed to radical, social transformation enabled, and even encouraged, those who participated in the collectives to put their experiences into context. The practical and ideological commitments of the movement provided language and concepts with which to understand and interpret their history. Activist respondents referred to classic anarchist writings or ideas to support their points, and discussed the ways in which the Spanish experience followed or differed from the ideal patterns. In addition, CNT membership provided them with concepts for, and an understanding of, the processes of participation and social revolution. They emphasized transformations in their own behavior and consciousness which they experienced through that participation. Perhaps even more important, organizational affiliation and the personal-communal associations it fostered created deep emotional ties. Few activists of either sex could talk about their experiences in the CNT or FIJL without being moved by the memories.

Perhaps the clearest sense in which continuing connection with the anarchist movement has affected people is in the support offered by organizational and personal networks. The fear that paralyzed many in the post-war period, and even today, is a product of the repression that began during the war and continued long after it. Even during the war, Franco's victorious troops engaged in massive executions and imprisonment of "traitors." In the aftermath of the war, thousands of people went to France and suffered severely in refugee or concentration camps (Falcón 1979; Mera 1977; and Stein 1980); others remained in Spain and were executed or jailed for their participation, or suspected participation, in revolutionary activities.[15] Thousands of others lived in fear that they would be arrested. Under such circumstances, isolation can be nearly fatal.

Those who remained in Spain and maintained connections with the anarchist movement all reported that those connections were crucial in sustaining them through the years of fear and isolation. In some cases the "sustenance" was material—saving people from abduction or facilitating escapes to France. Conversely, the sense of having a support network was singularly lacking on the part of those who were unconnected with the CNT or other resistance organizations. The fear many of these people exhibited, their hesitation to speak at all about the past, was often disproportionate to the actual roles they had played in the collective; but they felt themselves isolated in dealing both with the past and with the present.

In addition to providing some protection against paralyzing fear, organizational membership provides an important antidote to a sense of futility, the feeling that all the sacrifices made during those years and since were for naught. The sense of futility was strongest among those who had no continuing organizational ties. Such people also demonstrated little desire to identify themselves in any way with the process of collectivization. Among non-activists, women were often most ready to express such feelings—perhaps because of the very real fear that, if the men were taken off to jail, they would be left to manage household and family. Not only were the changes ephemeral and barely relevant to their lives, they also existed outside any meaningful context. Without either some permanence or a community for interpretation, the experiences were essentially de-politicized, and came to lack any real meaning.[16]

Of course, not only ties to the organization and the community of people it represented account for these perceptions. For many, an evaluation of the events also reflects a commitment to the goals and values of the movement. In general, for example, those who maintained ties with the CNT in the years following the war had been the most active at the time of the revolution. It is possible that positive memories and evaluations reflect a sense of commitment to the "mission" of the movement, but a number of important exceptions are worth mentioning.

It is not true that all who maintained ties with the CNT were those most centrally involved with the collectives or the movement. Nor did all the most active collectivists maintain membership in the organization. Over time, in fact, organizational ties may be significant not only for the personal loyalties they generate but also for the framework of analysis they provide. Direct action was—and is—an important element of the anarchist perspective on the world and social change. Continued involvement in a movement committed to direct action surely affects how one views one's own participation during those early years.

Conclusions

The economic and social revolution which took place in Spain in 1936/1937 was not a single, monolithic phenomenon, either in content or impact. What constituted "the revolution" differed significantly among regions and economic sectors, from one workplace to another, and to an extent, between the sexes. At least some of the seeming variations in the perceptions of change stem directly from the actual differences in those changes; but examination also shows important differences in perception even among those who lived in the same village or worked in the same shop.

Revolutionary change implies not only structural change but also transformations in people's understanding of themselves and the world around them. The data from Spain suggest that there is no simple and direct relationship between these two types of transformation, but that one cannot take place without the other. On the one hand, the revolution occurred because there were, already, groups of "prepared," self-conscious, and self-confident people. These people had an understanding of what revolutionary change entailed, namely direct action and self-organization, and they did not hesitate to act. On the other hand, their participation in direct action to take control over public services, workplaces, and even entire communities affected the people and institutions around them; it also contributed to their own empowerment. Others who were drawn into the range of revolutionary activities were, under certain circumstances, changed themselves. The degree of their transformation seems to have depended on the extent to which the change altered their daily lives, the degree to which they took an active role in bringing it about, and the extent to which they had a network of people to rely on for support—both then and in the aftermath. Even when there were substantial transformations in the structures of economic and political power, many people remained immune to them when their daily lives were unchanged. And given the specific context in which Spanish women lived, if change was to affect them, it had to have an impact considerably beyond the workplace, at least as traditionally defined.

In addition, while it is important to examine, for example, the sexual division of labor and the different ways it structures the lives of men and women, we have seen that the division of labor is not the only measure of women's status in a society. Nor are changes within it the only ones that matter. What made the most difference to women were those changes in cultural norms and values that allowed for much greater personal freedom—such things as easier access to education and information about birth control—changes in what would seem to be the most personal arenas. Conversely, it is important to examine the ways in which women, however subordinate they may be, act to change both their society and the social movements in which they take part. In fact, given the differences in the lives of men and women, the very forms of revolutionary activity in which they engage may differ (Ackelsberg and Breitbart 1984; Kaplan 1980 and 1982; and Levy and Applewhite 1980).

One of the ways in which women's oppression manifested itself in Spain was the denial of the opportunity to determine the course of their lives. "Involving" Spanish women in a movement over which they had little control—or leaving them aside to benefit later from changes made by others—could easily be seen as a simple reinforcement of their traditional dependence. Conversely, those who became involved, who participated in activities whose goals and means they defined for themselves, experienced a transformation of self-concept which was deep and long-lasting.

Revolutionary change that affects people's lives and consciousness must speak to the particular situations in which they live, and also engage them in the transformation of their own lives. When both of these conditions were met, change in Spain had a marked and lasting impact. When they were not met—as was the case in some collectives—change had much more limited impact. In many cases, the collectives not only failed to address issues of crucial concern to their members, they also failed to involve them directly in activities to bring about those changes. As a consequence, many people experienced the revolution going on around them as yet one more storm buffeting them about, and over which they exercised little control. Most dramatically, in the absence of a network of support, the repression and fear of the ensuing years denied many people the opportunity to reflect on or share those memories. In such a context, change that may have been, at the time, of considerable significance becomes unmentionable history—lost not only to neighbors and children but, perhaps, even to oneself.

108

Notes

This study represents part of a long-term project on the anarchist movement in Spain during the civil war years, and draws on information from archival sources, as well as on interviews conducted in 1979, 1981, and 1982. My research in Lerida and Fraga was made possible by the assistance of Ana Cases and Bernard Catlla. Research was funded, in part, by an AAUW post-doctoral research grant and, in part, by the Project on Women and Social Change, Smith College. I am particularly grateful for the help of Susan C. Bourque, Donna Robinson Divine, Verena Stolcke, and participants in the 1982 Summer Workshop of the Project on Women and Social Change for comments on earlier drafts of this paper.

1. The problems were most severe for working-class women; but middle-class women, as well, suffererd from inadequate information. See Bosch (1947, especially pp. 43–50); Comaposada (1982); Nash (1976, pp. 172–174; 197–227); and Nelken (n.d.r., p. 119).

2. The "Tragic Week," 26 July–1 August 1909, began with demonstrations (largely on the part of women) in protest against the calling up of Catalan troops to fight in Morocco. Much of Barcelona was shut down in the industrial strikes that accompanied the street demonstrations. Many churches were burned and looted. Ullman (1967) is the best source on the events.

3. The CNT, the anarcho-syndicalist trade union organization founded in 1910, had an estimated 850,000 members in May 1936 (*Congresos Anarco-Sindicalistas* 1977). Other organizations that formed part of the libertarian (or anarchist, in a loose sense) movement—and shared the goal of a non-hierarchical society— were the FAI (Federación Anarquista Ibérica); the Iberian Anarchist Federation, a "pure anarchist" organization, founded in

1927; the FIJL (Federación Ibérica de Juventudes Libertarias); the Iberian Federation of Libertarian Youth (also known simply as Juventudes); and Mujeres Libres, an organization of and for women dedicated to the liberation of women and their incorporation into the anarchist movement.

4. *Women* workers viewed that change—one heralded by the CNT as one of the most significant achievements of the revolution—as, at best, a mixed blessing. It left them with less control over the hours and conditions of their work, and forced them to make more formal arrangements for child care.

5. This information was confirmed in documents supplied by José Costa, who was secretary of the textile union in Badalona (just outside Barcelona) at the time; and in salary reports which can be found in the Archivo de Servicios Documentales, Salamanca, Spain, Sección Político-social de Barcelona, Carpeta 626. Attempts at wage equalization were not always successful however. Note, for example, the frequently-repeated story of the Barcelona opera house. For a short while, wages in the industry were totally equalized. But the singers objected. Finally, one day some of the leads announced to the ushers that, if they were so equal, the ushers and ticket-collectors should fill in for the singers. The experiment in equality soon ended.

6. Data on wage equalization on rural collectives can also be found in "L'Enquesta de la Consellería" (1936 and 1937). Some information on Fraga (Aragon) comes from Chiné (1979). Leval, who reports on the collective in Fraga in considerable detail, states that not everyone was a member and that some 700 families of "individualistas" remained outside the collective, cultivating crops and raising animals for their own use. Beyond what they needed for themselves, they were "advised" by the local council what to plant, etc. (1972, vol. 1, pp. 116, 119).

7. Information about birth control was supplied by an informant who wished to remain anonymous, who had participated in the collective in Albatarrech, Lerida, in an interview with the author in Lerida, 4 May 1979. On Mujeres Libres and its activities, see Ackelsberg (1985); Nash (1976), and Kaplan (1971 and 1977). Sources on the ateneos are numerous. For a moving account of the influence of one such rationalist school on one young man, see Pons Prades (1974, pp. 15–17, 23–34).

8. It is not clear just what proportion of working-class women knew of, or took advantage of, legalized abortion. A team of re-

searchers in Barcelona, including Mary Nash and Verena Stolcke, is attempting to gather data on this and other aspects of family life and sexuality during the years of the Republic and Civil War.

9. See, for example, Pons discussion (1974, pp. 94–102) of the development of "free union" ceremonies in the wood-working industry. Archival evidence suggests that the practice of "marrying" in union offices was fairly common ("Acta de unión libre . . ." 1936; and "En Barcelona" 1932). These perspectives were confirmed in interviews (Carpena 1981; Guillén 1981; Iturbe 1981; and Rovira 1981).

10. Relatively few people, whether men or women, recognized women's contributions—in the household or in revolutionary activity—as "work" equal in value to that of men. Many women interviewed were critical of men for *not* recognizing the value of household work. As one put it: "All that enormous organization which was the CNT, with its one million members, all that organization would not have existed if those companeros had not had, in their houses, the women they had" (Iturbe 1981; see also Ocaña 1979). For parallel findings of differential understandings of what counts as "work," see Bourque and Warren (1981, pp. 118–119).

11. The classic study of this changed consciousness is Thompson (1968). Chafe (1977), and Piven and Cloward (1979) discuss parallel sorts of changes in self-perception as part of the feminist and black power movements in the United States in the 1960s and 1970s and as part of "poor people's movements" more generally. See also Hinton (1966); Rowbotham (1973); Wellstone (1978); and Yates (1976). In our own day, consciousness-raising groups which formed an essential component of the early women's movement attempted, in parallel ways, to re-conceptualize experience as a basis for action.

12. Not all collectivization was voluntary: few large landowners wished to give up their estates! Nevertheless, there is reason to believe reports that a substantial proportion of small holders and laborers who took part in the collectivization in Aragon did so voluntarily, and had a strong sense of their own contribution to the change.

13. It is not simply a matter of perception. The extent of social transformation in many of the Aragon collectives was much greater than that achieved in Lerida. The stronger roots of the anarchist movement in the Aragon communities contributed, in large measure, to the difference in the depth, as well as breadth of change.

14. These findings are not inconsistent with Gilligan's (1982) claim—based on interviews with women and men in a very different culture (the contemporary United States)—that women tend more than men to be oriented to other people and to structure their identity through interpersonal networks.

15. In the village of Fraga, alone, for example, 260 suspected anarchists and leftists were jailed in one of the more wide-ranging "round-ups" in 1946 (Chiné 1979). See also Tellez (1974).

16. A number of those who had been participants in a collective in Lerida, a town approximately 180 km. from Barcelona, either minimized their roles, denied participation, or made it clear that they preferred to forget the entire experience—often, apparently, out of a diffuse sense of fear. Wives were frequently the guardians of the home, protecting their men from questioning with statements such as "he was young and didn't know any better," "he was just doing what he was told," or "he has nothing to say." Both men and women—particularly those now living in areas which have benefitted in the intervening years from the introduction into Lerida of irrigation—said that they would rather not discuss the events of that period at all: "The past is the past. . . . Let's leave it well enough alone." Interviews in Lerida: May, June, and July 1979.

References

Ackelsberg, Martha A. 1981. "Revolution Begins at Home: Women's Participation in Anarchist Collectives in Civil War Spain." Unpublished manuscript, Smith College, Northampton, Mass.

———. 1984. "Mujeres Libres and the Role of Women in Anarchist Transformation." In Elaine Baruch and Ruby Rohrlich, eds. *Women in Search of Utopia: Mavericks and Mythmakers*. New York: Schocken Books.

———. 1985. "'Separate and Equal'? Mujeres Libres and Anarchist Strategy for Women's Emancipation." *Feminist Studies*.

"Acta de unión libre . . ." 1936. Barcelona, 1 Diciembre. Archivo de Servicios Documentales, Salamanca, Spain. Sección Político-Social de Barcelona, Carpeta 626.

Bakunin, Michael. 1970. "Federalism, Socialism, and Anti-Theologism." In Sam Dolgoff, ed. *Bakunin on Anarchy*, pp. 103–147. New York: Anchor Books.

Balcells, Albert. 1972. "Condicions Laborals de l'Obrera à la Industria Catalana." *Reçerques* no. 2: 141–159.

Boletín del Sindicato de la Edificación, Madera y Decoración. 1936–1937. Barcelona.

Bolloten, Burnett. 1980. *The Spanish Revolution.* Chapel Hill: University of North Carolina Press.

Bookchin, Murray. 1979. *The Spanish Anarchists: The Heroic Years.* New York: Free Life Editions.

Borrás, Jacinto. 1981. Interview. Perpignan, France, 14 August.

———. "Lo Que Ví y Como lo Ví" (memoirs).

Bosch Marín, Juan. 1947. *El Niño Español en el Siglo .* Madrid: Gráficas Gonzalez.

Bourque, Susan C., and Kay B. Warren. 1981. *Women of the Andes.* Ann Arbor: University of Michigan Press.

Breitbart, Myrna M. 1978. "The Theory and Practice of Anarchist Decentralism in Spain, 1936–1939." PhD. dissertation, Department of Geography, Clark University, Worcester, Mass.

Brademas, John. 1974. *Anarcosindicalismo y Revolución en España (1930–1937).* Barcelona: Ariel.

Carmen. 1979. Interview. Lérida, Spain, 4 May.

Carpena, Pepita. 1981. Interview. Montpellier, France, 30 December.

Carrasquer, Felix. 1979. Interview. Barcelona, 16 February.

———. 1981. Interview. Barcelona, 31 July.

Cassañes, Rogelio. 1981. Interview. Sta. Coloma de Granamet, Barcelona, 6 August.

Catlla, Bernard. 1976. *Problèmes de la Construction et du Logement dans la Révolution Espagnole, 1936–1939.* Saillagouse, France.

Certificats de Treball [Work Certifications from "Adelante"]. Archivo de Servicios Documentales, Salamanca, Spain. Sección Político-Social de Lérida, Carpeta 5.

Chafe, William. 1977. *Women and Equality.* New York: Oxford University Press.

Chiné, Valero. 1979. Interview. Fraga (Aragón), Spain, 11 May.

Chomsky, Noam. 1969. "Objectivity and Liberal Scholarship." *American Power and the New Mandarins,* pp. 23–158. New York: Random House.

Colectividad Campesina "Adelante," CNT-AIT. 1936. *Libro de Actas* [Minutes of Meetings]. Archivo de Servicios Documentales, Salamanca, Spain. Sección Político-Social de Lérida, Carpeta 3, registro no. 3.

Comaposada, Mercedes. 1982. Interviews. Paris, 3 and 5 January.
Confederación Regional de Aragón, Rioja y Navarra, CNT-AIT.
1970. *Comarcal de Utrillas (Teruel): En lucha por la Libertad,
Contra el Fascismo (1936–1939)*. Toulouse: Ediciones 'Cultura
y Acción.'

———. 1971. *Comarcal de Valderrobres (Teruel): Sus Luchas So-
ciales Revolucionarias*. Toulouse: Ediciones 'Cultura y Acción.'

Congresos Anarco-Sindicalistas en España, 1870–1936. 1977.
Toulouse: Ediciones CNT.

Costa, Josep. 1979. Interviews. Barcelona, 12 and 19 February.

———. 1981. Interview. Barcelona, 4 August.

Dolgoff, Sam. 1976. *The Anarchist Collectives*. New York: Free
Life Editions.

"En Barcelona, a Veintitres de Octubre de Mil Novecientos Treinta
y Seis . . ." [Document Recording a "Free Union"] Archivo de
Servicios Documentales, Salamanca, Spain. Sección Político-
Social de Barcelona, Carpeta 1392.

Estorach, Soledad. 1982. Interviews. Paris, 4 and 6 January.

"L'Enquesta de la Consellería Sobre la Collectivització de la Terra."
Butlletí del Departament d'Agricultura 1, no. 3 (Diciembre
1936): 21–30; 2, no. 4 (Gener 1937): 75–78.

Falcón, Lidia. 1979. *Los Hijos de Los Vencidos*. Barcelona: Editorial Pomaire.

Federación Nacional Mujeres Libres. 1937. "Actividades de la
Federación Nacional, Mujeres Libres." Barcelona.

Fraser, Ronald. 1979. *Blood of Spain*. New York: Pantheon.

Gilligan, Carol. 1982. *In a Different Voice*. Cambridge, Mass.:
Harvard University Press.

Guerin, Daniel. 1970. *Anarchism*. New York: Monthly Review
Books.

Guillén, Sara. 1981. Interview. Béziers, France, 28 December.

Hinton, William. 1966. *Faushen*. New York: Monthly Review Press.

HOY. 1936–1937. Monthly magazine of the Sindicato de la Edificación, Madera y Decoración de Cataluña. Various issues.

Iturbe, Lola. 1981. Interviews. Alella and Barcelona, 3 and 4
August.

Kaplan, Temma. 1971. "Spanish Anarchism and Women's Liberation." *Journal of Contemporary History* 6: 101–110.

———. 1977. "Other Scenarios: Women and Spanish Anarchism."
In Renate Bridenthal and Claudia Koonz, eds. *Becoming Visible*,
pp. 400–421. New York: Houghton Mifflin.

———. 1980. "Women and Mass Strikes." Paper presented to

Smith College Project on Women and Social Change Summer Workshop, 9 June.

———. 1982. "Female Consciousness and Collective Action: The Case of Barcelona, 1910–1918." *Signs* 7, no. 3: 545–567.

Kropotkin, Peter A. 1913. *The Conquest of Bread*. London: Chapman and Hall.

———. 1970. "Expropriation." In Martin Miller, ed. *P. A. Kropotkin, Selected Writings on Anarchism and Revolution*. Cambridge, Mass.: MIT Press.

la Souchère, Éléna de. 1964. *An Explanation of Spain*. New York: Random House.

Leval, Gaston. 1972. *Colectividades Libertarias en España*. 2 vols. Buenos Aires: Editorial Proyección.

Leval, Gaston. 1975. *Collectives in the Spanish Revolution*. London: Freedom Press.

Levy, Darline Gay, and Harriet B. Applewhite. 1980. "Women of the Popular Classes in Revolutionary Paris, 1789–1795." In Carol R. Berkin and Clara M. Lovett, eds. *Women, War, and Revolution*, pp. 9–35. New York: Holmes and Meier.

Matilde. 1979. Interview. Barcelona, 16 February.

Mera, Cipriano. 1977. *Guerra, Exilio y Carcel*. Paris: Ruedo Ibérico.

Mintz, Frank. 1970. *L'Autogestion dans l'Espagne Révolutionnaire*. Paris: Bélibaste.

Nash, Mary. 1975. "Dos Intelectuales Anarquistas Frente al Problema de la Mujer: Federica Montseny y Lucía Sanchez Saornil." *Convivium*: 73–79.

———. 1976. *"Mujeres Libres" España: 1936–39*. Barcelona: Tusquets.

———. 1981. *Mujer y Movimiento Obrero en España, 1931–1939*. Barcelona: Editorial Fontamara.

Nelken, Margarita. n.d. *La Condición Social de la Mujer en España: Su Estado Actual, Su Posible Desarrollo*. Biblioteca de Cultura Moderna y Contemporánea. Barcelona: Editorial Minerva.

Ocaña, Igualdad. 1979. Interview. Hospitalet (Barcelona), 14 February.

Peirats, José. 1971. *La CNT en la Revolución Española*. 3 vols. Paris: Ruedo Ibérico.

Pérez-Baró, Albert. 1970. *30 Mesos de Collectivisme a Catalunya*. Barcelona: Ariel.

———. 1979. Interview. Barcelona, 14 July.

Piven, Frances Fox, and Richard A. Cloward. 1979. *Poor People's Movements: How They Succeed and Why They Fail*. New York: Pantheon.

Pons Prades, Eduardo. 1974. *Un Soldado de la República*. Madrid: G. del Toro Editor.

————. 1981. Interviews. 31 July and 6 August.

Realizaciones Revolucionarias y Estructuras Colectivistas de la Comarcal de Monzón (Huesca). 1977. CNT, Confederación Nacional del Trabajo de España. Regional de Aragón, Rioja, y Navarra: Ediciones 'Cultura y Accion.'

Rovira, Enriqueta (Fernandez). 1981. Interviews. Castelnaudary, France, 28 and 29 December.

Rowbotham, Sheila. 1973. *Women's Consciousness, Man's World*. Harmondsworth: Penguin Books.

Simoni, Encarnita, and Renato Simoni. 1977. *CRETAS: La Collectivisation d'un Village Aragonais Pendant la Guerre Civile Espagnole (1936–1937)*. Mémoire de Licence en Histoire Contemporaine, Présenté à la Faculté des Lettres de l'Université de Genève.

Stein, Louis. 1980. *Between Death and Exile*. Cambridge, Mass.: Harvard University Press.

Tauber, Walter. 1977. "Les Tramways de Barcelona Collectivisés Pendant la Révolution Espagnole (1936–1939)." *Bulletin d'Information, FIEHS* 1, no. 2: 8–54.

Tellez, Antonio. 1974. *La Guerrilla Urbana I. Facerías*. Paris: Ruedo Ibérico.

Thompson, E. P. 1968. *The Making of the English Working Class*. Harmondsworth: Penguin Books.

Ullman, Joan Connelly. 1967. *The Tragic Week*. Cambridge, Mass.: Harvard University Press.

Wellstone, Paul. 1978. *How the Rural Poor Got Power*. Amherst: University of Massachusetts Press.

Yates, Douglas. 1976. "Political Innovation and Institution Building." In W. D. Hawley ed., et al. *Theoretical Perspectives on Urban Politics*, pp. 146–175. Englewood Cliffs, N.J.: Prentice Hall.

II

The Individual Woman Confronting Change

4

Marx and Mary:
The Individual, Identity,
and the Development
of Social Consciousness

by Penny Gill

Mary Baker

In 1923 a young woman wearily climbed out of a train compartment and picked up her two small children and an old cardboard suitcase. People jostled by as she looked around what must be Union Station. She had made it to Chicago: Chicago, where there was work; Chicago, the biggest city she would ever know except for a year of her childhood in New York; Chicago, a place where her son and daughter might be able to go to school. But it was not work, urban life, nor education that had drawn her north from Alabama.

119

A Salvation Army worker believed she had tracked Mary's husband Thomas, the father of her children, to Chicago. For months she had had no word from him. Now she stood in Union Station, desperately hoping the slow bleeding, which had begun the morning she had left her Alabama farm house, would not soil her old coat and did not mean she would lose this third child conceived in that brief week she and Thomas had been together. For months, six and one-half to be precise, she had had no word from him. She would try one more time, have it out with him one more time: would he or would he not help to support his family? Would he leave those loose women and stop having a "gaiety time"?

Twenty-one years earlier Mary's young mother had also arrived in a strange city with a two-year-old in her arms. The child, Mary, had been born in Germany in 1900, several months after her father's departure for the United States to find work. Mary and her mother followed him to New York two years later, in search of work, education, and a better life than could be "scuffled together" as beet farmers on the Rhine. Occasionally Mary's father found day work unloading ships in New York harbor for a dollar a day. But it was Mary's mother who paid the rent and bought bread and baloney with the money she earned as a janitor. Children were born, often were sick, and one of them died. Mary, the eldest, took care of the little ones and learned English on the busy streets.

Mary's father soon gave up looking for work in the urban north and traced the string of mining communities down the Appalachians. Ultimately the Baker family settled as tenant laborers in a small rural community in Alabama. Mr. Baker worked in the coal mines when work was available. But most importantly, Mrs. Baker had a small cabin in the woods with room for a vegetable garden and a milk cow. Mary grew up there, her childhood shaped by caring for her smaller brothers and sisters, milking the cow, gathering old railroad ties for firewood, and carrying her father's midday meal to the head of the mine shaft. She says she was tall and skinny for her age; she must have been quick and help-ful as well. She was never permitted to attend school, and her parents arranged for her marriage to a friend of her fa-ther's, when she had just reached fourteen.

When Mary embarked on that train ride north, she had joined a great movement northward. Another dimension of immigration had been added to her mother's trek from Ger-man to American shores, as Mary tried to escape the rural poverty embedded in the red-soiled south. As she stood in Union Station, she faced an epochal transition, from peas-ant to factory worker. Her very physical survival would be threatened by poverty, hard work, and illness, as she experi-enced in her own life powerful forces of economic and so-cial change. Familiar social roles, her every-day movements through a known social environment, had been left behind in Alabama or were soon to be shattered in the crucible of Chicago in the 1920s. Mary's response to these threats is instructive. During the early years of World War II, Mary Baker left Chicago for work as a waitress at a Texas airfield. She married and moved to Holyoke, Massachusetts at the end of the war, this her third husband. In Holyoke she eventually bought a tiny cafe-restaurant, serving breakfast and lunch to the mill workers across the street. At sixty she married her fourth husband, sold the restaurant because her health was threatened by the long hours of backbreak-ing labor, and "retired" to her simple tar-papered cottage in the Berkshires, where I met her in 1974.

Identity and Consciousness

Observers of political life—kings, police, journalists, and grass-roots organizers—have recognized that conscious-ness, each individual's sense of him or herself, is an extremely important determinant of political action. Whether one wishes to encourage or inhibit certain forms of political behavior by certain members of society (e.g. organize a strike, terrorize peasants, continue low levels of voter registration by Blacks, or keep women in the home "where they belong"), one would be well-advised to pay careful attention to the shape and intensity of self-consciousness among the target group. What someone thinks of him or herself, who one knows oneself to be, will sharply affect one's political behavior.

There are two typical strands of such political analysis: one concentrates on the individual's sense of personal competence, even social potency, the person's sense of his or her ability to act meaningfully in the political arena. The second focuses on social dimensions of identity such as ethnicity, class, region, and nationality. Each reflects salient social cleavages and group identity which can trigger sustained political activity by those so identified. We have been supplied with a wide range of both theoretical analyses and painstaking empirical descriptions of the rise of new groups conscious of sharing ethnic, religious, class, regional, or national identities and demanding increased political participation and power.

Most such analyses tell us little of why so many lack consciousness and remain distant from the predicted types of political activity. Which factors inhibit the formation of certain types of group identity? And more specifically, which mute the impact of work in the formation of working-class identity?

Of all such analyses, Marx's theory of working-class consciousness is the most intellectually dominant. I will discuss this theory briefly and counterpose it to Mary Baker's own story as a factory worker in Chicago in the 1920s and the 1930s. I wish to advance a more complex answer to the question of what mutes, or clouds, the centrality of work in the formation of identity, among those centrally placed to be exposed to its severest hardships: factory work, low, unsteady wages, economic marginality, and substandard housing.

Most women's lives are structurally more complex than those of men because of women's dual responsibilities for home and market labor. A theory of the development of consciousness must take account of women's two spheres of activity: work in the economy and child-rearing. But even adding the second exterior source of identity, child-rearing or work in the home, when it is understood as a social role analogous to market labor (and thus: gender), will not fully capture the richness of Mary's experience of being a mother, of knowing herself as the mother of her two children, Tommy and Mary. For Mary, mothering reflects a profoundly interior sense of herself, quite apart from her social role as mother. It is sufficiently vivid and central to her identity to subsume almost completely her social role as a factory worker.

In short, to understand fully the formation of identity, we must be prepared to consider exterior sources of identity, such as work and the social role of mother, on the one hand, and gender and interior sources of identity originating in deep feelings, dreams, introspection, value and image, on the other.

Marx's Theory of the Development of Consciousness

Marx made a very significant contribution to our understanding of the development of a group-based consciousness. And although much of his later work as a mature scholar is devoted to an historical analysis of changes in the mode of production, he repeatedly links his economic studies to the associated shifts in class consciousness, ideology, and other cultural "products."

We might understand Marx's views on the emergence of revolutionary consciousness as consisting of a series of questions: How do workers learn they are workers? How do they learn to recognize themselves as the proletariat? How do they build social organizations, such as unions and cooperatives, that reflect their emerging group identity? And ultimately, how do consciousness and organization change history and society?

In short, Marx was interested, both normatively and empirically, in how workers first entered public life and eventually restructure the economic and political community. Because his theory of the development of class consciousness rested securely in his analysis of the development of capitalism, only under the specific conditions of factory life intrinsic to a mature form of industrial capitalism and characterized by a very high degree of concentration of private (productive) property in the hands of a few, could working-class consciousness emerge. Marx seems to have recognized that workers could well be workers before they knew themselves as workers, but that worker self-consciousness is the necessary factor for sustained proletarian political activity.

Marx argued that social consciousness reflects in two ways the individual's relationship to the economic system of his or her society: 1) The level of development, the very structure of the productive process of a person's society shapes in the most profound way the values embedded in consciousness, as well as its possibility.

> The sum total of these relations of production constitutes the economic structure of society, the real foundation, on which rises a legal and political superstructure and to which correspond definite forms of social consciousness. The mode of production of material life conditions the social, political, and intellectual life process in general.
>
> [Marx 1977, p. 389]

124

2) The individual's relationship to property within the specific developmental level of society even more sharply delimits the basic values and perceptions associated with particular forms of consciousness. In Marx's most familiar passage on this subject he writes that it "is not the consciousness of men that determines their being, but, on the contrary, their social being that determines their consciousness" (Marx 1977, p. 389).

It is too simple a reading of the *Preface* to call this economic determinism. It is more properly viewed as a theory of how consciousness is shaped, of how parameters are set in ways that both reflect and sustain the fundamental economic system. But we must remember that those parameters are wide, very wide, as Marx would be quick to admit, for they contain all the products of consciousness. For example, competing political ideologies, religious systems, and aesthetic styles reflect contradictions, or deep faults, developing between the economic system and the network of derivative social relations, and provide the arena within which those contradictions are fought out. Marx warns us to distinguish between "which can be determined with the precision of natural science, and the legal, political, religious, aesthetic or philosophic—in short, ideological forms in which men become conscious of this conflict and fight it out" (Marx 1977, pp. 389–90).

Even though Marx's analysis focuses on epochs in human history, explaining the macro-level shifts from agrarian to feudal and then industrial economies, one can read Marx as instructing us to begin our inquiry into social life by examining specific individuals. In part I of *German Ideology*, he suggests:

> The social structure and the State are continually evolving out of the life process of definite individuals . . . as they *really* are; i.e. as they operate, produce materially, and

hence as they work under definite material limits, presuppositions and conditions independent of their will.

. . . We set out from real, active men, and on the basis of their real life process we demonstrate the development of the ideological reflexes and echoes of this life-process.

[Marx and Engels 1976, pp. 35–36]

While Marx is not recommending biography as a research method, he is suggesting a way of analyzing individuals as acting in the world, working, reproducing, speaking with other such "concrete individuals." He emphasizes "real" individuals, suggesting material, hard, specific, boundaried, people, engaged in "sensuous activity."

For Marx, "consciousness" carries with it the basic assumptions of mid-nineteenth-century mechanical science: reality is physical and material, and it can be known and understood by a properly trained scientist. Ironically, Marx, the graduate student, once intrigued by the philosophical problems posed by religious consciousness, eventually must proclaim his own mode of analysis to be objectively true and non-ideological, as he criticizes "ruthlessly" other philosophical systems as ideological. Marx must reject interiority as a source of consciousness, in order to maintain his epistemological argument. One might well argue in response that interiority sneaks back in through his concept of consciousness, but his empirical method does not allow him to include interior sources of self-consciousness as evidence. Self-reflection, dream, and introspection are excluded from "sensuous activity." In words Freud might have been willing to claim, Marx urges his reader:

The reform of consciousness consists *only* in enabling the world to clarify its consciousness, in waking it from its dream about itself, in *explaining* to it the meaning of its own actions. Our whole task can consist only in putting religious and political questions into self-conscious human form.

. . . Our motto must therefore be: Reform of consciousness not through dogmas, but through analyzing the mystical consciousness, the consciousness which is unclear to itself, whether it appears in religious or political form.

[Marx 1972, p. 10]

From this point of view, the significant content of consciousness is one's sense of connectedness, of identity with the others of a social group, because of shared membership in that group. Marx argues that the progressive line of development in human history is essentially the gradual enlargement of the group with which people identify: from tribe and clan to class and nation, and ultimately, as we read in the *Early Manuscripts*, full species consciousness: this is to achieve non-alienation, to become a fully human member of communist society.

Consciousness, then, can and must be analyzed from the "outside," from the vantage of the viewer with the true viewpoint, Marx contends that consciousness is clearly visible in language:

> The production of ideas, of conceptions, of consciousness is at first directly interwoven with the material activity and the material intercourse of men, the language of real life. Conceiving, thinking, the mental intercourse of men, appear at this stage as the direct efflux of their material behavior. The same applies to mental production as expressed in the language of politics, laws, morality, religious, metaphysics, etc. of a real people.
>
> [Marx and Engels 1976, p. 36]

But it is worthwhile to stress Marx's point that even language is an exteriorally-visible, social product.

> Language is as old as consciousness, language IS practical consciousness that exists also for other men, and for that reason alone it really exists for me personally as well; language, like consciousness, only arises from the need, the necessity of intercourse with other men. . . . Consciousness is, therefore, from the very beginning a social product, and remains so as long as men exist at all.
>
> [Marx and Engels 1976, p. 44]

According to Marx there seems to be no possibility of private language, of language spoken-with-oneself, and hence consciousness. Marx's theory does not appear to admit private reflection, introspection, feeling-responses to the outer and inner worlds—in short, any individual's experiences of life not materially visible and connected to an outside world.

As we turn to Mary Baker's account of her years in Chicago, raising her children and working in Chicago's burgeoning factories, we might keep in mind Marx's observations about the formation of consciousness, and his instructions for studying the relationship of consciousness to economic and social structures. "We set out from real, active men, and on the basis of their real life process we demonstrate the development of the ideological reflexes and echoes of this life-process" (Marx and Engels 1976, p. 36). We will listen to Mary Baker, and her own words. We will show how her accounting, reflects both her experience and her consciousness.

Mary Baker in Chicago

Mary was very poor those years in Chicago. Her account of the 1920s and the 1930s, spanning her own twenties and thirties, concerns two subjects: work and poverty, and child-bearing and child-rearing.

She describes two jobs she had in Chicago, both assembly-line work in huge factories: one was filling jars with preserves, the other was a line manufacturing radio tubes. Although she had been employed for nearly ten years by the time she moved north, she had never been exposed to factory work before. She had worked on her mother's tenant holding doing agricultural chores and tending the smaller children, from the time she was six or seven years old. Her first paying job outside her home, at age ten, was working for a Chinese man who owned a laundry. Later she sold milk to the neighbor Black women, and soon began waitressing in a nearby town. She would return to waitressing whenever she could throughout her adult life. She had never liked factory work and was relieved when other kinds of work were available. But her first job in Chicago was working at the jelly factory.

The Jelly Factory

One place I was working . . . you know your preserves? Like your strawberries and pineapple and all that? We had a kettle that holds fifty pounds; you got to take it, go fast while it's hot. There's a truck there, with I think two dozen jars, and you don't realize how fast you gotta go, because they tell you, it will harden right in your what-do-you-call-it. But I got on to it. I got $18 a week. But brother I earned it. Many a time I would go home and that arm would be so tired. . . . Fifty pounds is quite a bit . . . to just go fast with.

Well, at that time, you did consider it good pay. [But] $18 is nothing . . . if you work from seven to six. You get half an hour. We worked long hours. Half a day on Saturday.

The Radio Tube Factory

Although the work in the jelly factory was heavy and exhausting, it was not dangerous, and Mary considered it relatively well-paying, especially in comparison to the tiny tips she had saved from waitressing in Mobile, Alabama. The radio tube factory was a dangerous place to work, although she seemed not to have known so until too late. Again, she had been lured by the promise of some education.

First when the TV's and the radios came in, and I was learning. He was going to send me to school, but what happened? . . . I worked there a little while, . . . ooh, I felt rich! To get that money, instead of working for $18, as I was getting here. You have to go out, and punch your card coming back in. It's the overtime that push me up. But you weren't allowed to work but so many hours. Instead of that, you turn your card over, and he puts the marks and pays you those. I had work good there. I found out I was pregnant. And I guessed—then, I guessed. Then we blew gas for making tubes. . . . The gas was there. You have to blow it, to make those, and that inhaled, and it made my . . . and it made me lose my baby.

Instead of vocational training or education, Mary suffered another miscarriage from the toxic gases in the factory. Even her language seems to falter under the weight of the miscarriage; her voice drops, and there are long pauses in the narrative. We hear the depth of the suffering, though it is not translated into political rage.

Work Environment

Marx argues that the necessary, although probably not sufficient, condition for the first appearance of working class consciousness is widespread factory work. Not only are workers brought together in very close physical proximity for most of their waking hours—often twelve hours a day, six days a week, doing the same repetitive, unskilled tasks that the people right next to them do—but also, factory work creates dense urban environments. Factory workers and their families live in tightly-crowded neighborhoods, often several people to a room. Social life is in neighborhood taverns, spilling onto the streets and porches of what will soon become a slum. At work, home, and play, urban proletarians are surrounded by people in exactly the same situation. They are poor, oppressed, propertyless, and dependent upon unpredictable wage-labor for their very survival. Marx suggests that ultimately they come to recognize a common oppressor and begin to feel, to know, and to articulate a common identity as workers.

But with the development of industry the proletariat not only increases in number; it becomes concentrated in greater masses, its strength grows, and it feels that strength more. The various interests and conditions of life within the ranks of the proletariat are more and more equalized, in proportion as machinery obliterates all distinctions of labour, and nearly everywhere reduces wages to the same low level. Thereupon the workers begin to form combinations [Trade Unions] against the bourgeois; they club together in order to keep up the rate of wages; they found permanent associations in order to make provision beforehand for these occasional revolts.

[Marx and Engels 1976, pp. 492–493]

An exterior-based identity or social consciousness would seem to be virtually over-determined by such an accumulation of socioeconomic factors.

To be certain that we understand the epochal shift this represents, Marx reminds us of peasants, similarly poor and oppressed. But their work is within the framework of a single tenant farm, and their co-workers are limited generally to members of their own household. Other such poor peasants are essentially competitors. Group consciousness can reach only to the limits of the household, the tenant holding. It is extremely unlikely peasants will develop any broadly shared sense of their own condition, the basis of a shared identity. In fact, Marx insists in the *Eighteenth Brumaire*, there is no such thing as peasant class consciousness.

The small peasants form a vast mass, the members of which live in similar conditions, but without entering into manifold relations with one another. Their mode of production isolates them from one another, instead of bringing them into mutual intercourse. The isolation is increased by France's bad means of communication and by the poverty of the peasants. . . . In this way, the great mass of the French nation is formed by simple addition of homologous magnitudes, much as potatoes in a sack form a sackful of potatoes.

[Marx 1979, p. 187]

Mary's stories suggest that, although women formed a significant part of the work force of both factories, they were divided by language and ethnicity. Necessary communication was apparently so simple it could be signed. And although we have no direct evidence, it might be reasonable to infer that management was quite happy not to have other kinds of conversation, social or political, underway. As Marx observed in the great European industrial centers of Paris, Brussels, and Manchester, the linguistic and ethnic diversity of factory workers sharply inhibits the formation of any sense of community, shared oppression, or common identity.

At work you didn't have friends?

No, not with Italians, the Polish, there. Couldn't understand one another. Try to motion all of it. And when you go there, you don't . . . at lunch time . . . most of the time I just grab something and go back to my work, that had to be out. You know, you get orders.

. . . That's right. You go fast, because it jells. You do, you lose your whole can. Bawl you out, too. They give you those foreign people and you try to talk with them. I don't want to talk with someone. I had enough to try and show them there! I don't want to have them for neighbors! Especially the Italians.

Within the factory, ethnicity was used to accentuate divisions between foremen and line workers such as Mary. Apparently she had no thought of righting any such "unfair" labor practice as she describes here, although her tone of voice echoed her old rage.

Were there lots of women working there?

They were working down on the first floor, packing and shipping. Most of them were Italians there. I was the only German there. That's the time I told you about that woman, who was going around with the boss, and I was doing her work, and my work too. And she getting paid just to talk around with him! And I got to do double work!

With a very quick sketch, Mary paints a picture of a good deal of violence, in her mind all related to conflicts among the several immigrant groups. The Italians seemed, to her, to be the most difficult to get along with. In other places she describes her ease with Greeks, Blacks and Irish. But not the Italians.

Tricky there. There is different kinds of Italians there, some of them would just as soon stick you with a knife. They always carried knives.

The women too?

Yes! The knives were all in there, colored people too. There were some colored people there too. You were mixed in there.

. . . They don't believe in it [a union] there. When I got to being a waitress, I tried to form one; I didn't last on that one either . . . in Chicago. But it didn't last long because it was in a neighborhood too mixed up, and I knew how to wait on tables, because I learnt it down in Mobile, you see.

The Irish women were willing to work for lower wages. Mary is still angry, and her face still flushes, sixty years later, when she recalls returning to her work blowing radio tubes after a miscarriage induced by inhalation of the poisonous gas:

So, all right, and I had to lose again, a few days. The doctor checked me; when I come back they had a boatload of them Irish women, from over there, and they cut us half. . . . We were getting eighty cents an hour; they cut us to forty cents. That's all he was paying them. So, brother, that was hard! After we learned! They are learning, and we already experienced! We still had to work just like they did.

Did anybody ever try to organize a union?

Most of them were foreigners, and they just went grabbing
for a job. They didn't need to worry about the union. . . .
Yes, I was the first. . . . When I was even a waitress, I did
that.

Life in the factory, its conflict, squalor, force, and violence, reflected social life outside the factory walls. Violence
is the key word.

Anything, just to get a job. The worst of it was, when you get
your envelope, your money is in the envelope. You had to put
it, hold your hands in your pocket, because they would hit
you and take it away from you. Oh, Chicago! Gangland
there. Brr . . . When I think about all the things I have seen.
When I went to church, even in the morning he had a force
there. Church was right across the street from there. I heard
the guns shoot, but then, I am so in worry with my children,
I didn't pay attention to it. They killed that guy right there,
and I was going into the church. But you dasn't look. Because I was always told: don't look, because they just as
soon kill you as . . . So I just went to the church and prayed.
There in the paper was a body killed, and took their money.

Again I asked her, wondering what gave her the strength to
go on under such conditions.

Did you have any women friends?

You didn't have no time for no women friends. The only one
I had is the sister-in-law, and she didn't care. She was just
. . . oh, I don't know, she had ways she could get around her
husband, drink with him, and I didn't. She's still alive too,
but I'm five years older than her. A lot of times I'd be trying
to sleep, and they had the music on, dancing. Oh boy. But I
couldn't say nothing.

She reflected on having come to Chicago. The difficulty
was not the poverty, not the hard work, but that there was

no way to make a garden, and that she had to live on a third
or fourth floor. And it was so very difficult with two small
children.

> Chicago. I hated it. Been there twenty-five years too. I still
> hate it. My son's there fifty years or more now. No, it was too
> much excitement going on! They bring bodies from Califor-
> nia and put them in somebody's car in Chicago. Boy, I'm tell-
> ing you, you read all kinds of things in the paper. I thought,
> it's terrible! I said to him, "Well, why in the dickens are you
> coming here to Chicago? We're better off down south," I
> said. "At least you can make a garden, but what I got here?
> Upstairs, three, four floors up, drag the kids there, drag one
> at a time, drag the other one.

Political Consciousness

Mary describes in passionate detail what scholars have told
us were the very blood and bones of urban politics in the
years between the two world wars: wage gangs, ethnic conflict, immigrants, sweat shops, dangerous working conditions, and establishing workman's compensation for work-
induced injury. Yet, Mary never considered these issues to
be political problems, disposing her to resolve them through
politics. Nor did she think *she* might have an impact on
correcting these problems in her city. Furthermore, she
seemed to have no information about national political life.
In the following excerpt, she paused a long time, then
fumbled for Roosevelt's name, and then it was not accurate.
She did not know what the New Deal was, when I asked
directly. There simply is not a shred of evidence that she
had any shared sense of herself as a worker, as a factory
worker, as a woman worker. Once she describes herself as
"the only German," but the "only" is probably as significant
as the "German." When I asked her about friends, she men-
tions only her sister-in-law. Her recollection of the Great
Depression in 1929 is that she was working good just before

it, earning $60 a week making the life-endangering radio tubes.

Those are the days, honey, I don't mean maybe! There was good meat and everything, but you couldn't touch it. It was as high as it is now, but . . .

Was that during the Depression, Mary?

Yes, during the thirties. Poor what's his name . . . Roosevelt? When the banks were closed. . . . Wait a minute . . .

That would be later . . .

Yeah. That's later. No, it was somebody else there.

Hoover was President.

Hoover. That's it. He went and took the . . . he had the . . . England there, but let us starve there. As far as Roosevelt, well, that guy was bad enough too.

Do you remember 1929, when the stock market fell?

Yeah. But I was working *good*, just before that! I was getting then sixty dollars a week!

Work, Mary's direct relationship to the economic system, occupied virtually all of her waking hours. It was *the* social role which structured her concrete, material existence. Yet there are no traces of work consciousness, or of providing the kernel of a larger social consciousness. And so, we are not really surprised, to find Mary uninformed about conventionally-understood political life, disinterested in political activity, and—according to those conventional definitions of life political—non-political herself. Others have argued ably that this reflects a marked male bias in our very conceptions of political life and political activity, disallowing much of what women do in their own families and communities as genuinely political. That line of argument is not usefully applied in this case. I wish instead to move in another direction; to ask: Why does work sometimes fail to produce any dimension of social identity and eventually political identity and activity?

The Dual Role: Worker and Mother

Mary Baker was barely able to discuss her work in Chicago at all, as a separate phenomenon. In the midst of a sentence she would shift her attention to her children, to the difficulties of finding adequate care for them, suitable housing, sufficient food, and always, fresh air. It is as if her very sentence structure reflected the course of her conscious attention while at work pouring jelly or blowing radio tubes; her mind was with her children. Even now, sixty years later, as she tries to describe her actual work day, her very speech flows into a description of her worries as the mother of two young children. Here are just two of many possible examples:

> Jelly and stuff, there. Blackberry, raspberry, they made it. . . . And I had to do the big twenty-five pound can, pour it fast there. I mean, you gotta go! Then you seal it, and somebody there on that machine would take it and stamp it. Then it goes in the box. And down it goes. I worked there about two years. Meantime, while I was working, as you are speaking about, the children had diptheria. They had to be sent south, because Chicago did not agree with them. . . .
> Most of them were Italians there. I was the only German there. That's the time I told you about that woman, who was going around with the boss, and I was doing her work and my work too. And she getting paid just to talk around with him! And I got to do double work! So this day I didn't feel good, cause the children, somehow, were not up to [unclear]. You change three cars there, you tired, pushing, pulling the crowd there. I was pushing Mary [her daughter] there, and I

said, Tommy [her son], push Mary, keep going. And then I
have to hang on there, until finally, here's a man to help me
push them. That's how we went there, three cars. Have to
change three times.

Mary worked to support her children. Her entire conception of work, her experience of it, her recollection of it, and
her description of it are all through the lens of being the
mother of Thomas and Mary. Travel to and from work is told
as a part of a three-car (street car) journey to take the children to the nursery the Sisters ran on the other side of
Chicago.

I took them to a nursery where the Sisters were. That's why
I had to take three cars there: one went to where the nursery
was, then from there I had to change to another line, and
then the other one would take me to work.

How old were they?

Well, they were not ready for school . . . Little. Well, Thomas
went to kindergarten, he couldn't then, cause I had to work.

Did you have to pay to have them in nursery school?

Yes, you do. The Sisters do charge. But I think it was twenty-
five cents a child, fifty cents a day. But you had to get them
out of there at six pm. I told her, by the time I get the bus, I
may be a little late, cause the crowds. So, all right, fifteen
minutes, but no more. Boy, you should see how we had to
. . . I just pray . . . but boy, I just don't know why I'm blessed
like this.

Wages are evaluated by the quality of food she could provide
for the two young children. Work-induced poisoning resulting in a serious miscarriage is conceptualized as a lost
child, with no shadow of thought about being able to return
to her former job at the same pay or how she might receive
compensation or a benefit through disability insurance.

The only mention of housing is in terms of needing to leave the tenement to take the children out for fresh air and exercise every day.

Mostly lived on the north side. I lived close to the Loop. On Erie Street. We used to walk, it was about half a mile to the Loop. The kids, I would take them, window shopping. Then we would walk back home, cause we had light housekeeping. I figured they need the air. I did too. Get the air, see. I wouldn't take them to park; when you take em to park, they want all kinds of stuff to eat, and I figured, well, this is not good. Cause then they don't eat their meals. So this way I make them walk, get their exercise; I remember poor Thomas would say, 'Mama, my legs hurt.' He had a little tricycle, see. 'Don't give up,' I said, 'the worst thing in the world if you get a cripple in your leg.' So, I take him and push him. Then I go back of him, making him laugh and thinking I'm pushing him. But he is peddling, he's peddling and he's screaming, 'It's so hard.' 'I do know, Son, I do; I went through it myself. Listen to Mama,' I says.

They have to sit down there, and they have a few toys, and they don't get exercise that way. See, so on Saturday and Sunday, I got a tricycle. Some man there who knew my husband, he brought it to me. Worked in the store. He got it and brought it there to us. That's how we got it. So on Saturday and Sunday and on evenings, I would take 'em out; that's how it was, exercise.

Even the children's father is invisible in her story, and I did not realize she had ever traced him in Chicago, until I asked directly. "Oh, yes . . . working, but he was drinking it up," she said. "He would work one or two days, and then he wouldn't work."

So you were paying for the rent and the nursery. Were you paying for food too?

How much do I have left. I had to have carfare too. But the food wasn't like it was today. Well, the Sisters would give you

140

a loaf of bread. And I think I used magarine instead of but-
ter. And I get a little oatmeal, or I get farina or something
there. That's what we did. . . . Or an egg. I don't remember
that we got any meat there.

[the house where we lived] that was damp there. Low, and it
had no basement. We all caught pneumonia there, again. It
was damp, very damp. Very damp there. So the three of us
got down again with it. That's when the measles come,
chickenpox, so I had to stay home again. Nobody there to
take care of anybody.

What would happen, when you'd get sick and stay home?

Well, somehow or 'nother, I got another [inaudible]. If I had
an egg or something, I'd stretch it with, make it with something, fill in your stomach. As long as I get milk for them, I
always figured you could manage, with milk and slice of
bread. In fact I got bread from the Sisters, I told you, or finally after a while, Thomas. I take him there where they
give you the bread, the bakery you know, if you go early in
the morning, they give it to you. Cause they send it to the
Sisters anyway. So they give it. Make either bread pudding
or something. Just anything I could think of, that's all.

    Mary's relationship to the economy is not the dominant
source of her identity; her relationship with her children is.
There is a strong dimension of social role to the mother/
child relationship, which we call "gender." And this we
would consider an exterior-based identity or consciousness.
It is tempting to suggest, here, that the extent to which the
mother/child relationship is an intimate one between two
persons, it will resonate with and reflect interiority. It might
be experienced, as Mary has, as an unavoidable imperative
arising within her very sense of herself. Overwhelmed by
the stresses and marginality of her life, I once asked her,
"Mary, how did you manage to do all this?" And she replied
without a second thought: "My mother made me do it." She
then reflected on how her mother had told her stories, over

and over, when she was a very little girl, about her birth in Germany, her arrival as a "veiled child" and all that portended, her grandmother's role in her actual survival as an infant, and so on. It is a powerful birth story rooting her in a line of female ancestors and oral tradition. An interior sense of self can also be nourished by impressive dreams, a chance poem, the habit of introspection.

In summary, then, work may not be the most salient category of identity, particularly for women burdened with the double responsibilities of work and child care. Our attention has focused on the significance of gender, in this essay; but we would do well to remember that interior sources of identity may be critically important for understanding the development of consciousness for both women and men. Ironically, it has long been assumed, that interiority is a normal consequence of economic privilege, a result of education, culture, and the gifts attendant to a spacious life. But Mary Baker's story, and undoubtedly the stories of many like her, reminds us that interiority, self-reflection, and personal maturation are not only possible for the poor and uneducated but, more importantly, they can be the overwhelming and dominant forces shaping their lives.

Last Questions

According to conventional definitions, women participate less frequently than men in political life, are less likely to be well informed about politics, and are less likely to have well-articulated political identities. Yet paradoxically, according to Marxian analyses, the significant factors contributing to political consciousness and ultimately political and even revolutionary activity among working class people are as omnipresent in women's lives as in those of men.

We have listened to a poor woman describe her life in

Chicago in the 1920s and 1930s, a time of intense political turmoil in a tumultuous city seething with ethnic conflict, competing gangs, and articulate anarchist and communist groups battling armed cadres of police and guardsmen. This entire period of Mary Baker's life was a time of very hard work and continuous poverty; yet Mary describes those two decades of virtually complete social and economic marginality, almost exclusively, as the years during which she bore, raised and educated her children. What we have heard is that Mary's very identity as the mother of Thomas and Mary was so strong that it became the lens through which she perceived and experienced every other aspect of her life: her work in the factories, her struggle for housing, her marriage to her husband, her relationships in the community, her very existence. "Mother," including both the social role and the deep sense of her own self, subsumes, it seems, the economic and social dimensions of consciousness.

That may indicate that the consciousness of women develops in more complex ways than that of men, because so many women are mothers as well as laborers in the market economy. A theory that adequately explains both men's and women's processes of consciousness must allow for different processes. If Marx's theory is adequate for men, it appears to be too simple for women. It has relied too heavily on one variable, the objective structures associated with factory work, and ignored another, child-raising. If men's identities were as fully shaped by fatherhood as women's are by motherhood, men would not fit Marx's theory either. But, men, in general, do not define themselves through relationships as women tend to do, and so consciousness for men may be more compatible with Marxian theory.

Interestingly, Mary's story instructs us that gender, itself, is a problematic category. For if Mary's life in Chicago were in fact "simply" a question of gender role, then Mary's narrative should reflect a more important sense of herself as wife; since the role of wife, too, is central to the definitions of a woman's role in our culture. Although Mary ascribes her difficulties in many places throughout her entire narrative to alcoholic husbands, she very rarely even acknowledges her marital relationships or herself as wife.

143

Is "mother" a social role in some ways comparable to occupation, such that we might be able to stretch Marx's categories to include (as Marx occasionally suggests we do, and as contemporary feminist socialists often do) reproductive within productive tasks? That would allow us to maintain, with Marx, that consciousness is fundamentally derivative, a reflection of exterior institutions, structure, and relationships. It also allows us to restrict ourselves to the "concrete," definite individuals behaving in socially observable and sensuous acts—"real," as Marx labels it.

Mary knows herself as "mother of Thomas and Mary." "Mother" is assuredly both role and institution, as Rich and many others have pointed out. In addition, though, "mother" is also the core interior image of Mary's personal identity. It is "mother" who works in the jelly factories; it is "mother" who grabs her pay envelope against the shoot-out on the street; it is "mother" who tells the story of the Chicago years; it is "mother" who reflects back on the continuity between her life and her mother's life; it is "mother" who seeks the wandering father of her children; it is "mother" who suffers one miscarriage in Union Station and another in the radio tube factory.

It may seem we are a long way from Marx and Mary. But what first led Marx into social and historical analysis was his interest in religious consciousness, and its relationship to citizenship as full membership in civil society in his mid-nineteenth-century Germany. He quickly chose one side of that intellectual tension, the perceptual and methodological side—articulated by science and favoring observable phenomena—material, sensuous, and real data. Religious consciousness—the experience and articulation of an interior identity which can be used to elaborate a meaningful social environment—then had to be "read backwards" as derivative of certain social and economic formations peculiar to a particular state of historical development. Mary's story reminds us of the part Marx left behind—people's subjective experiences of social life, interiority, and the creation of image, symbol, and meaning. Our difficulty, in this essay—weaving together both the exterior and interior accounts to enrich and inform each other—is a measure of our own boundedness in time and space, of our own culture's ideology about objectivity, knowledge, and reality. Marx left Mary behind, and explained the easy part.

Notes

"Marx and Mary: The Individual, Identity, and the Development of Social Conciousness," by Penny Gill, first appeared in the *Southern Humanities Review* 17, no. 2 (Spring 1983): 148–189 (copyright 1983 by Auburn University).

I am very grateful to Eva Hooker, CSC, and Kay Warren for their careful critiques of an earlier version of this essay. There is no way to thank Mary Baker (a pseudonym) sufficiently for her generosity in telling me her story.

1. This and all subsequent quotations are taken from a series of conversations with Mary Baker, taped by the author in 1976 and 1977.

References

Marx, Karl. 1972. "For a Ruthless Criticism of Everything Existing." In Robert C. Tucker, ed. *The Marx-Engels Reader*. Translated by Ronald Rogowski. New York: Norton.

Marx, Karl. 1977. "Preface to the Critique of Political Economy." *Karl Marx: Selected Writings*. Translated by David McLellan. Oxford: Oxford University Press.

Marx, Karl. 1979. *The Eighteenth Brunaire of Louis Bonaparte. Marx, Engels: Collected Works*, vol. 2. New York: International.

Marx, Karl and Frederick Engels. 1976. *The German Ideology*. Part 1. *Marx, Engels: Collected Works*, vol. 5. Translated by W. Lough. New York: International.

Marx, Karl and Frederick Engels. 1976. *Manifesto of the Communist Party. Marx, Engels: Collected Works*, vol. 6. Translated by Samuel Moore. New York: International.

The Dilemma of Polyculturalism
for a Moroccan Woman

by Stephen William Foster

Tangier, Morocco strikes the casual urban geographer as haphazard, an orchestrated disjunction of cultural, economic and linguistic groupings, distributed within an irregular, mosaic pattern of settlement.[1] It is a disjointed agglomeration of heterogeneous neighborhoods held together by the gravitation of the business core and port. A disintegrated approximation of community, it is not held together by a continuity of social networks but by a somewhat abstract notion of local identity. Like an aggregate of puzzle pieces from different boxes, it resists an altogether coherent pattern. In Tangier, one has the impression that no matter how long people from different parts of Morocco or different parts of the world live together, they will continue to speak their own languages and to pursue their own ideas of life. They make partial accommodations to those around them while regarding one another as curiosities to be marvelled at and to be exploited. Partial integration, pervasive ambivalence and persistent diversity are all hallmarks of the city. This complex milieu was the locus of the early experience of the woman whose life history I discuss in this essay. In Tangier, Samira (as I will call her)[2] encountered the ironic and ambiguous cultural counter-currents which have been the legacy of Moroccan political history.

Tangier is an overgrown small town. Its present shape and structure is in part a product of its geographical location—African, Mediterranean, and Atlantic, perched on the edge of Europe. The city's character has also been formed by the episodic presence of Romans, Portuguese, English, Spanish and French. These diverse influences are directly inscribed in the city's architecture and layout. America, too, took a strategic interest in Tangier, given its situation on the Straits of Gibraltar. In each case, that interest was parlayed into an economic advantage of some kind.

The origins of the town are obscured in a mythological past stretching back beyond the Roman period, frequent references being made to Hercules, Antaeus, and Ulysses. One can imagine an original sea-side or bay-side village which grew by slow accretions and was codified and fortified by successive efforts of self-defense. There were Phoenicians and Carthaginians as well as Romans who were, in turn, followed by Vandals, Byzantines and Visigoths. The city was governed by Byzantium when the Arabs arrived in 682 A.D. Soon after that date, the Islamic domination of Tangier became routinized.

In 1906, a conference among European powers occurred in Algeciras, Spain, across the Straits of Gibraltar from Tangier. The resulting treaty gave these countries (including France, Spain, Britain and Germany) considerable economic and political powers in Morocco. Tangier and environs became an International Zone in 1912, about the time that the French Protectorate was imposed on much of the rest of Morocco. The city's international status lasted until the declaration of Moroccan independence in 1956. At that time, the city was integrated into the Sherifian Empire as the Province of Tangier.

The broad social and cultural ramifications of the international administration of the city were and are complex, and their details are beyond the scope of this study.[3] The multi-national colonization of Tangier brought diverse and sometimes conflicting cultural influences. Traditions co-existed but did not blend except uneasily for those born and raised in this polyglot atmosphere.

The city's population increased significantly as a consequence of the International Zone resulting, for the most part, from an influx of Europeans. These diverse segments of the population—dominated by the French and the Spanish—formed national "communities" which were loosely structured social networks. They were only partially differentiated from one another by patterns of daily interaction, although each retained a distinct cultural identity. The colonists built the European quarter adjacent to the old town (*medina*) in order not to disrupt the extant pattern of settlement.

These diverse constituencies and the territory they occupied were governed by an international board, which maintained the political boundaries of the International Zone, sponsored a police force and judiciary, and regulated economic activities. The city experienced considerable economic growth during the International period not only as a result of the European population but also because of its status as a free port. The political, economic, and social climate made for conditions under which Tangier's lurid reputation for intrigue and indulgence was given further impetus. One could find anybody and anything in Tangier, or so it was said. Yet gambling remained illegal, ruling out a major attraction for the prospective tourist population.

Because France dominated much of the remaining Moroccan territory outside the International Zone, the French influence in Tangier became increasingly evident during the International period, although the Spanish presence qualified the French pre-eminence. The German and Austrian population was expelled from Tangier during the First World War. Yet the city's population remained culturally diverse throughout the International period and continued to be so for sometime after Moroccan independence. The Italian, Spanish, French, and American schools were founded early on in the International period, and continued in operation after its close. They continue to operate at present although, unlike in the past, most of their students are Moroccan.

The Place de France is the hub of the city's European quarter. Moving away from this central area with its shops and sidewalk cafes are diverse neighborhood enclaves. The *medina* is composed of tightly packed houses of considerable antiquity. This district also contains the traditional bazaar (*souk*) and is crowned by the *kasbah*, the ancient walled citadel that occupies a promontory above the straits. To the west, the Old Mountain Road winds up into a suburb of tree-shrouded villas, the residences of rich widows, artists, and would-be novelists—expatriates from England, France, Hungary, and America. The shantytowns hang about the periphery of the city and have swollen rapidly with formerly rural peoples. They consist of miserable huts of pressed tin and teem with witchcraft, unemployment and discontent. Extensive tracts of government housing have sprung up in previously unoccupied areas. In some of these live Berber peasants recently migrated from their villages, while others provide housing for the families of Moroccan migrant workers employed for part of each year in European industrial centers (Jelloun 1977). The house of Samira's family is located near the beginning of the Old Mountain Road, a mile or so from the Place de France. In this sparsely populated neighborhood are a few other large homes of Moroccan-middle class families and former *colons*. Nearby is the Spanish cemetery and a shanty-town enclave of country people.

An atypical (Moslem-Jewish) family constellation[4] in concert with polyculturalism, encouraged Samira to question and to revise creatively the traditional Moroccan woman's role.[5] Paradoxically, these same factors made it difficult for her to fashion for herself an alternate position in Moroccan society. The history of Morocco during the generation prior to Samira's birth resulted in a cultural situation that persisted into the 1960s and continues, in an attenuated form, into the present. This essay delineates the dilemmas of polyculturalism that Samira experienced and how she took advantage, as well as became a victim, of these exigencies.

In interpreting and editing Samira's life history, I do not offer anything approaching a "complete" biography. What follows is, instead, a thematic rendering of Samira's discourse about herself placed in the context of her historical situation. Her own recitations stress this mode of contextualization, which I follow in interpretation. By referring to "her historical situation," I do not mean "objective conditions" as such, but her own perceptions and articulation of her circumstances. Interpretation, here, is not a question of giving an "accurate" version of Samira's biography since, as Crapanzano suggests, that would be to mistake the "real" for the "true."[6] In Samira's recitations, as in those of the Moroccan man portrayed by Crapanzano (1980), the real and the true are brought together under a single set of terms. Samira's discourse is a bid for authentication—a rhetorical event, an occasion both for articulating herself and for constructing her world. [7] My interpretation goes forward on the basis of that understanding of Samira's words and attempts to impart something of the experience intimated or insinuated by what she has to say.

Samira's father, Abdellah, was born in Algiers and came to Morocco as a young man when France administered both Algeria and Morocco. His grandfather was the Dey of Algiers. Ester, Samira's mother, was born near Fez in a town called Sefrou, nestled in the foothills of the Middle Atlas mountains. Ester's father became an important figure in the Jewish community of Salé. Samira's parents met in Rabat, where Samira was born ten years after they were married. Samira's mother did not want to have children. She worried that in a Moslem country their lives would be made difficult by her Jewish background.

Abdellah had had five sons and a daughter by his first wife. [8] His sons often came to visit their father. Since Ester had no children of her own, she played with the boys and mothered them. But when she became pregnant, personal objects began to disappear which could be used to cast spells against her to abort her pregnancy or to cause a difficult birth. Witchcraft was probably being performed by Abdellah's first wife, who saw offspring from her husband's other marriage as a threat to her and her household. It was a difficult pregnancy and labor went on for forty-eight hours. Ester told her daughter that during the birth, she could hear the other children knocking on the door, asking if the spells had worked, if Ester had died. [9] Samira was born in 1955 in Rabat, one year before the declaration of Moroccan independence. Two brothers followed, one born in 1960, the other in 1963.

Early photographs often show Samira with her father, attending public events and state dinners with him. As a toddler, she became the "darling" of the Tangier police force with which, as a high government official in the city, Abdellah worked closely. Home movies taken after the birth of her older brother show Samira competing keenly for center stage and for the lion's share of her father's affections. While the polycultural dimension of Samira's experience began at home with Jewish mothering and Moslem fathering, Samira's father's public visibility and partial Europeanization elaborated the diversity of cultural references which Samira encountered. Working as part of the Protectorate bureaucracy in Rabat until the French brought the Moroccan monarch out of exile in 1956, then in the small town of Souk el Arba before being transferred to Tangier in 1957, Abdellah probably had as many contacts in the European community as with Moroccans during much of Samira's early years. The polycultural social ecology of Tangier in which Abdellah participated, combined with the dominant authoritative influence of the father mandated in Moroccan kinship ideology were important factors leading to Samira's own polycultural identification. In the family context at least, some cultural elements were stressed over others. Moslem identity seems to have gained some ascen-

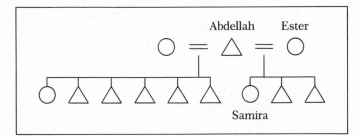

FIGURE I. FAMILY CONSTELLATION [10]

dency. Despite Abdellah's responsibilities for the households of his two wives, he resided exclusively with Samira's mother and her children. Samira's father was more of a constant presence for her than is usually the case for a female child in Moroccan families. I will suggest that this factor helps to explain her self-identification as Moslem.

Near the home of Samira's family was an Anglican church where Sunday school was held every week.

> I used to play outside in the street. One day, I walked into the Sunday school. I started going there secretly when I was three. I was just dragged there by the rest of the kids in the neighborhood. I saved my 10 francs and gave them every Sunday for tithing. Six months later, I came home and told my parents that I wanted to celebrate Christmas. My parents didn't know exactly what to make of it. [11]

They did allow Samira to have her Christmas celebration, and by then she was speaking English as well as French and Moroccan Arabic. She learned street Spanish from the Tetouani children she met outside at play. Her parents enrolled her in the British nursery school near their home and later, when she reached the age of five, in the American School. [12] The summer prior to her enrollment in the American School, her family spent in France, leaving Abdellah in Tangier.

> We spent the whole summer speaking French with Jewish friends of my mother. We were put under the pressure of meeting far-away relatives and friends who were Jewish. I went around saying I was Jewish too, since we wanted to be accepted.

Once she began going to the American School of Tangier, she remained there until she received her high school diploma. In the early years, Samira had to confront the tension between conformity and the cultural cross-currents of her background.

I had more expensive clothes than the Moroccans and a more European style of clothing than they did. But I didn't have casual, colorful clothes like the Americans had. That didn't help me to fit in with the Moroccans or with the Americans.

The food she brought with her to school was scrutinized by her classmates. When the Moroccan children saw the pistachio-filled dates which her mother had given her for her morning snack, they threw them on the ground shouting, "Jewish food! Jewish food!"

The Moroccan kids wouldn't associate with me because my mother was Jewish. The American kids wouldn't associate with me because I was Moroccan, and it wasn't their habit to befriend Moroccans. I found it very hard to explain to them that I had brothers who did not live at my house, but who were my father's other wife's children. It was an embarrassing situation, and I started lying about it.

Arabic class was the most trying period in her daily routine. Samira did not speak the Tangier dialect because her father spoke the Algerian dialect to them at home and her mother was from further south in Morocco. She also used many French vocabulary words when she spoke, since that was the mixture spoken at home. She was familiar with many idioms and colloquial usages. Her oral recitations in class were yet another source of her classmates' ridicule and of her distinctiveness.

The Arabic teacher was appointed by the Moroccan government to the American School. The school was not high in the Moroccan government's priorities, so the teacher was not closely monitored. He knew that Samira's father was a public figure and apparently used the classroom as an opportunity to question her about him.

"Is your mother Jewish?" he asked me. "Yes." "Did she become a Moslem?" "No." "So that means you're a Jew by Jewish law. Does your father pray?" "No." "He doesn't pray?" This would go on throughout the class.

As she grew older, the "rumblings" in the Middle East, as she calls them, began in earnest. Seventh and eighth grade were very political years in her recollections. Her mother's family had gone to Israel. Her mother's brothers were in the Israeli army, and her mother was often distraught. At the same time, said Samira:

> My father was fighting to keep my head where his was at politically. He wanted me to be definitely Arab and not to have Zionist tendencies, so he'd fill my head with all this nationalism talk. Then my mother would fill me with this teary, heartbreaking talk about her brothers and the Arabs who were killing them. I'd go to school, and I wanted to prove that I was like everybody else. Every time I opened my mouth, the teacher would tell me to shut up because my mother was Jewish and I didn't have the right to say anything.

Having identified herself as Moslem in the course of informal conversation, Samira once provoked me to challenge her with the statement: "But the children of a Jewish woman are Jews." Samira's indignant response followed immediately: "I am a Moslem!" This presentation of her identity was elaborated and given context in the following exchange among a number of persons including myself. We were talking with Samira specifically about her own family.

> Is it true that in Morocco, a Jewish woman must convert to Islam in order to marry a Moslem man?

> No. Not by the law in Morocco. But if she doesn't convert, there will be no inheritance for her. Marriage is all about inheritance. [13]

> But your mother never converted?

No, she didn't. She's racist (regarding Moslems), don't you think? And prideful. She's a Moroccan Jew. My brothers and I are very definite about Israel. If she goes there, she knows we'll never talk to her again. When she married my father, her family had the death ceremony (in Hebrew, the *kezazah*) for her.

She became a real *persona non grata* for them.

Yes.

Would her siblings talk with her now?

They're in Israel.

Yes, but if they weren't so far apart?

I don't think that they would talk with her.

Are the children of a Jewish woman Jews.

In a Moslem country, the children of a Moslem man are Moslems.

Samira is clear about how she regards her Moslem-Jewish background. Neither her father nor her mother is outwardly a religious person. Samira, in the above exchange, uses religious identification to situate herself relative to each of her parents. Her mother appears to have spoken little with Samira about being a Jew, or Samira disavows what her mother may have tried to teach her. This under-rating of her Jewish background is consistent with Samira's recollection of her father's attitude to Islam and how it affected her orientation.

I was very serious about religion [at the age of twelve], and I wanted to memorize the *Koran*. My father helped me along. The way he'd do it was to tell me a story and then tell me a verse [*sura*]—a prayer built into the story. Then we'd memorize it. He'd repeat it, and I'd repeat it after him. I even use to pray, especially in sixth and seventh grade, five times a day. I use to fast [during Ramadan]. I've never been in a mosque. My father has been in a mosque once or twice. My father doesn't pray, he just observes Ramadan. He's not a religious man. He's into religion as an identity thing. He says he's a Moslem because it's a way of living, his philosophy of life. He gets very upset if you have any pretenses of being anything other than Moslem.

Samira's religious enthusiasm waned as she grew older, but her description of her father's regard for Islam also serves for Samira herself. On the other hand, she situates her mother's attitudes not only in terms of Judaism but also in terms of Moroccan folk beliefs.

All the old women who hung around the house, the gardener and everybody, were always telling me stories about genies and supernatural powers. I was curious about these things. But they really drove it too far. It tormented me. They told me about Aisha Qandisha (a female demon with goat's feet). They were always scared somebody would put the evil eye on me because I was such a special child. Whenever we'd go to a party and I'd have an extra piece of cake, or I'd drink too much coke and I'd come home sick, my mother would be sure that it was the evil eye. She'd take her precautions and go through the ritual that would protect me, where you put incense in a brazier. It heats up and makes a bubble—an eye—and then it pops and they pass you over it. They were always putting things around my neck, hands of Fatima, quotations from the *Koran* written on little pieces of paper (*hjuba*) pinned to my underwear. The evil eye is not particularly Jewish or Christian or Moslem. It's North African, present in all these religious groups; you find it everywhere. I don't think it's a trend with ignorant people. Of course, my mother would never put a cross on me.

At this point I asked her, "What did they think of you going to church and celebrating Christmas?" She replied:

They didn't take it seriously. My father would make fun of me, saying, "My daughter comes home singing songs about Mary and Jesus!" He thought it was funny, which really upset me at the time. I did it, I think, because there really was no religious foundation at our house. We had a Moslem life style in that we never ate pork or had wine. My father fasted during Ramadan; the children didn't. Here I am at school with all these kids who pray and go to the mosque or the synagogue or to church. I wanted to fit in somewhere, it didn't matter where.

Samira seems to have learned little about her parents' courtship and marriage. Their marriage could be legitimized since a union between a Moslem man and Jewish woman is recognized by custom and allowed by Moroccan (Malikite) law. Their marriage was duly registered with the local officials. [14] Talking about her mother, Samira says,:

I really don't know the details of how she met my father or how they got married. All I know is that he is twenty years her senior and that her father was some sort of high official in the Jewish community in Salé.

As Samira mentioned, her mother's family performed the *kezazah* upon their daughter's marriage to Abdellah. This rite declares the severence of a member who marries someone seen by the family as an inappropriate spouse. It is a public statement of the family's disapproval and their decision to disavow kinship with and recognition of one of its members. Samira talked about her mother's family at some length:

My mother's father was born in Fez. He married a woman from Sefrou. She died in childbirth with my mother. My grandfather remarried after that, had eleven other children and moved to Salé. My mother grew up very, very spoiled. She had a step-mother, an aunt, and a lot of brothers and sisters. Although she was older than they were, they all took care of her. She told me that in her adolescent years in Salé, there was a sort of outdoor fair every Saturday night. She'd go with all her girl friends. Usually, the girls would dance together. Sometimes, they'd dance with the boys. They would dance the tango or the polka. Every week, she would have a new dress to go to the fair. That's one of her fondest memories. Apparently, she was very, very beautiful when she was young. She was tall. She was rare. She had long hair. She had good teeth. She had good skin.

Samira has a strong and somewhat critical opinion of her mother's character which is expressed in the next passage:

My mother is more jingoistic than my father. She is by character a sort of martyr. She's a Jewish mother in that she loves giving up things for other people. She loves wallowing in that sacrifice. She looks down on Moslems and Arabs. It's not blatant but it's there. She doesn't trust them in the street. She doesn't really want me to have any connections with Moroccans. She's very wary of them. It's justified because she gets attacked by them a lot. The Moslem women will invite her to their parties, but they will exclude her in other ways. She has managed some solid friendships with some Moslem women.

Yet Samira also recognizes that she made her mother's relationship with her difficult on frequent occasions, particularly during her fiery adolescence.

I have put my mother through some very, very difficult times. I have attacked her very, very violently many times. It started early when she'd scold me and I'd kick her. And she'd scold me and I'd bite her, scratch her. I was not at all afraid of her. She's very lenient in her punishments. She forgives very easily. She forgets when she gets mad at you. She forgets ten minutes later. She was devoted to me in a way that overlooked anything I did. She spent all her life sewing clothes for me. Clothes that I didn't ask for, but making sure that I had the nicest things, that I had a dress for every party. She spent her life going to antique sales and picking out little pieces and putting costumes together for me, making special little foods for me, taking very, very good care. That is something that I have never really thanked her for.

Abdellah lived in urban North Africa his entire life and had frequent contact with non-Moslems, formally and informally, Jews not the least among them. Samira delineates his style of approach and attitude towards Jews at some length:

> I don't know if his ties with the Jewish community grew out of knowing my mother, but I have the feeling that they existed before he met my mother. He's always had a painting of rabbis saying their prayers in a mosque. Apparently in Algeria, synagogues were often old mosques which were no longer in use. He is very fond of the Jewish people. It's something that although my mother's a Jew, she doesn't have. It's that Jewish mother thing, that body language, that mixture of French with Yiddish words or Arabic with Yiddish words. A kind of earthy vitality. Jews, in Morocco and Algeria anyway, like to have a nice spread for dinner. He likes their love of life, their love of food, their love of good things. As far as he's concerned, our religions are not very far away from each other. He doesn't believe in any sort of messiah. He makes jokes about it all the time. But the life-styles are not so different. He knows that religion for Moslems and Jews in North Africa is a way of life that's very similar. Maybe that's what gave him tendencies to marry a Jewish woman, because he was looking at that rather than at other things.

Samira's recitations are sprinkled generously with such speculations about the context of her and her parents' experience. As she recounts and gives shape to her life history, she again and again contends with diverse and contrasting cultural elements—or rather elements that she knows others understand as being in opposition. She attempts (struggles) in her speculations to harmonize and integrate them. The Moslem-Jewish milieu of her family may be seen as prototype and paradigm for many of the other situations she encountered—social, moral, religious, and academic. From this perspective, polycultural Tangier was merely the biculturalism of her family on a larger scale. In her attempts to "marry" diverse elements, to fashion them into a coherent whole, her identity as a Moslem remained a dominant theme during her adolescence, and I think indicates the primary significance of her father's influence.

Samira had few close friends until she entered her high school years. There was an American girl whose Mormon parents had come to work in Morocco (she later named her daughter after Samira). At home, the Berber maid washed Samira's hair for her, helped her to dress, straightened her room, and provided informal, gossipy companionship. The house was often filled with her mother's friends or with Europeans whom her father had come to know through his business connections. Abdellah's elder sons (Samira's half-brothers) were intermittently present to have dinner with their father. The house was a cultural pastiche as was the external urban environment. Samira acknowledges that she was readily tolerated and indulged by her family. Before the birth of her younger brothers, her father's sons were her frequent playmates. As she entered her high school years, Samira developed a diversified, flexible, heterogeneous social style partly in response to these varied social contacts. She enjoyed her family and a lively social life. Her interactions typically involved frequent code switching, just as talking with other Tangerines invariably involved switching from language to language, not just in speaking with one person then the next, but even switching in mid-sentence, depending upon the linguistic competence of those interacting, as well as on the vocabulary appropriate for the topic at hand.

Samira was recognized by relatives and family friends alike as a poised and articulate young woman, self-assured and quick-witted, though at times somewhat contrary. She could be counted on to do the unexpected. She remained social and family-oriented. Time out from the constant testing of her social adaptability came when Abdellah took his family—Ester and their children—to his brother's farm. Abdellah's brother's family was rather more culturally homogeneous than Samira's own and fairly "traditional" by Tangier standards—Moslem, kinship-centered, agrarian, self-possessed. Samira saw them as demanding considerably more conformity of her cousin Lillia than was demanded of her by her own parents.

As a teenager, the constant testing of her identity continued, particularly in the public domain and at the American School. Among her family's friends, whatever their cultural affiliations, she seems to have been expected to be charming, exotic. She dressed in a way that reflected her unique status on the social terrain, a bit stylish, a bit eccentric, a bit Euro-American, making no concession to traditional women's garb, much less the veil (*hezaam*). Her casual way of comporting herself, particularly influenced by her time at the American School, caused her some pains when she appeared on the boulevard. Moroccan men are opinionated about how "their" women act and appear in public. "Their" women include any woman identifiably Moroccan. When Samira was so identified (and she was not always), she suffered the sanctions of the Moroccan men to whom she must have appeared anomalous, desirable, and less than respectable. At times, they would have some trouble placing her ethnically and would question her about her identity. These encounters became something of a routine as she got older, making it difficult for her to be comfortable in her own "home town," and premising a certain measure of hostility on her part against those who questioned her.

While the American School was not a less comfortable social setting than others, it provided her with a certain amount of shelter (as did being at home) from the derision and intrusive intimidation she frequently encountered in public and a partial escape from the implied pressures to conform to "tradition." To a large degree, being at the school complemented the familial setting, for in both, she found legitimacy for her own, hybrid identity which she had synthesized for herself.

Samira continued to go to parties and social gatherings with and without her father. For eight years, she took piano, dance and riding lessons. On one of her birthdays, a teacher at the American School gave her a copy of *Alice in Wonderland*. She took part in school plays, taking the role of Antigone in *Oedipus Rex*. When the production was over, she went home and wrote her own version of the play. She began reading Sophocles and Euripides. She had had to try on various social roles and cultural identities, one after the other, even as a small child. Now as an adolescent, taking dramatic roles was perhaps an inevitable next step. She took these roles very seriously; for her it was more than merely "playing" a role. About playing Antigone, she says:

> I went up there and I was really demented. I went up there really convinced that I was Antigone, or that I had been Antigone in some other life, or that this was my real identity. I fluctuated between hysteria and tears, it was quite genuine. My mother said that there were two Moroccan women sitting in front of her in the audience, saying, "That girl, she frightens me. I can't look at her face." It put off a lot of people. That's when parents stopped letting their children come over to my house. That's when I stopped being invited to parties.

By all accounts, Samira became something of a maverick, a dissenter, someone who did not buy into any of the culturally standardized styles of being which went on about her. Her political ideas were one aspect of her critical, possibly defensive stance against the world. She had reservations about the Moroccan crown. She says that after her performance in *Oedipus Rex*, some people may have questioned her sanity. People may have feared that Samira might be possessed by a *jnun*, or demon (Crapanzano 1977c). Her mother told her that the jealousy of others was also a factor. Her mother's support at such times, like that of her father, seems to have validated Samira's activities in her own regard and to have allowed her to discount the critical opinions of others. In this respect, at least, her parents seem to have made her feel that she had their leave to become the person she would, to inhabit the identity she was devising for herself.

165

> I was an honors student. I was everybody's standard at the school. These girls were dumb, super-dumb. I did weird things. I walked home when we had a chauffeur. I wrote stories. I had costume clothes. I was very honest—straight-forward. When I was small, all these things were cute, but not when I got older. I wasn't doing them to be cute but because they were true, like telling the French Ambassador that he was a thief and that all Frenchmen were thiefs. My parents catered to all this, until the other parents began questioning it. Now I'm still doing it with bigger words and a more serious look on my face. It had started to frighten them.

Samira continued to put much of her energy into her roles in the productions of the Dramatic Society at the school. She became involved with an American young man who was also a student at the school. Together they plunged into literature, drama and poetry. She says that she was never invited to parties. But when an invitation did come for a party at the governor's house, Samira tried to stay at home. It was a dinner party, and her mother encouraged her to go. When she arrived, the governor's wife told her, "It's impossible to have a party without Samira. She's such a clown." This statement did not endear her to Samira who seems not to have been taken seriously, though she was recognized as a unique phenomenon.

Samira's family could be categorized as part of the relatively affluent Moroccan bourgeoisie. Abdellah had worked for the French during the Protectorate and then became an employee of the Moroccan government. He was part of the fairly Europeanized upper-middle class. Both as a result of the family's socioeconomic status and of their urban residence in Tangier, Abdellah's children were exempt to some extent from the social constraints to which they would have been subjected in a rural village. To be Europeanized, particularly in Tangier, meant to live in a relatively permissive milieu. To be affluent meant, for a family such as Samira's, to be somewhat insulated from the scrutiny of society at large. Urban permissiveness and family privacy were for Abdellah's children by no means absolute; Tangier is still a "small town" in some ways with many of the social controls that stereotype implies. But for Samira, these factors loosened the expectation that she would remain in the home (and therefore receive little education) and play out the traditional woman's script of obedience to husband, devotion to children, and restriction for the most part to the informal company of other women.

One of Samira's close friends was also a student at the American School; Malika was a Moroccan woman whose parents became friends with Samira's parents. One of Malika's brothers was a drug abuser and had been in a mental hospital. Malika's mother had a tea party and invited Samira's mother. At the party were

> all these ladies of the same social status, big shots. Malika's mother said to my mother across the room, "At least it's a relief to know I'm not the only one. Your daughter and my son are of the same grain." That really upset my mother.

What sustained Samira through her high school years was a selective set of relationships, with an instructor at the school, with her friend Rich whose father was in the diplomatic corps, and with Malika. Samira's cousin Lillia, who was only a few years older than Samira, had difficulties attending the French School. So Samira persuaded her to enroll in the American School instead. Samira surrounded herself with a sympathetic set of social others. Her parents remained tolerant as always in spite of their worries.

> When I was a senior in high school, I forgot to eat. I wasn't conscious at all. I was not trying to be dramatic. I had no audience. I was all alone. I would stay at home in my room for forty-eight hours at a time. My room was a jungle of books and papers. I was reading Dostoyevsky. I wrote a seventy page term paper. I was studying very seriously then, studying literature at home. I didn't go to school. I really enjoyed all that work. It was like a fever.

Rich had graduated from the American School at the end of Samira's junior year. He departed for the United States. He and Samira had read D. H. Lawrence together, *Sons and Lovers*. Their relationship, according to Samira, was "very much of a platonic relationship at the beginning." This relationship may have been keyed to those she had with some of her instructors, particularly with her English instructor, Mr. Cavett. He appeared to have been an inspired teacher and clearly recognized Samira's talents.

> My teachers, for example, couldn't bring their sexuality out in the open. They had an apparent nobility and purity about them. That's what I was aiming for. The only relationships I saw were intellectual relationships; also because there were no man-woman relationships I could see, not in the street or among my parents' friends. Most of them were married, not something that I thought was very important.

What did seem important to Samira and what was a definite departure from the usual pattern of relationships for
Moroccan women were her relationships with men mainly
in the public sphere. As had been indicated, the relationship between Samira and her father was the foremost
among these. Because Abdellah had two sets of children
and two wives, his attentions were keenly sought after, and
his children competed for his time. Because of the aura of
emotionality surrounding Abdellah and partly as a result of
the symbolic ascendency of the man and father in the Moroccan family, he was a powerful socializing influence for
his daughter. She received a considerable portion of his attentions. In talking about Abdellah, Samira refers to his relationship with his inferiors in the bureaucracy in which he
worked:

> He had two thousand men under him. They all called him
> "Papa." In a very discrete, uncalculating way, he seemed to
> establish that he was educated, wise, that he was good, that
> he would help them.

While Samira seems to be describing her father in this passage, she is also mythologizing him, and abstracting his (to
her) positive attributes. Samira's relation with Rich, which
she describes as "platonic in the beginning," and with Mr.
Cavett duplicated in varying combinations the mild, authoritative charisma of her father. These mostly non-sexualized
relationships with adult males (other than her father) were
Samira's most atypical relationships—atypical, that is, from
the standpoint of traditional feminine modesty and appropriateness. Correlatively, I think these were the relationships to which Samira assigned the greatest subjective
importance.

But the women in Samira's life were just as important as
the men. Samira's mother was not a traditional Moslem
woman, and so Samira had no opportunity to observe and

be socialized to that role. The presence of her mother was not only nurturant, but also served as the bi-cultural wedge for Samira's polyculturalism. Her women friends, which she would often dismiss as unimportant, may have provided her with an informal support network outside the domain where she was expected to "perform" or to be "on stage." It is important, therefore, to qualify carefully the dominant significance of the men, which Samira emphasizes in her recitations; it may be an artifact of the identity that she ascribes to herself as a Moslem woman.

When Samira graduated from the American School of Tangier, she came to a prestigious American university, which gave her a scholarship and provided an institutional umbrella for the continuing pursuit of her literary and social interests. Each summer of her undergraduate years, she made the trans-Atlantic crossing to Morocco, often taking American friends with her and inviting others to come to Tangier for a visit. In this way, she provided herself with some continuities in spite of her summer migration. Each autumn, she returned again to the university. The style, both personal and social, portrayed in her recitations is that which she had codified and continued to follow as a young adult.

During her undergraduate years, she continued to act in dramatic productions such as *The Trojan Women* and *Midsummer Night's Dream*. But she gradually lost interest in acting on the stage and has increasingly turned to her work as a translator of French and Spanish poetry. Her translations have been much admired by well-known writers and poets, though none have yet been published. Being a translator may be seen as an iconic recapitulation of Samira's polyculturalism, a vivid image of her manipulation of symbolic materials from various traditions in order, figuratively, to make a statement about the complexities of polyculturalism and of her own situation.

I really think it would be better for me and better for Morocco if I didn't live there. If I lived there, I'd have to mold myself to all those values. That wouldn't be honest for me. Ultimately, I would bother the people around me since I would disagree with them all the time. My mother always says, 'I feel you're safer when you're in the United States. If I didn't miss you so much, I'd let you stay there all the time.' When I'm home, they're always scared that something's going to happen to me. Very small things can get you implicated. As my father says, 'The next time you go to the airport, who's going to stop them from taking your passport away from you?' They don't have to give you a reason. If they want to do it, they'll do it. If they want to take you down to the prison and break your shoulder, they'll do it and nobody's going to stop them. Nobody's going to give you a reason. They don't owe you anything. In a country where everything is set up so that 'you owe everything to Them' with a capital T, I just don't want to live like that. I just don't want to owe anything to anybody. So I don't see where I fit in at all. Even the work I want to do, I wouldn't do there. I'm going to be able to borrow from Morocco. This is what bothers me sometimes. I want to do translations of North African writing. But I don't feel that it belongs to Morocco as it stands now. So what I want to do is to untie. . . . It's not tied to the cities, it's not tied to the government. It starts where the French roads stop.

Samira is presently pursuing graduate studies and continues to travel back and forth between Morocco and America, spending the summers in Tangier. Her father died a few years ago. Her two brothers are attending college in the United States.

The precarious political status and economic demise of the Sherifian Empire in the late nineteenth century made European intervention in Morocco at first conceivable, then possible, and finally probable and inevitable. The demographic changes that accompanied the International administration in Tangier, and the French Protectorate in much of the rest of Morocco brought many Moroccans into sustained and protracted contact with diverse cultural influences. Post-protectorate Tangier remained for some time the scene of both social fragmentation and cultural polymorphism; it was a smorgasbord rather than a melting pot. Thus, broadly speaking, emerging political forms premised demographic changes which, in turn, premised certain social forms and cultural possibilities. Interpreting Samira's recitations with this backdrop in mind reveals considerable concordances between the macrocosm of Moroccan political history and colonialism—particularly as it was visited upon Tangier—and the microcosm of Samira's experiences. She exercises remarkable (perhaps not so remarkable under the circumstances) rhetorical skills in posing a Moslem identity. While it may be convincing, that pose belies Samira's essential polyculturalism. Her rhetorical efforts are motivated by the prospect of achieving a fuller authenticity than her history has conferred upon her; hence her concerns about "fitting in."

Samira is not only Moslem. She denies, in large part, her mother's Jewish identity. [15] Samira speaks French, English and Spanish as well as Arabic. She comes from a partly Europeanized and colonized family. She has also been Americanized. These cultural counter-currents are intrinsic to Samira's history and thus constitute *for her* inevitabilities in her surroundings. The realization that cultural multiplicity may pose fewer conflicts in Samira's awareness, than in the sensibilities of those who regard it as problematic, helps to ameliorate the dilemmas of polyculturalism for Samira herself. It may be easier for Samira to see the many facets of her polyculturalism in concert, falling under a single rubric ("being Moslem"), than it is for those who do not share this background. From the outside, her history may seem heterogeneous, but for Samira it is a continuous, if diverse fabric.

Yet her recitations demonstrate how acutely Samira recognizes the anomalies she presents to other Moroccans, even to Tangerines who are better adapted than many to take polyculturalism in stride. And it is clear that she is somewhat at odds as to how to delineate her identity and to integrate her persona. One of the many ironies of her situation is that she cuts such a striking image in her social encounters. As for many Moslem women, particularly those educated in the Western tradition, Samira does not follow and does not wish to follow the traditional script mandated for her. Indeed, she would be ill-prepared to do so. She made a point of defending herself against the adverse opinions of others, which did so much to cause her discomfort and at times anxiety. In her dress and social style, I have indicated that she appeared to the average Moroccan as odd if not improper. Once in a while, she would go to a café in Tangier's European quarter, but she would not sit at a sidewalk table. She was never entirely free of the discomfort of the wandering eyes that seemed to question her presence. Her acute sensitivity to gossip and decorum in Tangier suggests her intention to guard herself against the approbation she was apt to encounter in the town.

In her intellectual pursuits, Samira perceived others as thinking of her as a deviant or eccentric. In both the Moslem and Jewish traditions, intellectual endeavor is highly respected, but is associated primarily with men. Moslem women may achieve a Koranic education and, particularly among the elite, may become proficient in classical Arabic; for these women, instruction occurred at home. Some women now get a European education. But traditionally, men rather than women are the teachers and scholars. Women who were to adopt these roles would be in a position to have regular and sustained contact with men in the public sphere. The meaning of being a woman intellectual in traditional ideology is patent: such a role contradicts Moslem canons of feminine propriety and is in opposition to the expectation that women be wives at home.[16] Nevertheless,

Samira's parents both respected their daughter's academic achievements. Still, Samira's mother once told me that reading too many books can "make you go crazy," a possible reference to her daughter's reclusive senior year at the American School.

For Samira, being something of an outsider had its price and its compensations; it also had a familial precedent. Samira's mother was a Moroccan Jew. Stillman suggests that "On the whole, Moroccan Jews accepted their enforced humility philosophically. They considered it, after all, to be part of the burden of a people in exile, and they adhered punctiliously to the restrictions imposed upon them" (1979, pp. 84–85). This characterization applies, I think, to Samira's mother in particular. She was an exile's exile and having been severed from her own family for marrying a Moslem, then being an outsider in a largely Moslem family and milieu. One can speculate that Ester's exile and her seasoned role as outsider pre-adapted Samira to being an outsider in other ways and in new contexts. As a woman in Morocco, she was an outsider to public life as was her mother. Yet through her intellectual pursuits she partially entered into the company of men. For that, her father had prepared her, taking her along with him to the many dinners and official gatherings, introducing her even as a child to his colleagues. These familial continuities in both her mother's and her father's experience prepared Samira for rejecting the typical feminine scripts. She was, if indirectly, encouraged to ignore them.

Most of the men whom Samira encountered (students and teachers) were from the American School. The Moroccans among them, whether at the school or elsewhere, often had difficulty categorizing her (Was she Puerto Rican?), let alone seeing her as a feminine other. She was assertive, forthright, and no nonsense. Thus Samira was something of a threat to the Moroccan men who knew her.

She would not be easily kept under control, a major concern for the Moroccan man. Moroccan sexual ideology defines femininity as powerful, and a source of *fitna* (anarchy/disorder), if not constrained by rules and male authority (Mernissi 1975). The more Europeanized men in Samira's milieu were less threatened than the traditional Moroccans and were better able to establish a rapport with her. At least in this regard, Tangier provided a far more permissive social environment than was to be found in a less cosmopolitan or less colonized setting.

The American School broadened Samira's social alternatives and sheltered her from some of these difficulties while being in part responsible for them, since it was being at the School which Americanized her. (The irony of this situation is but one manifestation of the double-bind that is cultural colonialism.) On the positive side, the School served Samira as a sort of conduit through Tangier society. When she came out the other end, a scholarship was waiting for her in America. Thus, education provided a route through and out of Moroccan society and then continued to serve her in a similar capacity upon her arrival in the United States. [17]

These multiple cultural influences, which have come to bear on Samira, could be seen as broaching for her the issue of identity choice. The outsider may easily see polycultural Tangier as providing a wealth of options and opportunities. But for Samira, it comprised a heterogeneous social field in which her experience was and is deeply embedded, and which has become internal to her history and identity. Making exclusive and free choices was therefore largely precluded and, I think, would only have served to deepen her alienation.

The political history of Tangier operated to pattern demographic "gating" for the city, allowing the entrance of a culturally diverse population and premising a culturally heterogeneous base. For Samira, a workable response to this situation was not to articulate her identity in cultural terms, but to differentiate herself from the various cultural traditions that came together in her. Her conceit has been to try to stand apart. In her subjective view, her situation is not, for the most part, a cultural situation at all. She does not interpret herself to herself or to others in terms of cultural specifics, diversity or heterogeneity. Culture and cultural difference is not, for her, an idiom of personal identity. While pigeon-holing herself in the abstract as a Moslem woman, she knows that such a categorization has its rhetorical aspects; it poses an understandable facade to Americans. It also articulates her primary allegiance to her father.

Thus, by and large, Samira eschews cultural identifications, though she knows they are part of her. Instead, she presents herself in terms of the politics and theatricality of her singular history and biography. Uniqueness often translates as "anomalous" for Moroccans and as "exotic" for Americans.[18] Samira thereby eludes straightforward cultural identification and altogether secure social placement. This situation requires that she negotiate anew a comprehensible persona for each social encounter. But she is consummately practiced at this task, drawing upon the diverse cultural resources at her disposal. This process is what I referred to earlier as Samira's creative synthesis of an identity for herself (Wagner 1981).

This creative, if uneasy, synthesis disallows Samira from readily situating herself in Moroccan society. At the present historical juncture, there is an increasing frequency of this experience of polyculturalism. But perhaps, in part as a reaction against cultural colonialism and against the colonial regimes of the past, polycultural identities may be seen as inauthentic or may become the subjects of political critiques. There may even be a social fantasy among some Moroccans that polyculturalism *not* exist, since it runs contrary to and may thus threaten the ideal of cultural purity, which is at times an adjunct of post-colonial nationalism. Persons with biographies like Samira's have to face difficult ambiguities. They must somehow fit into social arenas in which polyculturalism is mistakenly (if wishfully) seen as on the wane. The social identity and social recognition of persons with such backgrounds thereby become ever more problematic.

Samira's situation suggests that there may be no real "solution" for the dilemmas of polyculturalism which clearly have their painful aspects. She attempts to override these lived dilemmas by raising her own discourse to a meta-level at which various cultures, the experience of polyculturalism, and the politics thereof become matters for reflection and for constant, controlled manipulation in light of moment-to-moment social circumstances. Because the heterogeneity of these circumstances does not adjust to her, she has made adapting to them into her art and style of life.

Notes

I would like to thank Alfred M. Brown for many indulgences during the writing of this essay. Paul Rabinow, Kenneth Brown, and Sue Freeman were kind enough to read this work, and they provided much appreciated encouragement.

1. In addition to many of the stories and essays written or translated by Paul Bowles (for example, 1981), works on Tangier include Beyer (1978); Landau (1952); Steward (1977); Stuart (1955); and Vaidon (1977). A revealing novel of Tangier and Morocco is written by Hopkins (1972).

2. The "ethnography" which is the basis for this essay was collected haphazardly, if intensely, over a period beginning in 1973 when I met Samira and continuing into the present. Lengthy taped conversations between Samira and myself, journal entries,

and diary fragments form the bulk of this corpus. In addition to more or less continuous contact with her over this period, I lived in her family's house in Tangier for a total of six months during the summers of 1974 and 1976. In posing an interpretation of this material, I stress the embeddedness of perspective, description, and theorizing in the encounter between Samira and myself and in the resulting, shared milieu (Rabinow and Sullivan 1979, pp. 4–5). Thus, my description is not a detached sociological analysis, but a portrayal that has, as any rendering of human activity, grown out of actual interaction, the resulting social discourse, and each participant's conceptual apparatus. This essay is a continuation and artifact of this discourse (Crapanzano 1977 a and b). I have fictionalized some details of the histories in order to preserve a modicum of obscurity and privacy for the persons mentioned and to preclude exact identification.

3. For additional information on the recent political history of Tangier and Morocco, see Bernard (1968); Burke (1976); Harris (1921); Laroui (1977); Scham (1970); and Stuart (1955).

4. For ethnographic background on Moroccan kinship and family systems, see Geertz (1979).

5. The anthropology of women, sex roles, and sexuality in Morocco is considerable. A rich description of the world of the Moroccan woman is Fernea (1975). The culture and ideology of sex roles is described by Dwyer (1978 a and b), and concepts of sexuality and sociology of sex differences is interpreted by Mernissi (1975). Other ethnographic material can be found in Davis (1977 and 1978); Kramer (1971); Maher (1974 and 1978); and Rosen (1978). Historical material broadly relevant to the present study can be found in Vinogradov (1974).

6. Crapanzano's exact words are as follows: "I did not . . . understand that the real was a metaphor for the true—and not identical with it. . . . I had been listening only for the real, which I mistook for the true. The truth was for me masked by the metaphor. Such was my cultural bias" (1980, p. 130). With Samira's recitations, we do not have the telling of a life according to a canon of historical facticity (the "real"). I would suggest that she speaks, instead, in a figurative mode of her own experience which may be at odds with our cultural bias. That bias leads us to read life histories as "accurate" (or inaccurate) in some sense. That expectation of discourse and presumption about it need not be shared by Moroccans.

7. Fatima Mernissi told me that the women she interviewed in Morocco did not retrospectively recognize themselves in their recitations. She suggested that Samira, too, would not recognize herself in what she said. I believe Mernissi's conjecture to be accurate, and it speaks both to the ephemeral and proximate nature of the encounter and the recitations.

8. Here "first wife" refers to Abdellah's earlier, Moslem wife as distinguished from Samira's mother. Both of these women married Abdellah after his arrival in Morocco. He had been married and then divorced earlier while still in Algeria. This early marriage was without offspring.

9. Samira says she was really born in two places, in Salé and in Rabat: "I got stuck after my head came part way out. They put me and my mother in a car with the midwife. We went to a clinic in Rabat. The delivery was made with forceps. The doctor told my mother that I might turn out to be stupid."

10. The marriages and offspring of Samira's half-siblings are not shown in this diagram.

11. All indented quotations from Samira's recitations are taken from the author's verbatim transcriptions and journals.

12. The American School of Tangier is organized along the same lines as American public high schools in terms of curriculum, faculty, architecture, and cultural focus. It feeds many of its graduates, regardless of nationality, into American colleges and universities.

13. Although under these circumstances, Moroccan inheritance laws did not provide for Abdellah's wife, he provided for her indirectly. He signed all his property over to Samira and her brothers prior to his death. Thus Ester's children were able to provide for their mother after their father's death. Abdellah's children by his other wife inherited nothing. In addition, the Moroccan crown offered Ester a generous allowance at her husband's death for his many years of government service.

14. For a description of Moroccan marriage customs and ceremonies, see Geertz (1979, pp. 363–370); Maher (1974, pp. 164–170); and Westermarck (1914).

15. For material on Jews in Morocco, see Rosen (1972); and Stillman (1979).

16. Rosen summarizes the traditional set of expectations and realities for women as follows:

In many respects the men and women . . . in Morocco live
in separate worlds, their relationships are more intensely
cultivated within distinct realms of activity than in direct in-
terchange with each other. . . . It is often remarked that
women's lives are largely restricted to the private realm of
household, family, and kin group while men lead public lives
in the workplace, the market, and the sphere of political relations [1978, pp. 562–563].

Samira's early experience in the public domain with her father
continued and was broadened when she began school. Although
the restrictions on women in Tangier are not as carefully maintained as in the past, the descriptions of those restrictions which I
quote next give some idea of the sort Samira would face, would be
expected to face, and would no doubt find anathema in a fairly
non-Europeanized conjugal situation. These descriptions are
taken from life history materials from a rural Moroccan woman,
and she means to delineate past social conventions rather than the
more lenient ones of the present. My impression is, however, that
even among Europeanized Moroccan males, their notions as to
the appropriate restrictions on women have changed significantly
less than their attitudes about other domains of their experience.

If I came to visit you, I can't come unless my father-in-law
gave me permission or someone came with me. I won't go
even if we were out in the country. We use to live in tents,
we don't have rooms or anythings. For the women her boun-
dary is the edge of her tent. . . . When a woman was still
young, it was shameful for her to go to the *suq* (market). . . .
I never ever saw what the *suq* looked like [Davis 1977,
pp. 214–215].

17. A poignant fictional account of a Moroccan woman's experience, curiously similar to Samira's, can be found in Bowles
(1981). The woman in this story leaves Morocco and ends up marrying an American. But the woman in the Bowles story remains
entirely naïve of the educational and other possibilities available to
her, unlike Samira.

18. For an extended analysis of the social meaning of the exotic
in the Euro-American context, see Foster (1982).

References

Bernard, Stephane. 1968. *The Franco-Moroccan Conflict, 1943–1956.* New Haven, Conn.: Yale University Press.

Beyer, William. 1978. *Tangier.* New York: Dutton.

Bowles, Paul. 1981. "Here to Learn." *Midnight Mass.* Santa Barbara: Black Sparrow Press.

Burke, Edmund. 1976. *Prelude to Protectorate in Morocco.* Chicago: University of Chicago Press.

Crapanzano, Vincent. 1977a. "The Life History in Anthropological Field Work." *Anthropology and Humanism Quarterly* 2, nos. 2 and 3: 3–7.

———. 1977b. "Mohammed and Dawia." In Vincent Crapanzano and Vivian Garrison, eds., *Case Studies in Spirit Possession.* New York: John Wiley.

———. 1977c. "On the Writing of Ethnography." *Dialectical Anthropology* 2: 69–73.

———. 1980. *Tuhami, Portrait of a Moroccan.* Chicago: University of Chicago Press.

Davis, Susan S. 1977. "Zahra Muhammad, a Rural Woman of Morocco." In Elizabeth Warnock Fernea and Basima Qattan Bazirgan, eds. *Middle Eastern Muslim Women Speak.* Austin: University of Texas Press.

———. 1978. "Working Women in a Moroccan village." In Lois Beck and Nikki Keddie, eds. *Women in the Muslim World.* Cambridge, Mass.: Harvard University Press.

Dwyer, Daisy H. 1978a. *Images and Self-Images: Male and Female in Morocco.* New York: Columbia University Press.

———. 1978b. "Women, Sufism, and Decision-making in Moroccan Islam." In Lois Beck and Nikki Keddie, eds. *Women in the Muslim World.* Cambridge, Mass.: Harvard University Press.

Fernea, Elizabeth W. 1975. *A Street in Marrakech.* New York: Doubleday.

Foster, Stephen W. 1982. "The Exotic as a Symbolic System." *Dialectical Anthropology* 7, no. 1: 21–30.

Geertz, Hildred. 1979. "The Meaning of Family Ties." *Meaning and Order in Moroccan Society.* New York: Cambridge University Press.

Harris, Walter. 1921. *Morocco That Was.* Boston: Small Maynard.

Hopkins, John. 1972. *Tangier Buzzless Flies.* New York: Atheneum.

Jelloun, Tahar ben. 1977. *La Plus Hautes des Solitudes*. Paris: Seuil.

Kramer, Jane. 1971. *Honor to the Bride, Like the Pigeon That Guards Its Grain Under the Clove Tree*. London: William Collins.

Landau, Rom. 1952. *Portrait of Tangier*. London: Robert Hale.

Laroui, Abdellah. 1977. *The History of the Maghrib, an Interpretive Essay*. Princeton: Princeton University Press.

Maher, Vanessa. 1974. *Women and Property in Morocco*. New York: Cambridge University Press.

———. 1978. "Women and Social Change in Morocco." In Lois Beck and Nikki Keddie, eds. *Women in the Muslim World*. Cambridge, Mass.: Harvard University Press.

Mernissi, Fatima. 1975. *Beyond the Veil: Male-Female Dynamics in a Modern Muslim Society*. New York: Wiley.

Rabinow, Paul, and William H. Sullivan. 1979. *Interpretative Social Science*. Berkeley: University of California Press.

Rosen, Lawrence. 1972. "Muslim-Jewish Relations in a Moroccan City." *International Journal of Middle East Studies* 3: 435–449.

———. 1978. "The Negotiation of Reality: Male-Female Relations in Sefrou, Morocco." In Lois Beck and Nikki Keddie, eds. *Women in the Muslim World*. Cambridge, Mass.: Harvard University Press.

Scham, Alan. 1970. *Lyautey in Morocco*. Berkeley: University of California Press.

Steward, Angus. 1977. *Tangier, a Writer's Notebook*. London: Hutchinson.

Stillman, Norman A. 1979. *The Jews of Arab Lands*. Philadelphia: The Jewish Publication Society of America.

Stuart, Graham H. 1955. *The International City of Tangier*. 2nd ed. Stanford, Calif.: Stanford University Press.

Vaidon, Lawdom. 1977. *Tangier, a Different Way*. London: Scarecrow Press.

Vinogradov, Amal Rassam. 1974. "French Colonialism as Reflected in the Male-Female Interaction in Morocco." *Transactions of the New York Academy of Sciences* 36: 192–199.

Wagner, Roy. 1981. *The Invention of Culture*. Rev. ed. Chicago: University of Chicago Press.

Westermarck, E. 1914. *Marriage Ceremonies in Morocco*. London: Macmillan.

6

Mara:
The Construction
of a Professional Identity

by Diedrick Snoek

Theories of social change tend to divide into those that emphasize the primary importance of economic and technological factors, and those that stress the impetus provided by people's changing ideas about themselves and their relationships to the world. Whichever factor one regards as the primary cause for social change, we need a better understanding of the links between them: what can be observed at a societal level and what is taking place in any given individual's life? We need to know more, for example, about the forces that move creative individuals to transform their personal conflicts and frustrations into a search for new options that initiate activism on the part of others. This question is highly relevant to understanding the origins and potentials of all sorts of liberation movements. How do these movements maintain or lose momentum by the ways in which they address the possibility of change in the lives of their potential adherents? The Women's Movement of the 1970s is a wellspring of ideas and experiences relevant to these questions. My aim is to examine what can be learned from a psychological analysis of the life histories of individual women who made significant changes in their lives under the impact of that movement.

The early writers of the Women's Movement stressed the significance of developing not only a political awareness of the many ways in which the social system consigned women to a place of subordinate status and power, but also a highly personal consciousness of the subtle ways in which existing gender roles function as ideological and practical supports for the status quo. Women's habits, motives, attitudes, and values, insofar as they had been made to conform to traditional gender roles, were to be reexamined as the result of sexist ideology, rather than as authentic expressions of self. Refashioning one's old attitudes by daring to act on new assumptions was thus to be viewed as a political contribution as well as an act of personal liberation. Such a formulation of course constitutes a two-edged sword: by defining the self as malleable, it offers the hope that one can transform oneself into an instrument for bringing about the kind of life one desires for self and others. The idea of personal liberation correctly assumes that a great many social arrangements are held in place by social norms, and that a refusal to conform generates significant pressure towards social change. But the theory of personal liberation also turns the individual into a significant arena for social con-

flict. Though it is a battle that carries the potential for transformative change, it challenges each individual to undertake an arduous effort at self-directed personal change. To
be sure, the invitation to personal change holds out a seduc-   185
tive promise: out of all the things people might wish to influence, their own lives lie most directly at hand. If they
themselves can significantly change the way they live, they
might by so doing bring about social change even where
other, more institutional change is stymied. On the other
hand, there are limits to how much change one can effect
in one's own life without a collective effort to change the
conditions under which all women and men live their lives.

To the social psychologist interested in attitude change,
the argument for revolution through personal change offers
a number of challenging questions. To begin with, how
much change is possible in attitudes that have been established since early childhood and that form a significant part
of the individual's self-concept? While a number of social
psychologists have emphasized the connection between social attitudes and more deep-seated aspects of personality,
the question of the limits of change in such attitudes has
not received much attention. Gender role attitudes, like racial attitudes, are established quite early during the individual's lifetime, and ordinarily remain quite stable. But research following the advent of the Women's Movement
made it clear that gender role attitudes were in fact changing rapidly among large segments of the adult population.
These studies included several panel surveys, in which data
from the same sample groups interviewed at several different times made it unmistakably clear that individual women
changed their attitudes in major ways between the early
1960s and the mid-1970s. (Mason, Czajka, and Arber 1976;
and Thornton and Freedman 1979). This conclusion, from
quantitatively expressed aggregate data, is corroborated by
personal observation that at least in some women the atti-

tude changes that were occurring went well beyond a rejection of traditional ways of looking at gender roles. Numerous women testified both in words and in action to a radical transformation in their view of themselves and their relation to society, a transformation that could not be adequately described by the existing stock of items on so-called sex-role inventories. Who were these women? What brought about the more extensive changes that accompanied their transformation into feminists? How do these women resemble or differ from others who became pro-feminist without undergoing such a thorough change in self-concept, or from those who resisted change altogether? What role did their transformation into "feminists" play in what others took to be the meaning of the Women's Movement? Such questions clearly call for interdisciplinary investigation. What psychologists can hope to contribute is some insight into the links between social movements and the dynamics of personal change.

Social psychologists also are divided about the relative order of importance of a change in behavior or a change in attitude. Starting historically from the assumption that a change in attitude would necessarily have to precede changes in behavior, both laboratory experiments and field investigations have led to the recognition that inducing a change in behavior is one of the most effective ways of bringing about attitude change. Social psychologists have also become more aware that attitude changes without accompanying behavioral commitments have a short life. These findings, plus the general behavioristic bias that has predominated in psychology, have sustained a conviction that ideology in general, and private attitudes in particular, are probably negligible factors in accounting for social behavior and thus for social change. But how long can this conviction be maintained in the face of numerous personal testimonies from individuals who say that it was a poem, a teacher, or a personal encounter that "unlocked" the beginnings of a new consciousness or that became the starting point for significant personal change rather than the conclusion of it? The role of consciousness and ideology in promoting or retarding social change remains open to questions for other social sciences as well. One approach to understanding the interplay between attitudes and action is through the examination of individual cases; but before turning to that approach, it is necessary to clarify the concept of personal change.

Personal Change

The most comprehensive way of describing personal change is by reference to the individual's self-concept. While this is notoriously difficult to define, let alone measure with any precision, it is nevertheless an indispensable way of describing this fact: people hold certain ideas about their own behavior, interests, values, and relationships to be true, while others are rejected as false. Most people's self-descriptions agree to a large extent with the descriptions that others would give. In fact, it is a tenet of one of the earliest formulations in social psychology that people learn who and what they are primarily from the "reflected appraisals" of others. And there is a good deal of evidence that demonstrates the interdependence of one's own self-estimates with the evaluative attitudes of those who interact with us. One way of recording personal change, therefore, is to focus on changes in self-concept, while paying close attention to concomitant changes in those with whom the subject interacts.

For convenience, one can say that self-concepts change in three ways: by a process of self-discovery, by a change in self-acceptance, and by personal growth. *Self-discovery* consists of becoming aware of things we believe, values we cherish, or capacities we possess when we had previously been unaware of these attributes. We may have remained unaware of them simply because we were never in a position to exercise choices. Alternatively, we, and those around us, may have had some emotional stake in preventing awareness. Self-discovery is a normal process in growing up. It is particularly evident during adolescence, for example, but the balance of awareness can shift at any time during one's life as the need for defending the status quo diminishes. *Self-acceptance* occurs when we evaluate what we have always done or wanted to do in a new, more positive way. It is a very significant aspect of personal change, because it allows us to come out of hiding and to be more direct and assertive about what we want. To the extent that the scale of values by which we appraise ourselves depends upon the values of those around us, entering into new relationships and encountering others with a different scale of values is probably one of the more significant ways in which such changes in self-acceptance come about. The assumption of new behaviors brings about *personal growth* in which we challenge or develop latent capacities or arouse new interests. Some growth also involves deletion, as in learning to drop unproductive or unsatisfying modes of behavior. It is not always easy to discriminate growth from self-discovery or self-acceptance; but the conceptual distinctions are important in that they direct one's attention to the different ways in which the individual's total way-of-being may change. People may develop new self-awareness, come to a new self-evaluation, or free themselves to take greater risks in the process of exploring new behavioral possibilities.

Change may be forced by circumstances as well as invited by new opportunities. *Forced* changes are likely to occur, for example, when people are widowed or divorced. Because old patterns or relationships are no longer possible, they are forced to explore new ones, and in that process considerable personal change may be set in motion. Change is *invited* when new opportunities present themselves; when, for example, a young person leaves the parental home. New occasions for the exercise of personal choice, new roles, and new behavior settings permit discovery and growth. When either a need or an opportunity for new behavior exists, people are probably most ready to be influenced by other people whose example they can observe. In isolation, one has no examples to follow, and change must come from one's own invention. But in social settings that permit close contact with others, the behavior and values they model may invite change quite readily. Whether change is forced by circumstances, permitted by new options, or invited by new examples, the next step is clearly up to the individual: one can refuse change as well as accept it. It is important to acknowledge both these possibilities in the actual lives of most ordinary people. All change involves loss as well as gain; and even if one's present way of life is tremendously dissatisfying, it may be difficult to let go of what was one's past "self." The widow can refuse to fill the gap left in her life by the death of her spouse; the college student can cling to her adolescent reliance on her parents and high school friends; anyone can encounter different values and alternative lifestyles, and yet choose to ignore or reject them. To understand why it is so difficult to let go of the past, one must first understand the sources of people's attachment to it.

Change may be difficult to accept because the past has been so attractive and fulfilling that one cannot bear the prospect of giving it up and moving into the present. Thus any change, even if it promises moving into a "better home" or an "improved job," tends to involve some *stress* associated with the feelings of loss and the necessity for new adaptations that come with it. Peter Marris, in his book *Loss and Change*, has made a very convincing case for the parallels in the emotional experience of undergoing changes associated with relocation, for example, and the experience of grieving (Marris 1974). Even if the past was not all that satisfactory, people have come to believe that it is necessary to continue to be the way they were if they are to continue to earn the rewards they used to value. If their self-esteem is shaky, the continued approval of known others may appear to be of critical importance, and change may be held off or unacknowledged for a considerable time. One aspect of emotional attachment to others is that people may come to believe in the illusion that the way they are now can not be changed, except at the risk of another's well-being. This is evident in the case histories of some victims of wife abuse, for example. According to psychologist Lenore Walker, wives may stay in an abusive relationship, despite an opportunity to move out, because they fear their departure would precipitate intolerable distress for the husband (Walker 1979). This fear is not entirely without basis in reality, because the same author presents data showing that, in cases where the abused spouse *does* leave the relationship, a significant number of their former spouses suffer breakdowns or attempt suicide. Nevertheless, the example is simply an extreme case of a more general tendency to forgo even desired opportunities for personal change, out of a feeling of obligation to another person. Finally, psychotherapists also recognize that unfinished grieving associated with past losses, particularly with losses suffered early in the individual's life, may constitute a powerful emotional obstacle to readiness to undertake change in the present situation. For everyone, therefore, attachment to the past acts as a strong impetus for conservatism. The forces that drive people to abandon their past selves and to embrace change must be powerful enough to overcome this built-in conservatism.

Catherine MacKinnon, in her book on sexual harassment, observed that of the relatively few lawsuits that have been brought on this issue, a disproportionately large number have been initiated by black women. She speculates on their willingness to litigate as follows:

> . . . since black women stand to lose the most from sexual harassment, by comparison they may see themselves as having the least to lose by a struggle against it . . .
> [MacKinnon 1979]

While it may be true that people with their backs to the wall are readier to recognize oppression for what it is and thus to opt for protest over acquiescence, that doesn't account for the fact that, among women active in the Women's Movement, many came from relatively privileged backgrounds (Mason, Czajka, and Arber 1976). So the question remains: Aside from those who are forced to fight for their survival, what forces are strong enough to inspire a desire for change, in those who would have an easy enough future if they acquiesced in the gender role system as it exists?

A desire to change is not enough. The courage to risk changing also requires hope, a sense that change is actually possible, and a vision of a future that seems worth changing for. The psychological concept of "sense of personal control" recognizes both the situational and the personal factors that influence people's willingness to consider themselves "in charge" of their lives, as opposed to viewing their lives as "being controlled" by various forces beyond their influence. Belief in personal control results in more intelligent behavior, more persistence in the face of problems, and better feelings about oneself than the lack of such beliefs. People prefer to maintain a belief in their own control over events, even in situations that are obviously controlled by chance. Because beliefs in personal control are so pervasive, people often react strongly to loss of control, whether perceived or real. Moreover, when people perceive that their freedom has been abridged, a state of psychological "reactance" is aroused that motivates various attempts to restore freedom (Wrightsman and Deaux 1980). The application of this set of ideas is very broad. In this particular context I want simply to note that active involvement in feminism is known to be associated with a greater than average sense of personal control (Sanger and Alker 1972). With regard to personal change, too, I would expect that those whose sense of control over their lives is increased, and those for whom it is already high will be among the individuals most ready to attempt changes when opportunities for growth occur. Access to education and the hope for opportunities for personal and vocational enlargement may have been the common strand in the lives of U.S. women in the post-World War II period which precipitated frustration with the rigid gender system and propelled some into the movement for Women's Liberation in the late 1960s.

In order to do justice to the complex interweaving of personal and sociohistorical forces, I shall employ the life-history approach to first recount and then reflect upon one woman's life. The life-history approach takes, as its primary data, an individual's own account of her life and the events that influenced her attitudes, values, and actions. A significant advantage of this approach is that it presents the person in the context of her continuous development, over a period of time and amid the full complexity of the personal, social, and historical circumstances that were meaningful to her. Ideally, such an account is produced as a result of a collaboration between the subject and an investigator in an open-ended, semi-clinical interview. The investigator attempts to facilitate the subject's openness to self and guides her to explore the implications of what is expressed. The success of the interview depends in important ways on the subject's willing consent. It also depends on the inter-

viewer's trustworthiness and understanding, as expressed
in body movement, facial expression, and verbal respon-
siveness as much as in the phrasing of the questions themselves. The text of such interviews can be explored not only
in terms of the content of what is said but also in terms
of how it was said, in what context, and with what kind
of emotional expression. Like any other method, the life-
history approach has some built-in limitations and disadvantages. What individuals say about themselves has, at
times, the unmistakable ring of authenticity; but the lis-
tener shall never be able to ascertain exactly how accurate
or complete the individual's self-observations are. The re-
quirement of informed consent necessarily limits the interviewer to individuals sympathetic to the aims of the study,
and the length of the interview limits the number of persons who can be included in such a study. The subject
probably tells her story differently at different times in her
life. In retrospect meanings may be discovered that were
not evident at the time. And the investigator is left with the
task of reconstructing her story in terms of what probably
happened, and must use clues that are widely dispersed
throughout the interview or evident only by implication or
inference. All of these problems are more familiar to the historian or bibliographer than to the social scientist. Nevertheless, despite its selectivity, unrepresentativeness, and
subjectivity, the life-history approach allows access to data
that are inaccessible to other methods (Erikson 1975).

Mara's Story

At the time I interviewed her, Mara was thirty-nine years
old, and working on a feminist project that had deep meaning for her. As the following story makes clear, however, this
sense of vitality and involvement was not achieved easily.

Our conversation focused on how she had come to commit herself to her current work and explored the personal and historical circumstances that had formed her convictions.

Born in 1941, Mara describes how she grew up in the post-war period and entered college in 1959. Mara's parents agreed to send her to college only if she would undertake nursing studies. As she describes it:

> I grew up in a family of five children with two boys and three girls. My parents, having little money, wanted their daughters to do very traditional work. They wanted my sister to be a high school teacher, and another one to be a medical technician. Meanwhile they were saving their money so my brothers could go to medical or law schools. . . . And they decided that I should be a nurse. It was partly economic, but it was also that is all they thought I was capable of. So I did go to nursing school for four years, and it was the most horrible, dreadful thing that could ever have happened. It just destroyed ten years of my life to recover from it. And I was, of course, aware that had a lot to do with my being female. And I was aware that part of my hate of being in it was being in a subservient position to doctors—and under the authority of domineering women. I mean, it was a very good way to see sex roles, being trained as a nurse in a hospital, but there was no ideology to explain it.

Eager to leave home, Mara looked upon nursing school as a necessary evil to acquire an education and a means of self-support; but although she did quite well in her courses, she hated the nursing program and determined that she would never work as a nurse. Upon graduation, her knowledge of medical terms was instrumental in landing her a job as a research assistant to a medical school professor. This experience, in turn, led someone to suggest to her a graduate program in community psychology. She was admitted there, approximately four years after graduation. That same year she married, but the marriage was unsatisfactory and ended quickly in divorce. While a graduate student at Co-

lumbia, a great deal of her energy was taken up by her participation in the growing anti-war movement. Her experiences there led her to start her dissertation research on
returning Vietnam veterans; and eventually she finished
her doctoral work and was appointed to the psychology faculty of one of the branches of the New York State University
system.

Although Mara had been aware of other women's involvement in the Women's Movement she had not felt drawn to
their activities at Columbia. Only at SUNY, as one of only
two women on its psychology faculty, did she begin to reflect on the difference that gender made in how she was
perceived and reacted to, by students and faculty alike.
Eventually she wrote a paper on this topic that was widely
circulated. Forming links with other women, a feminist perspective began to influence her courses and research.

During the next few years Mara studied the careers and
roles of faculty women. This research resulted in a book
that commanded attention from a national audience and influenced her department to grant her tenure. Shortly there-
after, aware that her interests were never strictly "academic," Mara was excited by the call she heard at a national
conference for academic feminists to create firmer links between their research and political feminists' activist strategies. Taking a leave from her academic position, Mara
began devoting her time to a new project to reduce or eliminate sexism in police work by changes in the curriculum
for training police officers. About this project Mara said:

> It was very rewarding to know that I made this project hap-
> pen, that I've put it on the map. I mean, in some ways, it's
> absolutely manic, and mad . . . but I'm convinced, and oth-
> ers have said it too, that I'm the only person that could have
> done this. . . . I'm convinced I am the only person who could
> have wheedled my way into these cold circles and could
> have made it happen. And that is a real satisfaction, that

somehow I did something that was true to myself, that really was the exercise of all my skills, from my personality to the kind of political shrewdness that I learned from the Columbia years.

The satisfaction that Mara derived from this work, however, came not only from the opportunity it afforded to harness all her skills and values to a project with great potential usefulness. At age thirty-nine, it appealed to her as well on a deeper level as "an affirmation as opposed to a negation which I've had all these years." To understand what this has meant to her, it is desirable to review her account of how and why she rebelled against nursing:

Interviewer: You were obviously unhappy [in nursing school]. Did you see yourself as having to do it this way in order to be in college at all?

Mara: . . . In order to be able to support myself. I mean, to have a degree that would let me go do something else. And, I think [I was] quite correct. There was no hippie movement, no drop-out movement. All of that came after my day [1959–1964]. There was no counter-culture. No one ever dropped out even for a semester—I mean there was no safety net; there wasn't any. I suppose I could have washed dishes or something, but there really were no alternatives. . . . So I thought, if I got my degree I'd at least be in a better position, which is exactly what happened. I knew I would never practice a day in my life and I didn't. Instead, I put everything into. . .well, it was more grandiose than that: I think it was the key to my survival—I'm sure I would have killed myself if I hadn't engaged in my project, which was to plan—it took me the whole year—a bonfire and an event.

Anonymously, I reserved a park. It's very funny, because in some ways it really was the first "Happening"—as we have happenings in art now—and there was only one person who knew what I was doing, a friend who also hated nursing. She helped me to implement it. I planned it, and I built a dummy, and I made up a poem, I can't even remember it now, but it was in the local newspaper. It was

called the "First Annual Fest of Florence." You see, I wanted
to put on this event and not have anybody know—make
them think it was some official thing. I had it all printed up
like wedding invitations, in all these envelopes, and it was
engraved and I think I got the printer, who thought it was
wonderful, to do it for free. I put it anonymously in the mail-
boxes of all 250 nursing students, and another 100 to doc-
tors, interns, orderlies. . . . It said to come and celebrate the
First Annual Fest of Florence and to bring—we had these
terrible uniforms, that had all these little buttons and studs,
a million studs, and you know, I hated that. I built a dummy,
ten feet high, and then of course dressed it on the day of the
event in my uniform and lashed it to a stake over the barbecue pit. And I built boats to put all these little buttons in,
that the invitation said to bring. . . . You know, [it said to]
bring the whole thing, the buttons, the uniform, and their
little strings. Of course it took me a whole year, because
every little detail was planned. And no one knew; they got
the invitations and no one knew! The papers came to find
out about it and of course no one knew. They went to the
Public Relations Department and, in fact, they asked all the
nursing students. They asked me, "Do you know anything
about this forthcoming event?" I remember I was wheeling
a patient into a cafeteria and I said, "No, I got the invitation,
but I don't know."

And so, on the day, I made a costume for myself which
was, ah, sheets and wings of tin foil, and I was [to be] the
Spirit of Florence Nightingale. I got a gong and I would be
behind the hill until. . . . What had happened was that one
of the things that just galvanized my hate of them was that
they forced us to go to a Gideon Society Tea—that's the Gideon Bible people—We had to go, it was mandatory, and
they gave us all these little white bibles, that had the Florence Nightingale Pledge in them. So on the great day of the
fire, I had this orderly carry out a purple pillow; on it I put
the bible in which I had practiced reading the Florence
Nightingale Pledge in such a way that it was slightly provocative, about serving the physician. . . . I mean the whole
thing was blasphemous from beginning to end and, oh, 350
people came. It was the day before graduation and the day
after classes were officially over. So I knew there was no way

198

they could do anything to me. And I knew I hadn't sent anything through the mail, because I had put it in [all the mail
boxes] by hand at midnight. Every detail was perfect, and
Mary kept hitting the gong, and all these people came,
mostly nursing students and medical students, and they put
their buttons in the boats and they stuffed their nylon uniforms into the barbecue pit. . . .

I was behind the hill. My friend started hitting the gong
and chanting. We had been listening to Gregorian chant,
you know, it was bizarre. And all these people watched as I
came over the hill with Gabriel, the orderly, with the sheets
and wings on. . . . Slowly it dawned on these people that
something terrible was happening. . . . I came down and
climbed on a picnic table, and I read [the Nightingale
pledge] to the gong's sound and the chanting. . . . It was a
very disturbing event. Then my friend threw the match on,
but I had called the fire department in advance, not wanting
to be thrown in jail or anything. Well, it all exploded. It was
nylon! The fire department was there, and then the police
came and—it wasn't bad for a while, but then people. . . .
No one knew how to interpret what had happened, but they
did know it was blasphemous and—I blotted out part of it—
but there was a sort of mini-race riot, because it was '64 and
there was a lot of trouble and people started drinking . . .
and they started fights and I ran away.

It was wonderful, because I just ran and to think it was all
going on and I was safe! And I was free! Then my parents
came the next day for graduation and there was this article
in the paper about how Florence would have turned over in
her grave if she had seen it! So then people found out, naturally [that it was I] who had organized it. I mean, I came over
the mountain and, obviously, it was me. And oh my parents
were just horrified, because it was graduation and people
came up to me calling me Florence. . . . I thought it was just
wonderful, and the university didn't know what to do with
me, because I was an honor student. Right? They couldn't
do a damn thing to me. And here I had done this horrible
thing. So they sent somebody to invite me to this—breakfast
the next day, and I just went to see what it was. There were
fifty-year old alumnae of the nursing school and the medical
school, and the president of the medical class, and the presi-

dent of the nursing class, and then me, the renegade, sitting there. Nobody said anything to me. Nobody did anything and as I was leaving, the Dean of the Nursing School just looked at me and said, "What graduate field of nursing are you planning to go into, Mara?" I just looked at her and I didn't say a word, and that was it. You know, there it was. I burned everything. I burned everything . . . my shoes even, my books, and that was it.

The glee with which she recounted this story, the careful plotting to make the Fest of Florence "blasphemous," yet to carry it off with complete impunity, and the open pleasure at offending both the nursing school officials and her parents on graduation day, tell us a great deal about the anger that Mara sought to channel into this rite of separation. It was an act of rebellion not only against the restriction of opportunities and the implied inferiority of women, but also an attempt to separate herself once and for all from her family and the role they had prepared her to play.

I came from a very . . . not just academic family, but one where the only thing stressed was brains. That was why being sent to nursing school was particularly important. Because, it's not as if I was from a working-class family. I was from a very sophisticated [family]: my father was a very well-known scientist . . . and there I was being sent to nursing school. [Interviewer: "What was your mother's education?"] Well, she went to college and started to do some writing. Got married when she was seventeen, finished college, and that was it. She later got work as a teacher, when my youngest sister went to college. [Interviewer: "I gather she had some intellectual values too?"] Oh, yes! She is an avid reader . . . oh, no, they're very intellectualized. Now my father is very highly trained and a scientist, well-known in his field. My mother has that kind of untutored—intelligence, but she's very bright and reads more than anybody I ever knew in my life. . . . So, on the one hand, all that counted was academic achievement, on the other hand I was being sent to nursing school.

About the decision to send her to nursing school, she said:

> My father acquiesced to it, and my mother was really the domineering force. . . . She constantly, all our lives, told her daughters her favorite saying [which was]: "A woman has to give ninety percent and a man ten percent to make it work."

But the rigid sex-typing that characterized her mother's ideas about what Mara should do needs to be understood at a still deeper level. Mara perceived early that her parents' relationship was a strained one and, even as a child, began to devote herself to holding the family together:

> Within the family *I* was the one who carried the burden of: Are they going to get divorced? . . . I was my mother's confessor, you know, I was her sustenance. I had that role. . . . I saw my mother, ah, as a rather unhappy person. Ah, I just hated her, but mostly I saw her as vulnerable, because I thought she loved my father very much, and it was quite clear to me that he didn't love her at all, although they stayed together in a bitter relationship that went on all their lives. . . . It was only later that I could sort of define the relationship in terms of social roles. I didn't have those categories, but it was very clear to me that she was . . . very unhappy as a woman, unhappy as a mother. . . . I saw my mother as a victim, and I felt that I was my mother's victim, and those two things are very powerful. . . . I think my own emancipation from that relationship was very slow and tortuous.

Here Mara touches on the painful core of her situation. A child who accepts the role of helping a parent carry great unhappiness is burdened by feelings of pity mingled with deep resentment, an anger that is usually deflected so as not to make the parent's situation even more difficult. Furthermore, the child's inability to alter the parents' situation in any fundamental way adds a quality of helplessness, anxiety, and guilt to such efforts. It is very difficult to separate oneself from such an overwhelming task, because leaving home is unconsciously felt to be an abandonment of one's parent. Going away to college was a first step, and rejecting the occupation chosen for her upon graduation was a second one, but Mara states that even after graduation she remained "caught up in that madness for many, many years."

In the period following her dramatic graduation gesture Mara found that

> . . . when I had burned everything there was nothing left to take its place . . . I had never developed because I had been consumed for four years in this horrible pit, and so it was a very long process to sort of come alive again.

She certainly had little sense of control over her own life. Her first job as a research assistant at a well-known mental health research center was found by accident and landed her in a complicated and demeaning relationship with her boss.

> I was being sexually harassed by my boss. That was my first encounter. And it was extraordinarily confusing. This was at ———— and he only hired young things, usually out of eastern schools, and he had buzzers for each—you know, two shorts and a long—and it was just insane. He had a real hold over me. I was really scared of him. He was a father figure. It was really, ah, frightening beyond belief. I was so confused. He had power over my life. It was a nightmare. I had many nightmares; [my experiences] were all nightmares for so many years. And so finally ah . . . but I wanted to leave anyway. He said he wouldn't write me a recommendation. You know, it was the *old* thing, but then he decided that—I don't know what happened—but he decided he wanted me out. He thought I might really collapse or something, so he actually did write me a good recommendation.

Going to graduate school first occurred to her as the result of a casual suggestion that the university might find her experience and training an asset in their new community psychology program. To her surprise, she was accepted there on the understanding that she would have to make up some undergraduate work. Later she learned that someone in admissions had recognized her father's name and considered her a good bet on that basis. At the same time that she entered graduate school, she married and a little later divorced. About that marriage she only spoke once:

> I got married I think to please them [my parents], a nice doctor, whom I then divorced a few years later.

Although she was aware of other women in the university beginning to organize around women's issues, she felt she had little in common with them. What did engage her feelings was the anti-war movement, and in time she turned her research activity into a study of returning Vietnam veterans.

> I was very involved in the Anti-War Movement. That was my main concern for many years—far more than anything in the Women's Movement. . . . I can't really remember when the Women's Movement started for me, because I do remember that when I got divorced, which was in 1968—In retrospect, of course, all the issues were exactly what was then beginning to be talked about. But I remember there was *no one* talking about those things then, or no one that I was hearing. . . . It felt like a totally alone venture: all the guilt and all the isolation. I had all this pressure, from in-laws particularly, to have a child and of course to stay home and be a doctor's wife—and so in everything I was doing, I was playing out a feminist role, but I had no words for it and I had no understanding of my situation.

What she did understand and have words for was her opposition to the war. When I asked what accounted for her interest in the Vietnam veterans, she replied:

> There may not have been that many people knocking on doors, ringing doorbells, going up and down talking to

people about the war and being told "You weren't there! What do *you* know?". . . . It was very clear that the only people they couldn't say that to was Vietnam veterans.

At the university, Mara remembers not wanting to associate with the first graduate students' women's caucus. She never felt she quite belonged there, was far "straighter" than the Cambridge crowd that was flourishing all around her, and most of all could not identify with the early campus feminists as people. She did notice, but without thinking about it, that many of her fellow students dropped out, especially the women:

> I was just one of the few that got my degree and got it relatively fast. I don't know how I did it. It was a sort of iron, self-punishing force that I had developed in nursing school, when I had decided I had to get all A's so that I could get a scholarship and transfer out of nursing. I did get all A's, and a prize, but then discovered that as an out-of-state student I did not qualify for the scholarship. I had also been told by my mother that I might fail academically. You can imagine what that sets up. . . . The only way out was to get all A's, but I was supposed to be dumb so I felt I might fail anyway. I trained myself to be *totally disciplined*, to be able to sit and not move for five hours at a time. I remember that as a goal, to sit for five hours straight in the library, and I did. I became this thing, you know, that just functioned like a machine. . . .

Mara started turning to feminist ideas only when she went to the state university and started to teach. It was her first job, and suddenly she found herself classed with other women faculty, who at that time were very few. Here is how she described her experience:

> How I developed as a feminist was pretty much as a loner. But I had a special sensitivity to those issues. I mean, I knew the truths were not hard for me to accept, because they all fit to interpret most of my life [slight laugh]. You know, it was a kind of natural affinity for that view, but it didn't come about

through any organized activity. And when I first taught, I didn't teach any women's courses, I taught a course on psychology and law. But I *did* write a paper a couple of years after I got there. I did begin to notice very early that students reacted very differently to female faculty than to male faculty; and that the women faculty were describing things that intrigued me in terms of women's roles, and I decided to survey those women and find out what they were experiencing and to analyze what the situation was. I think that's the first attempt I made to really use my training to analyze something from within a feminist perspective and to understand how questions of legitimacy and authority were affecting one's ability to enact male roles.

When I asked "Would you say that you fought against being identified as a woman?" Mara replied:

As a woman or as a feminist? They are very different. I want to look at how I ended my marriage and say, 'This woman is fighting being a woman, right?' But we could also look and say 'This woman is fighting to *be* a feminist.' Then I got into the psychology professional entourage. Was it safer just being a psychologist, never mind the gender? *Now*, when I look at my life [I would say] it was a striving to reject all of those roles that were stereotypically done, without any ideology to explain them, *except* the ideology of inferiority. That's really all I knew. What I *knew* was that I wasn't good enough to be, and I *knew* that I had to fight that.

The Construction of Mara's Professional Identity

Mara's life story seems to divide into three major parts. The first episode is her account of her unwilling subservience to her parents' ideas of what constitutes an education for a woman with intelligence. Wanting to get out from under their authority, but realizing that for a woman of her class some form of education was the only way of qualifying for a "decent" job, Mara submitted to a nursing school curricu-

lum that she deemed devoid of intellectual substance and to
an administration she experienced as arbitrary, restrictive,
and authoritarian. The nursing school forbade her to participate in the university's debate team, for example, on the
grounds that it would require being absent on weekends
when she was expected to do duty at the hospital. But sub-
mission comes at a price, and only Mara's vow never to
practice nursing stayed the course for her. Keeping her anger to herself, and making sure that she could not be pun-
ished for her Fest of Florence mockery of the school's oppressive ethos, she managed both to survive until graduation and to give such powerful expression to her feelings
that she feared the event might have turned into a racial
brawl.

The second phase of Mara's story covers the decade following her act of rebellion. It began with the discovery that
"when I had burned everything, there was nothing left."
Even in the highly condensed version of the story presented
here, it may be evident that she was far more reticent about
this period of her life than any other. She made it clear that
she was without plan or purpose and very frightened. No
doubt she was vulnerable prey for the sexual harassment
she experienced on her first job. Her account of how she
got into graduate school stressed her complete lack of control over the plan's conception (a friend suggested it), or
success (the dean admitted her only because he recognized
her father's name). In fact, of course, she must have written
her own application and presented herself as a sufficiently
credible applicant to gain the university's attention. Once
admitted to graduate school, her marriage was a last attempt to satisfy her parents' desire for a normal life for
her—one they could understand and endorse. But the marriage only reinstated the pressures she had fought so hard
to escape. She became pregnant and then recognized her
urgent desire to terminate the pregnancy and leave the

marriage. Once again she was completely on her own, dependent only on the one skill she had developed: the ability to discipline herself to study, which she describes as a "sort of iron self-punishing force." She felt alienated from those around her, cut off from both community and friendships. The terms she uses to describe herself convey both her sense of isolation and emotional hollowness. ("I was somehow quite dead inside, but it didn't stop me from being nice and carrying on my social role.") I received no hint about her relationship with her family during this period, except that ominous phrase that she used early in the interview to characterize it: "I was very caught up in all of that madness for many, many years."

Out of this phase she gradually shaped a new identity: that of activist-researcher. After her divorce, she felt drawn to Left politics and became active in the anti-war movement.

> My involvement with anti-war activities grew out of deep moral and political concerns soon after my arrival [in the East] in 1965. And although I did not join any group, I identified with the Left and became involved in activities sponsored by various groups. As a regional director of Vietnam Summer, I became aware of the importance of mobilizing veterans into the Anti-War Movement.

Mara combined these political goals with her research project on political consciousness among returning Veterans—a project about which she felt so strongly that she pursued it even after the government grant that made these studies possible was withdrawn.

> They wrote this lovely letter saying "Would you please explain how your research proposal fits into nursing?" . . . and, well, I had to give the money up, but that was all right.

I suggested to Mara that her strong feelings about this project might have derived, in part, from her feelings of identification with these men who, like her, felt embittered and betrayed. But she denied this interpretation and stated:

> My choice of veterans as a dissertation subject was strategic. I did not see them as "victims" though I later developed some compassion for their feelings of being "duped."

It nevertheless strikes me as significant that a person who described herself as "quite dead inside" felt drawn so deeply to this subject. The particular form that this research effort took came to characterize her research style in later years too: she chose a problem because it engaged her interests, because it was located in the practical realities of the everyday world, rather than dictated by theory. And she persisted in it despite her recognition that, in her own words, it set her apart from "real academics" and might jeopardize her career. All her subsequent research has tended to break new ground and to be based on problems that she herself, or those around her, have experienced in real life, rather than being primarily theory-based. And it has risked the adverse judgment of established scholars in her field.[1] In short, Mara's research has become a form of social and political activism, and her reputation as an investigator and writer derives from the success with which she has spoken to the condition of her readers.

Before this adult version of Mara's identity emerged full-blown, however, two other significant events appear in the story she tells. The first is her study of what it meant to be a woman on the faculty of a predominantly male university. Her observation was that male and female faculty, herself among them, were approached very differently by students. Typically, her first approach was an intellectual one: she constructed a role analysis in sociological terms and decided to collect some data. The nature of her interviews must inevitably have brought her into closer acquaintance with other women on the faculty. In trying to collect and interpret their experiences, she undoubtedly heard some feminist "truths" that applied to her own life. The experience of doing this project must also have served to bridge the gap she felt between herself and those other women. The evidence I have for this is only indirect: she wrote a paper that was circulated hand to hand and gained widespread recognition in the feminist community. In her present life, she counts many of these women as her friends and allies. Remembering her previous feelings of alienation from feminist women, this change seems a notable one. What might account for her newfound readiness to make common cause with other women is a certain degree of resolution of tensions in relationship with her parents. During the section of the interview in which she discussed her conversion to feminist thinking she sums up as follows:

> Now, when I look at my life, [I would say] it was a striving to reject all those roles that were stereotypically done, without any ideology to explain them except "the ideology of inferiority."

This same phrase, "the ideology of inferiority," occurred earlier in the interview when she was describing her parents' sex-typed ideas of "what a woman had to be," and in characterizing their reasons for insisting upon a "practical" education for their daughters. In the final section of the interview, she told me how she hears her parents' teachings now that she is an adult:

> I had a conversation recently, right before my father died, with my mother, and I was just astounded. They believe, I mean they would *say* that women are equal in intelligence, but that their *role* is at home with the children. I mean, not only that, but certainly they would not go along with [the idea] that men should compromise their careers as much as

women, or along with women [in order to] *share* these roles
with women. It was absolutely something they never believed in!

The astonishment in her tone of voice conveyed the adult
woman's delight at being able to hear clearly at last what, as
a child, she found puzzling and oppressive. As a child she
had resented her mother without understanding why. She
observed the emotional circumstances of her parents' marriage and saw her mother "as a pitiful person." She states:

> Mostly I saw her as vulnerable, because I thought she loved
> my father very much, and it was quite clear to me [that] he
> didn't love her at all; although they stayed together in a bit-
> ter relationship that went on all their lives.

This mixture of resentment and pity, as pointed out earlier,
makes it particularly difficult for children to give up their
emotional attachment to a parent, in this case the mother,
who is simultaneously experienced as a victim and an oppressor. Mara speaks of coming later to understand her
mother's life "in terms of the rage of women against their
children." Her explanation for the behavior that made her
mother angry stresses frustrated feelings of rage and so
takes her particular experience of oppression into the realm
of many women's shared experiences. But what about her
father? Mara voices no anger at him or at the role he played
in her mother's life. He appears to symbolize a life of intellectual freedom and moral privilege. In yearning for an education in the arts and sciences rather than in nursing, and
in becoming a professor "well-known" in her own realm,
Mara may be said to have emulated him and made his powers her own. But in her disdain for academic scholarship
without social relevance or sensitivity, she seems to be striking a new note.

The Social Context

I have lingered over the dynamics of personal change in Mara's life, at the risk of overlooking the very significant evidence of how she has been touched by social change. Her case is an interesting one, because she starts out resisting change (by ignoring the call of the Women's Movement and distancing herself from feminist women) and winds up an advocate of change. To attribute the sources of her anger solely to her difficult relations with her mother is to play into a stereotyped image of the movement's followers as frustrated neurotics. If there is a lesson to be drawn from Mara's case, it is only that anger is often the only emotion strong enough to motivate a decisive break with one's attachments to the past—not that the source of that anger is necessarily to be found in the dynamics of the family of origin. Even in Mara's case, it is *the structure* of that family's pattern of relationships, and the values encoded in that structure, that can be recognized as a universal element in her personal history. So too both *the desire* for an education as "a way out" and the *real opportunities* that were opened up to her by virtue of the underlying societal changes that touched the lives of many women (Holter 1970; and Mandle 1979). The path that she traveled in moving from ignorance of and resistance to the Women's Movement, to playing a leading part within its ranks may well be a common one: she is of the middle- or upper-middle class, living among people who have both money and time to spend at their discretion; she clearly sees the advantages and privileges of an education, yet she meets obstacles in gaining access to education and in realizing its supposed advantages. These obstacles are clearly linked to a gender role ideology that she has never learned to accept. Her early awareness of the inequities of that ideology may be looked upon as a "failure" in her socializaton, but Mara says that she looked upon that ideology as unconvincing and unjustifiable from the beginning. What she lacked, she tells us, was a social analysis that would help to explain her parents' attempts to force it upon her. Had her relations with her parents been less troubled, she might have questioned less and accepted her role in the gender system until much later in her life. As it was, she felt *they* prevented her from using the major opportunity she saw of getting out of the family and gaining financial and emotional independence. It would be inaccurate, however, to conclude that, "lacking a social analysis," she was instantly ready to accept the analysis that the Women's Movement offered. According to her own testimony, she resisted both its message and its proponents during the entire period of her graduate school education. She makes it clear that during this time she kept distant from other people in general, and from women in particular. The key to this distance, psychologically speaking, lies in the image of femaleness that she derived from her childhood. Seeing her mother as a victim, she experienced herself as a victim, and fought against that vulnerability by applying herself rigorously to her studies. She achieved a degree and a position in the academic world that guaranteed some standing in the ranks of academia, where the required skills in intellectual analysis and in forceful presentation of one's ideas suited her well. Her choice of topics, however, often seems to have served a double purpose: her studies of veterans, female faculty, and women who decide to have abortions were all inspired by a deeply personal interest. This approach seems to have allowed her both to enter deeply into the emotional issues surrounding each of these topics in her own life, and to energize her work by linking the demands of her profession to the values she has cherished. This work has permitted her to accept herself for what she is and has given her an increasing sense of self-confidence. This is what permits her to say of her current involvement, with such a sense of triumph, that it permits her a sense of "affirmation as opposed to negation." Instead of fighting her own feelings of victimization, she succeeds in this new work in putting her hard-earned skills to positive use on behalf of all women.

The life that Mara has shaped for herself bears witness to the social changes that took root in middle-class women in the United States during the early 1970s. Certainly the availability of opportunities for education and for a role in the workplace was a critical factor in her life. Her case does not suggest that a change in the social definition of women's roles, by itself, would have been sufficient to motivate the choices she made. Nevertheless, the changing ideological climate of the 1960s probably facilitated her success, in avoiding the roles of wife and nurse, and transforming her into an activist-researcher. The times were ripe for her admission to graduate school, and her work gained a recognition that it might otherwise have been denied, by an audience that was eager to hear her analysis of questions that bore directly upon other women's lives.

Education and opportunity have played an important role in Mara's life. It happens that education and opportunity were strongly linked during the 1950s and 1960s, more strongly than today, for example, when both demographics and economics conspire to make the future for women with higher education far more uncertain. Mara resolved, in her own unique way the strains that women of her generation experienced between what they had been led to expect of life as a daughter, wife, or mother, and what she aspired to in her life as an intellectual and a professional woman, realizing that her aspirations entailed several kinds of personal change. In rebelling against nursing school and the forces in her family that had sent her there, she discovered her anger and paid a price for burning her bridges behind her. In reconstructing her life during and after graduate school, perhaps the most significant change came when she accepted the freedom to choose her own subjects of study, in terms of what held personal meaning for her life. In so doing, she found her own voice and learned how her work could be sustained by her anger at what she perceived to be the failure of American public institutions to respond with justice and equality to the changes in U.S. society. This change towards an identity of activist-researcher was made possible also by increased self-acceptance, an attitude that needed to encompass both her attitudes towards her mother, in particular, and other women in general.

Notes

The complete text of this interview is on file with the author. I have tried, in so far as possible, to convey both the tone and the sequence of the portions quoted in my discussion.

1. The necessity for disguising the identity of the subject of this interview prohibits clear-cut identification of all research projects that "Mara" pursued.

References

Erikson, E. H. 1975. "On the Nature of Psycho-Historical Evidence." *Life History and the Historical Moment*. New York: W. W. Norton.

Holter, Harriet. 1970. *Sex Roles and Social Structure*. Oslo, Norway: Universitetsforlaget.

Janoff-Bulman, Ronnie. 1979. "Characterological Versus Behavioral Self-Blame: Inquiries into Depression and Rape." *Journal of Personality and Social Psychology* 37: 1798–1809.

MacKinnon, Catherine. 1979. *Sexual Harassment of Working Women*. New Haven: Yale University Press.

Mandle, Joan. 1979. *Women and Social Change in America*. Princeton: Princeton Books.

Marris, P. 1974. *Loss and Change*. New York: Pantheon.

Mason, Karen O., J. Czajka, and Sara Arber. 1976. "Changes in U.S. Womens' Sex Role Attitudes: 1964–1974." *American Sociological Review* 41: 576–596.

Sanger, Susan Phipps, and H. A. Alker. 1972. "Dimensions of Internal-External Control and the Womens' Liberation Movement." *Journal of Social Issues* 28, no. 4: 115–130.

Thornton, A. and D. Freedman. 1979. "Changes in Sex-Role Attitudes of Women: 1962–77." *American Sociological Review* 44, 831–842.

Walker, Lenore. 1979. *The Battered Woman*. New York: Harper and Row.

Wortman, Camille B., and J. W. Brehm. 1975. "Responses to Uncontrollable Outcomes: An Integration of Reactance Theory and the Learned Helplessness Model." In L. Berkowitz, ed. *Advances in Experimental Social Psychology*, vol. 8. New York: Academic Press.

Wrightsman, L. S., and Kay Deaux. 1980. "Social Influence and Personal Control." *Social Psychology in the 80s*, pp. 378–401. 3rd ed. Monterey; Calif.: Brooks/Cole.

III

The Complexities
of Consciousness

7

Women's Moral Dilemmas:
in Pursuit of Integrity

by Sue J. M. Freeman

Introduction

Moral choice is an attribute uniquely human. As a process, it is as intellectually puzzling as it is emotionally gripping. In psychology, efforts to define and understand morality have been disposed to universal formulations without respect to time or place. Given morality's transcendence as common and vital to human affairs, universals of moral development would seem preferable to a situational ethics that is neither predictable nor readily taught. Our search for universals of moral development, however, has resulted in inquiries and findings that isolate individuals' moral choices from their social contexts and from other aspects of their own development. [1] By challenging long-standing approaches to the psychological study of morality, we discover how women's notions of moral choice are informed by their changing social contexts.

Here social context refers to immediate, personal life circumstances and to larger considerations of time and place, that is, social and/or cultural influences characteristic of what is sometimes called an historical moment. How these broader structural circumstances, be they political, economic, or cultural, interact with one's personal life depends somewhat upon individual interpretation and translation. These interpretive processes, or perceptions, are shaped by one's current and previous psychological and social development which is, in turn, imbedded in immediate and broader social contexts, both past and present. In this study, women's moral notions can be seen as a function of their perceptions of their own evolving psychological development, which necessarily includes its history within a social framework and its current interaction with social change. [2]

My research begins to explore the relation between social change in the larger society and individual moral development. I am addressing the question of why personal change occurs, not in terms of a universal hierarchy of male-derived development, but rather as a concomitant of contemporary social factors. This approach implies that the changes people identify and the developmental patterns that researchers describe, are, themselves, subject to change.

Indeed, my evidence suggests that developmental patterns described here and by other researchers, such as Kohlberg and Gilligan, are much more tied to social context than has previously been assumed. To understand moral development we must go beyond examination of people's responses to real or hypothetical dilemmas. We must place those dilemmas and the responses generated by them within a framework that includes such questions as: What becomes a dilemma, to whom, and for what reasons? Without this kind of sensitivity to the social and historical circumstances of the group studied, psychologists cannot be certain that the cognitive distinctions they have drawn are truly gender-based.

This research suggests one way in which social context might be incorporated into psychological modes of inquiry. With increased emphasis on the processes rather than the products of human development, notions of context and the differences between actual and perceived change may begin to be refined. Such ideas as these become apparent when assumptions implicit to traditional modes of psychological inquiry are abandoned, in favor of fundamental questions such as what is a moral dilemma and what makes it so.

Conceptions of adult moral development are undergoing a revolutionary change. Well-established frameworks have been challenged and proved wanting (Frankel 1976; Gibbs 1977; Kurtines and Greif 1974; Simpson 1974; and Sullivan 1977); new frameworks are being articulated to address identified inadequacies (Gilligan 1977 and 1982). In the course of this re-examination, scholars are exploring the fundamental limits of analytic models and explanations customarily employed in the field of psychology (Freeman 1981). As yet, few have demonstrated concretely how inadequacies in the general views of moral development result from limits in conventional psychological methodologies. This chapter focuses on those fundamental limits that regularly occur in research on moral development, but that have not been sufficiently identified.

A central question here is gender, and the new types of research methods to be employed if its ramifications are to be considered fully. As with other approaches to gender in the social sciences, new questions and methods often lead to a different perspective on the way all questions are raised.

In the case of psychological research, the field has been dominated by male-defined inquiries that have confined the categories, methodology, and understandings to a narrow repertoire. Different trajectories of moral development for males and females are now beginning to be explored in a way that is more reflective of gender-specific conceptualizations. My research, in addition to contributing to that exploration, suggests the importance of grounding the notion of trajectories of moral development in the processes of social context and change.

Gilligan (1982) has brought to light the importance of a gender perspective in the formulation of psychological theories of human development. For many years such theories, based upon male experience, dictated the prototype for human development (Freud 1925; Kohlberg 1963; and Piaget, 1965). These theories at best were unable to account for women and at worst relegated them to an inferior position on various scales, hierarchies, and gauges of psychological development.[3] When women's voices are considered apart from male-established standards, however, an expanded understanding of the intricacies and complexities of human development is found.

Paradoxically, theorists of human development have measured both sexes according to the same yardstick, while implicitly assuming natural, and therefore legitimate, differences in characteristics and life direction by gender. Although Gilligan has departed from the standard methodology, her results confirm those implicit assumptions until later in development, when males and females manifest characteristics that have typified the opposite sex. Gilligan argues that the path of psychological development is indeed different for males and females. For males, the primary developmental progression involves separation, individuation, and an independent stance in the world of achievement. Females, on the other hand, travel along a road of personal attachment, connection, and relationship where caring is paramount and selfishness and hurting others are to be avoided. What is less explicitly delineated by her data, but certainly an important assertion, is her contention that both sexes move toward each other's paths in the course of development. Thus, males become more concerned with relationship to others and females with consequences to self as they approach psychological maturity.

These familiar differences tend to conform to established notions of what characterizes and distinguishes each gender's approach to intrapersonal development and interpersonal relationship. Here, as in other psychological research, it is important to examine the contribution of methodology to findings that support conventional understandings. Gilligan's data are drawn primarily from interviews with women in the throes of and subsequent to an abortion decision, and from a sample of males and females responding to questions about moral dilemmas. The abortion decision, one that is peculiar to women, invokes the most personal kind of reflection upon questions of self, relation to close others, and ramifications for future life. Here morality is expanded beyond the abstract, apersonal considerations elicited by hypothetical moral dilemmas that have been most commonly used in moral development research. The nature of the abortion choice itself, however, may "pull" toward issues of care and of self versus other that are traditionally associated with femaleness, particularly maternity. Further, the very existence of a legal abortion choice represents an aspect of context not central to Gilligan's inquiry; that is, the extent to which women's personal development affects and has been affected by broader social change in the form of the recent Women's Movement and associated legislation in the United States is not examined within her framework of analysis.

Dissatisfaction with a male model of moral development that consistently found inadequacies in females motivated my own initial research on adult development (Freeman 1974 and 1981; and Freeman and Giebank 1979). Calling both theory and methodology into question, I believed that the very starting point of a male-designed hypothetical dilemma skewed consequent findings. Thus, I began with the question, "What is a moral dilemma?" from the viewpoint of women's lives rather than from the researcher's construction. Believing further that moral development involved the whole of a person in thought, feeling and behavior, I posed questions designed to tap those aspects, instead of focusing only on detached thought about hypothetical problems. Also, in light of the absence of attention to contextual influences in psychological development, my inquiry included questions about interactions between both immediate and larger social context and personal development. Rather than seeking a smooth sequence of universally encompassing categories, I was interested in how individuals represent, psychologically, on their own initiatives, their sense of place in time and space, and how that might be understood and registered as variations in personal development.

While Gilligan provided the first viable, gender-based alternative to the established male-model of moral development (Kohlberg 1976), her approach also mandated that women respond to a particular moral dilemma that she, as scholar, defined, denoted, and categorized. Moreover, just as Kohlberg's methodology and use of hypothetical dilemmas encouraged certain kinds of responses as opposed to others, so the specialness of the abortion issue used by Gilligan tended to elicit from women disproportionately relational responses of "selfishness" and hurting. By way of illustrating the limitations inherent in even Gilligan's sophisticated work, I might point to women's self-defined moral dilemmas in which "selfishness" is a social and historical construction, defined and applied by circumstances and gender. Thus, individuals' responses cannot be judged free of the expectation each gender holds for itself and the opposite gender. What today constitutes "selfishness" in women is tantamount to an expected given in male development—independent achievement.

My research shows that women now see their separation from family, independence and individuation, which are ordinarily associated with male development, as the natural, but still problematic, outcome of social change. [4] The women I studied are still ill at ease when they recognize, acknowledge, and pursue their individual desires or rights; and for that reason they call such actions moral dilemmas. They tend to believe that individual and independent identity for women is a "selfish" function of a socially constructed belief system. Given the nature of women's socialization, their concern for others when making moral decisions is predictable. For women, commitment and responsibility to others have assumed a moral precedence over self. Self-interest is a male, not a female, prerogative, and women have been enjoined against "selfishness" as a moral dictum specific to their gender. That they now feel compelled to seek personal freedom and an independent integrity is a reflection of social change. That this search is fraught with personal anxieties and even anguish is largely gender-based. It is not accidental, therefore, that the abortion choice, itself caused by and reflective of social change, can precipitate a radical revision in women's thoughts and feelings about themselves and others. With further social change and another generation of women, we might expect displacement of these notions by different manifestations of interaction between new social contexts, gender constructions, and personal development.

Instead of presenting male-designed hypothetical situations for cognitive moral judgments, this study sought to investigate thought, feeling, and behavior in reference to women's moral issues. Connections between those issues and social change were explored through questions of women's perceptions of the relation of social context to their individual development. Interview questions began with the women's own definitions of moral dilemmas. What do women define as the moral questions with which they have struggled? How did they think about these? How did they feel about themselves at the time and after their resolution? What did they do to resolve the dilemmas? What effect did their personal life circumstance and the larger social context have on their thoughts, feelings, and actions? Here women were asked explicitly about the social circumstances of their decision making. Their perceptions of the influence of context, in immediate life situations and in the larger society, were explored in the interviews.

Thirty-one women were interviewed about the moral dilemmas or decisions in their own lives. The women ranged in age from nineteen to fifty-six; and most were white, American, and middle class, although three called themselves working class and three claimed economically privileged backgrounds. They come from various parts of the United States, and while two spent their childhoods elsewhere, most were raised in this country. They were housewives, working wives and mothers, students of college age and older, single parents, lesbians, single working women, widows, and a Catholic sister. Although they varied in income level, political and religious beliefs, the majority considered themselves middle class and were either already living in that stratum or striving towards it.

While demographic sampling variables were not controlled, this pilot study is revealing with regard to women's perceptions of their moral responsibilities, especially in light of the changing complexion of contemporary American family. In addition, the study demonstrates how useful it is, for a deeper understanding of the course and nature of psychological development, for people themselves to describe how their lives intersect with traditional and countervailing social ideologies.

Social Constructions of Women and Morality

True to their often imputed historical role, contemporary women have led the recent foray into questioning longstanding beliefs about individual rights and social responsibility. Women have discovered that they are in a paradoxical position. As mothers at home, they are to shape tomorrow's citizens by teaching them fairness, justice, and equality, while they themselves do not receive equal treatment by law or by custom. Their protected childlike status is in part a function of their position in the domestic sphere; but while women have been placed there by tradition, it is the male-dominated public sphere that is esteemed. When women move into the public sphere, they are often treated as though they are out of place and belong at home. Not only are they perceived and treated differently from men—and in many ways as inferior—but such women have also served as the objects of considerable recrimination for abandoning home and family. When they behave as if they are challenging the prevailing norms and disputing the established boundaries represented by public and domestic spheres, women as well as men begin to evaluate this behavior in highly-charged moral terms. When apparently conducting their lives in consonance with conventional mores, women are called moral teachers. When seemingly abandoning such conventions, women are blamed for moral disintegration within society. Such notions could not have emerged were it not for the fact that psychological development is simultaneously socially rooted and, to an extent, politically and socially directed.

226

Historically, women have been charged as caretakers of morality because of what was believed to be their inherent nature as well as their role in the family (Lasch 1976). As wife and mother in the home, a woman supposedly stood as guardian of consensually agreed upon moral values for her husband and children. Whereas men could normally be expected to stray from the moral fold, and children had to be initiated and tutored into correct beliefs and behavior, women were designated as "natural" moral mainstays (Elshtain 1974). As long as women were at the moral helm in the home, maintaining and reinforcing normative values, society's business was to proceed in the secure knowledge that its private morals were in reliably watchful hands.

The increase in women's mobility and freedom outside of the home, and their renunciation of characteristics traditionally described as inherent and gender-specific, also coincided with a resurgence in societal attention to morality. Large scale moral questioning over the past two decades parallels a social reordering initiated by women. Despite shared societal responsibility for moral maintenance among such institutions as church and state, it is the movement of women out of the home and the familial changes such movement appears to support that are associated with massive moral confusion.

How do women themselves view the transformation of their social and economic roles? How do they perceive their responsibilities to self and others during this period of rapid social change? How do they account for their changing relation to home and family, especially when these changes call into question the public (male)-domestic (female) dichotomy that has seemed so fundamental to sexual divisions of the moral order in America?

The research reported here indicates that women, at least these thirty-one cases, now want the right to make active, conscious choices about the course of their own development. Their freedom of choice is restricted when their identities and roles are predetermined by conventions, which the women themselves have internalized. Women's primary family commitments place very real limits on their individual exploration of self and social contribution, but these women are nonetheless compelled to become more instrumental in their own destinies. In order to do so, they struggle with themselves and with other upholders of traditions—be they parents, husband, or other women—to assert their right to independent achievement and sense of competence. Self-actualization is a moral imperative for human beings, and women are no exception,[5] but self-actualization implies self-determination, and women have been denied that right by virtue of a domestically confined definition of female fulfillment. Now, women are claiming their right to their own lives, to the freedom of self-pursuit outside of the family. That claim has become a moral one for women, who must defy a tradition that has denied them the right to pursue their own development in an unfettered way.

In theory and practice, women have been assumed to give precedence to the well-being of others and to interpersonal considerations over such individualistic concerns as their independent identities and life directions. My findings suggest that women's consideration of self as equal, rather than secondary, to others is a significant developmental achievement that must ultimately refer to social context. It is, after all, a social belief system that had shaped and maintained women's subordination of self to others, and another organization of values that now encourage women's self recognition and pursuit. Because of the long-standing

227

228

strength and pervasiveness of traditional social constructions, American, white, middle-class women have had great
difficulty claiming power or believing that they possess
power to determine their own self-images—to say nothing
of the direction of their lives. A woman's struggle is not only
against upholders of the traditional views but also against
herself, her socialization, self-image, and her formerly held
beliefs about her life paths.

Because of their socialization, then, women's claims to
power over self and life direction take on moral significance. What would seem to be an ordinary developmental
task has become instead a moral dilemma for women who
must overturn their socialization and their own self-images
to claim power over their lives.

The belief system that relegates women's primary responsibility to familial caretaking becomes an integral part
of individual and collective psyches. Such belief systems
help define the life paths of individuals through implicit, if
not explicit, assumptions about what is "natural" and therefore "right." Thus females have been designated as inherently suited to perpetuating the collective good by giving
precedence to the care and feeding of others. More than a
role, this life-calling gained legitimacy through its claim to
a natural, even biological, order that translated into a social
ideology with collective and individual psychological representations. To violate this image of social well-being has required a fundamental questioning of woman's essence, her
value, and her morality. Questioning in this case involves
overturning what has become a "natural" and "proper" order, which is not only externally imposed but also psychologically internalized. Challenging this social order and its
psychological representations serves as a source of new
moral dilemmas for individual women.

As suggested in interviews, these challenges have been
facilitated by the appearance of the new social ideologies

that have been disseminated by the Women's Movement in the United States during the past two decades. Increasing recognition of the tenuousness of assumptions about women's nature and destiny has promoted revisions of our ideas about the appropriate and necessary functions of the genders. Changes in ideas and social roles are encouraged in various arenas, on the individual and collective psychological level through "consciousness raising," and in apparent social change through the complex manifestations of society's institutions.

Even without consensus about the occurrence of social change or what it might consist of, protracted ideological challenge can influence psychological perception and awareness of possibilities. Thus, women have become aware of alternative social ideologies that sanction and promote their pursuit of new life directions. Perceptions of change are enhanced by the emergence of options, which are now legitimized by new institutions and role models. My point is not whether social change has occurred, but how the perception of it shapes individual development on the psychological and behavioral level.

Women's Moral Dilemmas and What Makes Them So

The dilemmas[6] that the women in this study term *moral* are diverse in content, but can be grouped together thematically. The themes include sexuality, marital commitment, issues of independence and individuation, commitment conflicts, and political assertion. In interviews about actual moral dilemmas of their lives, women discuss the kinds of issues that are easily recognizable as moral ones. As normally defined and understood by members of contemporary American society, sexuality, divorce, conflicts of commit-

230

ment and responsibility to self and other each carries a major moral connotation. Furthermore, these categories have become the particular province of women. That is, they fall primarily within the domestic sphere, where women have traditionally been posed as gatekeepers of society's morality. Most dilemmas of sexuality, divorce, and commitment conflicts invoke the familial woman whose consideration of consequences to parents and/or children (existing or yet to be born) is ever present. Where "blood" families are not foremost in a woman's conscience, her metaphorical family, usually a network of women, becomes her alter ego. In any case, both the origin and resolution of women's actual moral dilemmas can be traced to their perceived injunction to act as moral role model for their families.

An examination of the criteria that constitute a *moral* dilemma further corroborates women's customary orientation to others, especially family, to whom primary responsibility is assumed. Mothers serve as the most obvious examples of women whose family roles and responsibilities are central to their moral decisions. A fifty-five-year-old woman, who could not effectively combine work with child care, expresses what has been traditionally women's, as opposed to men's, charge:

> When you bring children into the world, they're your responsibility. As long as they're dependent on you. Until they are able to go out and fend for themselves, the buck stops with you. And you know, if you don't accept that responsibility, your children may not survive. Maybe you won't . . . lose them while they're children . . . but eventually you may when they're grown up, because you haven't made the right choices.

Implicit in this statement is the notion of women as blameworthy in the eventuality of children's waywardness. As family mainstays, mothers are held responsible for the development and well-being of their children, who are always a central concern when women contemplate divorce. Another woman expresses the views of several:

> [My daughter] was always a very important part of the decision making, and the part which always aroused a little guilt. What would happen to [the child] if the marriage dissolves? How will it be for [her] if she has to be a member of a divorced family? What will it be for her not to live with her father. . . . And I felt a tremendous amount of responsibility to give [her] a family.

Trained to sacrifice self for other, especially with regard to children, yet another mother learns to consider herself last:

> And you have this feeling of obligation that everybody else comes before you do.

The strength of women's moral obligations to their children is such that it begins before birth:

> [Natural childbirth is a moral decision] because of the child involved. See, if it were just a decision regarding me and my physical health, that would be one thing. But I have a moral obligation to, um, bring a healthy child into the world.

In a sense, those obligations can be said to precede a female's own entry into the world, in the form of the socialization that awaits her. Marriage and family have been the prescribed "right" path for women. Divorce, a serious break from that path, can be the occasion for reflection on the source of one's moral standards.

> I just assumed that wasn't the right thing to do. I should just stay home. I had a lot of moral "shoulds" and "shouldn'ts" for the way a wife and mother are supposed to behave. And I operated under them . . . [now] I'm suspicious of the word "should." Where does it come from? The world at large puts it there.

It is not only in relation to the family that women feel obliged to consider others and "not to hurt."

> The decision I made, how is it gonna affect people around me? . . . I don't think I could—I would never want to intentionally hurt anyone.

Even in reference to a job situation, a twenty-one-year-old believes:

> I still think that once you make a commitment to something that's . . . that affects other people, it's really important to secure [that is, hold fast to that commitment].

Moreover, an individual's action can positively affect others outside of family. A single woman who took a public stand against sex discrimination in employment did so not just for herself but for all women. Her identity is with a family of women:

> [moral] questions that are important to me personally but, which are not, that do not just involve myself. In other words, I am a woman, and therefore I am all women. And something that happens to me happens to all women, and something that happens to all women happens to me. And I can't separate myself out. That makes it a moral decision. . . . A moral decision to me is not just a personal decision, I guess. It's based on principles, it's based on values, it's based on ideals. . . . It involves concern not only for yourself but also for other people. It involves a broader scope than just personal one.

Thus for these women a common criterion of a moral dilemma is the effect of an action on others. The first group of others ordinarily considered by women is the family of origin and procreation. The primacy of family in a woman's life stems from a particular set of social mores that characterize females as inherently other-directed and domestically focused. Our society's division of labor has come to require that women assume full and often sole responsibility for the physical and spiritual well-being of others. Further, their caretaking role is widely celebrated as "right" for the individual woman and for society. The sexual division of labor which clearly defines and limits who and what women and men are to become has gained legitimacy and support of society's institutions—economic, political, educational, and religious—and has thereby been perpetrated as the moral order.

233

Women's mandate as caretakers is overdetermined by social institutions actively maintaining the traditional social structure. One of those institutions is the family itself which, of course, reflects and perpetuates the social order. Socialization begins at home and is continued outside of home at play, school, church. For the most part, the fundamental messages communicated to individuals from early childhood—or at least the ways in which they are conventionally received—appear consistent in spite of the many different institutional sources, and therefore are extremely powerful. Those messages derive ultimate power, however, from the fact that they are instilled in children in a formative state when they are fluid, dependent, and suggestible. The content of messages and their assigned value in turn, become formative as they are internalized, becoming part of the person's sense of self, reality, and the world.

Both sexes are socialized according to norms that specify personal characteristics and behavior held appropriate to the social beings they are destined to become. My findings indicate that a most crucial distinction between male and female socialization must be drawn between differential access to paths of normal development, specifically with respect to the process of separation from family, with all of its necessary implications for future physical and psychological independence. Whereas males, in adolescence, are expected to critically question society's most cherished tenets

(Erikson 1963), females have been expected to conform to and willingly accept the values transmitted through their own socialization. This turn of events is consistent with each sex's socialization prior to adolescence. In childhood, boys are encouraged toward self-sufficiency, instrumental competence, and emotional and intellectual independence. Their challenges to authority and behavioral divergence in adolescence are a logical outcome of childhood growing toward assumed, eventual leadership and maturity in the public arena. For girls, too, adolescence has represented a continuation of childhood preparation for a life suited to the limited scale of the domestic sphere. In this case, the aim has been not power, independence, or self-sufficiency, but rather an orientation to the welfare of others, dependence, and interpersonal responsibility. Even when a focus on the self would be normal in adolescent development, females have been deprived of the freedom to shape their own identities. The effectiveness of their socialization has worked either to curtail a period of free exploration and experimentation[7] or to replace it with an early marriage, which is both testimony to and continuation of that socialization.

The privilege of position in the domestic sphere is presumed to be protection and removal from the harsh realities of public life where power can corrupt. As moral teachers and guardians, wives and mothers are not to be concerned with power except in the case of control over those even more dependent—their children. Although women's authority over children is accepted as part of their role and self-definition, that authority is experienced as responsibility more than power. With those of equal status, women often express a moral injunction against "judging others" or being "judgmental." Adhering to their roles, women must eschew power over others. Most important, however, their socialization in many cases seems to render them powerless, and to instill in them a sense of powerlessness over their own identities.

Women's moral dilemmas and the criteria distinguishing them include both the expected and the extraordinary. It is not surprising to find women discussing sexuality, divorce, commitment conflicts, and political action as moral dilemmas that invoke guilt about responsibility and consequences for others. What is extraordinary, however, is that personal individuation and development of an independent identity are *moral* dilemmas for women. For some women, independence itself was the dilemma's name; almost all women classified other dilemmas as moral mainly because of their implications for independence. Criteria of responsibility, commitment, and consequences to others were commonly cited as constituents of a moral decision. Independence, consequences to self, and power and control over one's own life paralleled, and in the long run, overshadowed the more common criteria in determining women's moral choices.

The process of separation and individuation would seem to be normal grist for the developmental mill, not necessarily calling for moral decisions. Because of a foreshortened or delimited psychosocial moratorium, these women have not had the opportunity to forge their own separate identities and, in the process of doing so, to develop their independence and sense of competence to function as adults. Instead, they learn to accept socially determined identities of dependence within a domestic sphere. Consequently, their struggles for independence come many years after adolescence, when they themselves may be mothers, and are usually constrained by real responsibilities to others, a condition dramatically different from the normal psychosocial moratorium. In claiming their own lives, these women face two major obstacles: their extant and very real commitment and responsibilities to others, often dependent children; and their identities inherited from a tradition that is incorporated quite fundamentally into the notions women bear of who they really are.

Independence, then, is a *moral* dilemma because it requires women to deviate from their socialization and their long-standing identities. Rather than a naturally evolving development, independent identity must be *actively* pursued by women. Acting deliberately against tradition itself constitutes, psychologically, an attack on their own socialization. In deciding to act, these women feel themselves to be at risk, a condition not uncommon to moral dilemmas. Frequently, the first risk is experienced as one of physical survival. Having been dependent on others for physical sustenance, women face and fear their own incapacity to provide themselves and their children with the basics of food, clothing, and shelter.

> . . . economically I had no particular way to support myself at that point. . . . I knew it was gonna be tough. So, I was faced with having to work as well as trying to raise the child. . . . So, in a sense, it would have been much easier to kind of save the marriage, have the economic support, at least a father figure . . . and to stay in the situation with those kinds of comforts around.
>
> I had never done anything, you know, by myself. I got married at 17, and for five years I had a husband who did absolutely everything, including telling me what we were having for dinner, and what kind of clothing I would wear. . . . I went from that to living in my own place with my children. But my mother was always around the corner. . . . My parents, for most of my life, dictated my life.
>
> At the time, I was an extremely dependent person, probably absolutely devastated by . . . a break-up of the marriage. What was I going to do and how was I going to survive? This was the worst thing that ever happened to me, with three children to bring up. And I was just totally devastated by the whole thing, you know, to the point of near collapse. Because I didn't know how I was going to survive, and . . . but determined. The children were what, what made me, you know, say 'Look,' you know, 'pull up your bootstraps, you're somebody's mother. You can't really collapse, you have a job to do. There are three people depending on you.'

It took me a good six years to . . . achieve my own independence, psychologically.

Ironically, women's responsibilities to others, particularly
to children, impede their freedom to discover their own capacities for physical survival; and thus to explore, experiment, and follow the lead of their own developing identities.
Mothers, unlike adolescents and young adults, are simply
not free to do and become whatever they might, as long as
children are dependent on them. What they say they need
is a reciprocity of independence, such that the gradual
weaning of children's dependency coincides with a parent's
increasing freedom to pursue an independent self. Mothers
interviewed claim to purposely foster their children's independence partly because their own hinges so heavily on it.
They speak of enabling children to avoid their mother's dilemma and of simultaneously providing themselves with
more opportunity for independence. One divorced mother
of three is waiting until her children are more independent:

> It's a position [her job] I'm not particularly happy with, but
> it's something I have to do because I have my kids. It's kind
> of like I've put my own, put my own life off. . . . I'll probably
> wait til they're in high school, and when they're wanting to
> have a little distance from me, then I'll go back to school and
> do what I need to do.

Another woman who is experiencing her own self-reliance
tries to encourage her daughter's independence through
practice in decision making:

> I try to . . . just say . . . 'Here are your options of—whatever
> the situation is—you can either do this, or you can do that,
> or you could do this.' And kind of lay it out to her so that she
> can see what would be best for her at the time. Of course,
> her decisions are little ones, now.

While the practical risks to self and other are not to be minimized, it is the psychological risk that the women I studied characteristically emphasize. The awareness of an emerging self, which diverges from the long-standing traditional one, threatens a woman's relationship to herself and to others. She had accepted social definitions of her identity as her own, and she is surprised to find her adopted identity no longer suitable. The acknowledgment of a discrepancy between a woman's socially determined identity and an independently forged one appears to place women's lives in jeopardy. Such women face the censure of significant others and of the larger society. Moreover, such women are confronted by self-images that no longer sufficiently account for the persons they are in the process of becoming. Aware of the social response to their deviance and its impact on others in their lives, these women are ultimately concerned most by their sense of inner conflict.

If and when it comes—and it comes at different points in these women's lives—the urge towards individuation is arresting and finally irrepressible. Despite pragmatic exigency and social censure, women cannot deny their emerging selves. To do so would be a kind of psychological death, and indeed, women speak about their decisions, literally, in terms of survival.

> . . . either there was going to be a divorce or there was going to be a marriage which felt like death to me.
>
> I knew if I stayed that I couldn't survive, and I think that I had to choose for me to live. And I think that's a very, very, um, just about as basic a decision as you could ever make, and hopefully one wouldn't have to.
>
> Everything's much clearer to me now. In a way, I'm amazed that I could have even considered anything other than. . . . Anything else would have been suicide for me. [Now] I feel good about myself. No, terrific. I feel more whole as a person than I have ever been.

Although physical survival may in fact be risky, it is psychological survival that ultimately determines women's decisions. Deprived of what would seem to be the natural rights of an adult, women are compelled to undertake a more comprehensive set of activities as independent individuals. If a propensity for self-expansion, for "becoming" more of what one can be, is portrayed by our culture as natural and perhaps inherent in human beings—although, in effect, almost exclusively ascribed to men—conversely, the suppression of a developing self is generally considered a death blow. Thus by virtue of at least one of the cultured messages American society transmits, women would appear to have no choice but to pursue their developing selves. Periods of social change enable women to hear and act upon those messages as applying to themselves. But in so doing, they are claiming rights to self-determination and power denied them by their socialization and mitigated by the traditional social mores embedded in our culture.

Countering the relatively diverse content of women's dilemmas is a similarity of criteria for categorizing them as moral. Morality comes to mean personal integrity, whether the dilemma itself is one of divorce, discrimination, sexuality, political action, or independence. The dilemmas women choose to discuss are often described as "marker events" or "turning points," because they represent a significant change not only in their lives but also in their senses of themselves. The decisions represent a separation from socially determined identities and a move toward self-definition and independence. The degree to which women can achieve their new goals varies, of course, with their actual circumstances. For example, a fifty-two-year-old woman viewed her divorce and relocation to another state as essential to her survival despite the deviance and the consequent isolation she suffered. Living with dependent children, she still yearns for a moratorium that would permit self-exploration:

> I guess I'm, and this is a long range thing, needing—not just wanting, but needing—leading my own life more than I have in the last 52 years. And I've had very little opportunity. [My daughter] was gone for three weeks last summer. It was the first time I had ever been alone, and three weeks wasn't long enough to really find out what I was all about, and I really need that. I haven't had enough of that. I've had too much responsibility for too long a time. I need more time.

Self-discovery and the formation of an independent identity are rarely a once-and-for-all accomplishment, rather a continuing multiple process which women incorporate into their lives wherever possible.

The process requires that women distinguish between social prescription and what is right for them as individuals. Women are members of society, and society is also, in a way, embedded into their personalities. Their socially-defined identities are integral to their self-images and cannot be easily dismissed even when considered insufficient. Nor can women deny the emergence of new senses of themselves which may diverge from the old. Women are faced, then, with the substantial task of reconciling their old and new identities, a task exacerbated by the sexually-determined constraints that even contemporary life choices entail.

The degree to which women are able to integrate their long-standing and emerging identities varies with their life circumstance, their individual psychology, and social support. Caretaking abilities, usually an important source of women's pride and self-esteem, are retained as integral, but no longer exclusive or predominant, to self. Thus, a woman's decision to deviate from social norms is often cast in terms of both self-interest *and* benefit to others. Women's acknowledgment of self-interest, wherever it may lead, can threaten what had been a predictable family and social structure.

Individual differences notwithstanding, the processes of separation and individuation in the United States in recent years require a woman to declare her independence both privately and publicly. With the strength of their convictions, and with social support from some quarter—usually other women—women often return to their first families for validation of a new adult identity. It may seem paradoxical that women seek acceptance for a development that involves suspension of their customary concern with others' approval. When understood as women's movement toward personal integration, their return to family for self-acceptance represents the perfect circle—the ultimate consonance between old and new identities.

> But how could I talk to other people that I can talk to about it, if I can't even tell my parents. . . . It's like being frightened of saying who and what you are. . . . Like a Watergate, covering up mostly . . . that's like running away from what I am. It's running away from who I am . . . and I'm not going to live my life as a lie . . .
>
> My biggest pride was that both of my kids had graduated from high school, I mean that was no small account with my family. I did it myself, I mean, they did it but I, um, I kept us all alive.
>
> It's [relationship with her parents] better now. August was a real turning point . . . it was the beginning of my last year [of college]. And to complete that was to be breaking a taboo in my family. Commencement weekend, my parents came and stayed with me. . . . And it was okay. . . . I didn't have to suppress it.

Whether or not familial acceptance is forthcoming, there is no turning back. The women I have studied do not regret their decisions. Such decisions have significant implications for subsequent behavior, because they have involved a change in self brought about through thought, feeling, and action. Feelings can serve both as signals and criteria. Women often describe feelings about a dilemma as signaling the invocation of core personal values. Decisions are then evaluated against subsequent feelings about the self. Thought and feeling serve to test and corroborate each other; and feelings of congruence and personal integrity can be enhanced, if the resolution of a moral dilemma can be achieved. Finally, action or "taking a stand" is almost always essential to a *moral* decision. That stand may be as private as a declaration of an independent identity or as public as legal action, but the decision is not complete without some declarative behavior. Lastly, since moral dilemmas invoke one's entire being, their resolution can yield personal changes that significantly affect the shape of subsequent dilemmas and the individual's approach to them.

What becomes defined as a moral dilemma, then, is a function of both person and society. Women's claims to independence and power over their own lives are *moral* in that they may require women to deviate both from social expectation and from their own self-images. Moved by such principles as individual freedom and the right to self-determination, women are often finally compelled to choose personal integrity despite the risk of social alienation.

> . . . I could fulfill his expectations and be that wife, and give up me, give up my identity, give up my autonomy and have a happy family. . . . Or I would have to give up the relationship. I would have to give up the house. I would have to give up the animals, and I would have to give up the American nuclear family . . . which represented a tremendous amount of security and acceptance and belonging within the community, in order to maintain my integrity. And that's what I felt like—it was a matter of whether or not I was willing to give up my integrity.
>
> For me, realizing that I was going to have to live alone felt like my integrity, and I can't think of another word. I remember it felt that to maintain the relationship, I was going

to have to give up something that was so deeply implanted in me that if I gave it up, I wouldn't be a human being, then I would die. I wouldn't be anybody. And that outweighed the fact that it was right to be part of a family, but it was an excruciating decision to make. I had grown up with a certain set of values, and I was choosing not to adhere to those values or societal values, and making a decision totally on my own with really no role model. It was like jumping into a black hole.

   . . . this was a whole turning point for me. . . . I had all these other voices everywhere, you know, pushing me back—'stay in your home,' 'keep your mouth shut,' and 'what more do you want?' So I had a whole array, which made it harder for me, much, much harder. And for a while, I believed everyone and I went home and tried to cool it. But it just wasn't possible, I mean it was impossible. . . . I was no longer influenced by those voices, and you know, those sorts of things. I just knew what I had to do.

Striving for honesty and personal congruence in their lives, these women are attempting to provide their children, most notably their daughters, with expectations for self and future that were formerly not available to women.

They've [her children] done all their own thing and have made all their own mistakes. Even though I gave them rules to follow, I encouraged them to break them if they thought it was right. As long as they take the consequences for what they do. And as a kid, I never thought for myself. Even then in college, my father thought for me. Then I married and my husband thought for me.
   . . . [my parents thought] being an authoritative parent was right. . . . I certainly didn't believe that. . . . I was trying to get my own kids to make up their own minds—as to what they wanted to be so they wouldn't have this kind of a crisis at my age. Plus I was trying to make up my own mind.

If the socialization of females is truly changing, we may speculate that the moral dilemmas of daughters will differ from those of their mothers.

Women's moral dilemmas demonstrate the role of social ideology in determining what becomes a moral choice. Social ideologies have worked to structure women's dependency, and to precipitate their struggles for independence. Aware of the influence of a traditional socialization on their lives, women also acknowledge the importance of a countervailing social ideology in their realization of possibilities for self development. Reflecting upon her decision to divorce, a thirty-five-year-old woman states:

> I had to have some impact from the outside, in terms of even being able to view myself as a separate person, and that I did have some value myself; and that my daughter was a separate person, and she had her own individuality; and to be able to even think that . . . consider a better environment for us to become people, you know, in a real sense.

Women's sense of arrested development, personal and political, has been informed by economic and social shifts, as well as by the current Women's Movement, which has urged them to act in whatever ways they can. Their moves to change their lives and senses of themselves, be they tentative or bold, are supported by others with similar beliefs. That support is vital to women in their struggles to claim their own lives within and without the family.

Many women testified to the importance of support from others during periods of change. The range of women interviewed included those who identify themselves in some way as feminists, and those who clearly do not. Feminist consciousness notwithstanding, most of these women placed their life developments, dilemmas, and decisions within existing social and temporal frameworks.

> . . . at the time, statewide, nationwide, people were speaking up, I think. So it made it a little easier. . . . In our particular area we were . . . the first group that finally did speak up. . . . But a few people decided that they had to take a

stand. . . . It was a group. . . . But it was easier everywhere to speak up at that period of time. Society was changing that way, I think.

Another woman talks about the importance of support in her fight against sexual discrimination:

> I think that I wouldn't have made the decision on my own. I wouldn't have been quite so sure that it didn't matter how long it took, and it didn't matter how difficult [a] position [it] put me in personally . . . but the Women's Movement, and the politics within the community at the time, and the support that I got at the time from a lot of other women. . . . I would say at first it egged me on . . . by the community saying, 'Don't be scared. Be powerful.'

Social change has indeed fostered a reevaluation by women of their individual rights and their responsibilities to others. Roles and characteristics attributed to women were established as the moral order for a society based on a sexual division of labor. Women's claim to the freedom of their identities and to the power of self-determination is experienced, therefore, as a moral dilemma by the women themselves. Thus, principled morality is not the exclusive province of men, as the narrow view provided by Kohlberg's model would have us believe. Women are indeed exercising moral judgments that are based, ironically, on the "principles of justice" Kohlberg has described. Those principles, however, derive from a particular social philosophy and are responding to a discriminatory social ideology. Women's call for the right to self-determination and individual freedom, as essential to personal integrity and self-actualization, represents an egalitarian ideal consistent, on some level, with the general ideals our society upholds. That kind of individualism may be particular to American society and, as such, receives support from our economic and political systems. Hence, the philosophy of individualism cannot be dismissed even for sectors of the population to which it has never been fully applied.

Not surprisingly, then, real changes in our society have precipitated an expanded awareness of the discrepancy between theory and practice, between philosophy and the actual provisions the society makes for particular groups of people. A woman who did not leave her marriage talks about this discrepancy:

> I had a couple of good friends at the time who—we used to get together and talk. And everybody was pretty much going through the same type of re-evaluation. We were all trying to decide where we were going, what our roles were in the family, what the Women's Movement was doing for us. You're trying to figure out who you are . . .
>
> . . . But it was a conflict in the way that . . . was I doing the right thing leaving these children? Because nobody was doing it [work outside the home] at the time. Don't forget this was the sixties, the early sixties. It wasn't as common as it is, was in the seventies . . . and that is when I first realized I could be independent.

Recognizing the denial of free opportunity to them, women have actively claimed their individual rights while maintaining their customary responsibilities to others, just as Gilligan found in interviews of women considering abortion. Significantly, this research shows that what shapes these developmental progressions are not gender-based personality or cognitive traits, but past and current social ideals and realities. In reconciling a socially defined identity with an emerging independent one, women strive for personal congruence in which the socially defined "right" must stand up to the test of individual freedom and integrity. The words of a thirty-five-year-old woman make vivid this fundamental point:

> A moral decision? I define my morality by my own definition of what is moral and what is immoral. And morality, for me,

is synonymous with integrity. My morality is not an institutional definition. It is not a societal definition; it is a very personal decision. So was it [her divorce] a moral decision? Moral being synonymous with integrity, it was a moral decision.

Conclusion

Individual human development and social change are inextricably related to each other. While most academic disciplines study one or another aspect of the person or of society, this research begins the study of human development from a holistic perspective. We must look at the individual in relation to the social environment in which the individual was born and has developed. Research directed at the interactions of various social contexts with moral development must necessarily study the moral issues of people's lives, as *they* actually define them. We need no longer be confined to a scholarly tradition of assessing primarily cognitive judgments about hypothetical dilemmas. The interpretation of moral development as a cognitive, problem-solving task has segregated it from important personal dimensions (i.e., feeling and behavior) and from social context. When women have integrated thought and feeling with social considerations, they have been viewed by psychologists as inferior in their development. When moral development is viewed within social context, the alleged inferiority of women can be viewed as a strength. Social context is not a marginal variable for women; it is a central one. Women capable of abstract reasoning may prefer a more integrated resolution of moral dilemmas than the pure cognitive application of "principles of justice" would allow. Women insist on a resolution that incorporates behavior within a social framework. Abstract, asocial principles may be an appropriate ideal for narrow hypothetical dilemmas

248

which permit judgments rendered at considerable personal distance; but a more adequate resolution of real moral dilemmas would seem to require consideration of the complexities of self and social context.

It is not that theories of moral development (Piaget 1965; and Kohlberg 1969) make no reference to the social environment in which development occurs. They assume, however, that development merely requires normal interaction with an ordinary social environment. Active questioning about that environment and its variations have been all but precluded. Further, such theories place social and interpersonal criteria for moral problem-solving at a conventional level, which must eventually be superceded in order to attain a universal perspective and to be proclaimed the hallmark of moral maturity. To relegate societal and interpersonal considerations to a conventional mode within a developmental hierarchy is, in itself, of questionable legitimacy. Moreover, such relegations and the hypothetical dilemmas from which they are derived (Kohlberg 1958) contribute little to our understanding of the evolution and solution of real moral problems that are undeniably socially linked. This becomes absolutely clear in studying, holistically, the moral and psychological development of even a small group of women.

Popular views and traditional psychological studies have described women's morality; but rarely have women themselves had the opportunity to be the articulators of their own moral consciousness. Women's challenges to prevailing social and family structures have been interpreted by lay persons and by professionals as eschewing moral responsibilities. But women's own views of the changes in their traditional commitments to family and to self are much more complex—with morality not so easily situated in the carrying out or abandonment of prescribed conventional tasks within the so-called domestic sphere. In psychology,

male-derived constructions of the world are being challenged by those initiated and built by females, and by scholars who take seriously the use of gender as a primary category of analysis.

The study of moral dilemmas, as people actually experience them, will surely expand our understanding of human
development. Since human development always occurs in a
particular social context, it makes sense to uncover more
about what women and men in various categories of life
and under different historical and social circumstances encounter as moral dilemmas. What do they think and feel
about these dilemmas? And, not unimportantly, what they
do about them.

Further research should refine the notions of social context and change. The interactions between individual development and social change raise many questions about
perceptions of change and the language employed to describe it. Answers will remain distant if scholars are reluctant to take people's complexity seriously; to examine their
concrete experiences; and above all, to confront them in
terms of their living languages, shared feelings, and socially
shaped individual personalities.

Notes

The research reported here is part of the continuing work of the
Smith College Project on Women and Social Change, funded by
the Andrew W. Mellon Foundation with additional support from
the Monticello Foundation. This study represents the contributions of many individuals. I thank the late Anna Marie Armijo,
Margaret Dyer, Heather McGaughey, and Carol Rodley for astute
interviewing; Gina Hough, Ann Katsoulos, and Lise Lambert for
fine research assistance; Kathy Carbone, Elizabeth Cooney, June
Delp-Burdick, Carole DeSanti, Nava Grünfeld, and Bette-Ann

250

Rodzwell for stimulating analytical help. Finally, the sustained intellectual community formed by members of the Smith College Project on Women and Social Change has provided invaluable inspiration and support. I am particularly grateful to Martha Ackelsberg, Susan C. Bourque, Evan Daniels, Donna R. Divine, and Kay B. Warren for suggestions about this paper. And the women who contributed rich and wonderful interviews made it all possible.

1. Psychological inquiry has traditionally focused on the person separate from the social environment, leaving the latter to other disciplines. Moreover, different aspects of the person have been isolated for study in the interest of more precise and reliable measurement. Customary divisions among thought, feeling, and behavior are evident in the psychological study of moral development where the emphasis has been on cognitive moral judgments or decision making (Kohlberg 1969; and Piaget 1965). This approach to moral development is characterized by male-defined hypothetical dilemmas, predominantly male subject samples, and findings that place females at a lower stage of moral development than males. Recently, Gilligan (1977 and 1982) has presented a more integrated approach to the study of women's moral development, but even here we see a leap to another stage theory—psychology's categorizing tendency, which has put a premium on the end product rather than on the processes of human development.

2. The relation between moral development and social context is an analytic concept that does not correspond to the "conventional morality" of stage theory. Kohlberg (1976) described three levels of six moral stages: Level I—preconventional, Level II—conventional, and Level III—postconventional or principled morality. The conventional level includes: stage three, where moral judgments are based upon mutual interpersonal expectations, relationships, and interpersonal conformity; and stage four, where moral judgments stem from one's obligations and duties as defined by society. In contrast, the formulation here is an interactive one that can best be understood as process-oriented rather than content-oriented. Interactions between dynamic psychological development—sometimes referred to as consciousness—and immediate and broader social contexts, past and present, are seen as critical to the structuring of moral dilemmas as they occur in individuals' lives.

3. Freud (1959) echoed and perpetuated dominant cultural convictions about women's nature when his psychosexual theory of development disqualified females from civilization's higher concerns by virtue of weaker (than males) superegos. An underdeveloped capacity for sublimating sexual energy in the interest of achievement explained the absence of female contribution to culture and attested to the rightfulness of women's domestic station. Unlike men, whose maturity enabled them the separation of thought from feeling necessary for a society based on reason, women were generally believed incapable of executive and moral judgments because of their infusion of thought with feeling.

Continuing the Freudian view of women as men's moral inferiors, Kohlberg (1963) established a hierarchical sequence of stages of moral reasoning through which everyone presumably passed in the course of psychological development. Kohlberg's developmental sequence was derived primarily from males' responses to hypothetical dilemmas. Thus the male viewpoint became the standard for Kohlberg as it had for Freud. Using contemporary scientific methods, Kohlberg empirically found women wanting as moral decision makers, when their scores were generally arrested at a conventional, interpersonal morality halfway through the six stage sequence.

4. In this study, the women interviewed often cited the notion of independence as central to their lived moral dilemmas. Here independence is not meant in the same way as Gilligan and others have interpreted it in reference to more typically male development. That is, independence does not imply an absence of interpersonal relationship and/or singular, solitary functioning and achievement. Rather, independence refers to a freedom of identity formation with its attendant internal processes and open-ended external eventualities.

5. Humanistic psychologists (Maslow 1970; and Rogers 1970, for example) describe self-actualization as a basic force motivating human organisms. Maslow hypothesized a hierarchy of human needs progressing from the basic biological ones through psychological needs, such as love and belonging, and culminating in the need for self-actualization, or the development of full individuality with the various parts of the personality in harmony. Rogers explains self-actualization as ". . . the directional trend which is evident in all organic and human life—the urge to expand, extend, develop, mature—the tendency to express and activate all the ca-

pacities of the organism, or the self" (1970, p. 351). Thus, a tendency to strive to fulfill themselves, their potential, is viewed by these psychologists as inherent in human beings.

6. The dilemmas themselves are described in detail in another paper (Freeman 1982).

7. During adolescence, people are normally expected to "rebel," to challenge prevailing standards that have been inculcated by parents and other representatives of the normative social order. Erikson (1963) refers to this period of experimentation, when youth are trying different roles and lifestyles, as a psychosocial moratorium, because the young experimenter must be free of responsibility and commitments and, therefore, serious consequences. The key is freedom; psychological freedom is essential for a young person to develop and pursue independent notions. Paradoxically, that freedom must be granted since the adolescent is ordinarily still dependent upon the primary targets of the rebellion. It is precisely at this time when parents, fearful of their daughters' burgeoning sexuality, restrict their female adolescents while giving more rein to and expecting rebellion from their males ("boys will be boys"). Hence socialization of boys includes the expectation and license for their rejection of some of their socialization, whereas girls are socialized to stay that way.

References

Elshtain, Jean. 1974. "Moral Woman and Immoral Man: A Consideration of the Public-Private Split and its Political Ramifications." *Politics & Society* 4: 453–473.

Erikson, E. 1963. *Childhood and Society.* New York: W. W. Norton.

Frankel, J. 1976. "The Kohlberg Bandwagon: Some Reservations." *Social Education* 40: 216–222.

Freeman, S. J. 1974. "Individual Differences in Moral Judgment by Children and Adolescents." Ph.D. dissertation, University of Wisconsin, Madison.

———. 1981. "Integrating Self and Society: Women's Moral Choice." Unpublished manuscript.

———. 1982. "Women's Moral Dilemmas—Reflections of Self and Social Context." Unpublished manuscript.

Freeman, S. J. M., and J. Giebink. 1979. "Moral Judgment as a Function of Age, Sex, and Stimulus." *Journal of Psychology* 102: 43–47.

Freud, Sigmund. 1925. "Some Psychological Consequences of the Anatomical Distinction Between The Sexes," In J. Strachey, ed. *Sigmund Freud Collected Papers*, vol. 5. New York: Basic Books. 1959.

Gibbs, J. 1977. "Kohlberg's Stages of Moral Judgment: A Constructive Critique." *Harvard Educational Review* 47, no. 1: 43–61.

Gilligan, Carol. 1977. "In a Different Voice: Women's Conceptions of Self and Morality." *Harvard Educational Review* 47, no. 4: 481–517.

———. 1982. *In a Different Voice—Psychological Theory and Women's Development*. Cambridge, Mass.: Harvard University Press.

Kohlberg, L. 1958. "The Development of Modes of Moral Thinking and Choice in the Years Ten to Sixteen." Ph.D. dissertation, University of Chicago, Chicago.

———. 1963. "The Development of Children's Orientations Toward a Moral Order: Sequence in the Development of Moral Thought." *Vita Humana*: 11–33.

———. 1969. "Stage and Sequence: The Cognitive-Developmental Approach to Socialization." In D. A. Goslin, ed., *Handbook of Socialization Theory and Research*, pp. 347–380. Chicago: Rand McNally. pp. 347–380.

———. 1976. "Moral Stages and Moralization: The Cognitive-Developmental Approach." In T. Lickona, ed., *Moral Development and Behavior*. New York: Holt, Rinehart and Winston.

———. 1981. *Essays on Moral Development. Volume One—The Philosophy of Moral Development*. San Francisco: Harper and Row.

Kurtines, W., and E. Greif. 1974. "The Development of Moral Thought: Review and Evaluation of Kohlberg's Approach." *Psychological Bulletin* 81: 453–470.

Lasch, C. 1976. "The Family as a Haven in a Heartless World." *Salmagundi*, Fall.

Maslow, Abraham. 1970. *Motivation and Personality*. New York: Harper and Row.

Piaget, J. 1965. *Moral Judgment of the Child*. New York: The Free Press.

Rogers, Carl. 1970. *On Becoming a Person*. Boston: Houghton Mifflin.

Simpson, E. L. 1974. "Moral Development Research: A Case Study of Scientific Cultural Bias." *Human Development* 17: 81–106.

Sullivan, E. A. 1977. "A Study of Kohlberg's Structural Theory of Moral Development: A Critique of Liberal Social Science Ideology." *Human Development* 20: 352–376.

8

Gender, Power, and Communication: Women's Responses to Political Muting in the Andes

by Kay Barbara Warren and Susan C. Bourque

How can social scientists come to understand a woman who fails to bring a serious grievance to a public meeting, saying that no one would listen even if she were welcome? Why does an active but uncomplaining woman suddenly burst forth with a full-blown, private critique of women's exclusion from politics? Why does another woman react to crises in her family by withdrawing into a narrow litany of complaints rather than asking others for help? In this paper,

255

we argue that important answers to these questions reside in the politics of communication and the social contexts of women's lives.

256   In *Women of the Andes* our goal was to move past debates over the economic versus cultural roots of women's subordination, to a more integrated explanation of the forces that shape individual lives and collective experiences. Our model emphasized the interconnectness of sexual divisions of work, differential access to institutions, and cultural conceptions of "female" and "male" in forging distinctive life experiences for peasant women and men. We found that cultural meanings play a major role both in perpetuating women's subordination and in offering alternative significance for women's activities when they are devalued or undervalued.

In this paper we want to extend our analysis of the cultural construction of gender by examining the politics of communication in rural Andean communities. We are most concerned with the structural patterning of who speaks, who listens, who is heard or ignored. In addition, we explore the substance of what is communicated, left unsaid, or restated in distinctive symbolic forms. For this analysis, the political dimension of communication is revealed through the interplay of speaker, message, and action as they are influenced by peasant power structures.

This study begins on the theoretical level by examining the work of Edwin and Shirley Ardener, two Oxford anthropologists, on gender and muteness. Then we move to ethnographic case studies of communication and gender in agrarian and commercial settlements in the Peruvian Andes. Ultimately, we want to understand (a) why some individuals find a voice and others are silenced in community affairs, and (b) how patterns of communication reflect and affect change in peasant communities.

The Ardener Model: Women as a Muted Group

The Ardeners have formulated a provocative theory to explain why, although women speak, they are often effectively silenced in hierarchical societies. [1] Their work is controversial because it focuses on communication—on values, perspectives, and visions of reality—rather than on resource distribution, labor force participation, and economic dependencies, which have been the concern of much new research on women. What is particularly promising in their approach is the structural concern with the creation, communication, and suppression of cultural meanings in ongoing social life. The questions posed by this framework need to be addressed both by those who would cast women in system-confronting roles, as well as by those who find surface passivity and non-action in need of explanation. Thus this inquiry is central to our discussion of why some women are motivated to seek change, while other women remain indifferent or resist.

The Ardener model is concerned with world views and the forms of discourse through which people express their experiences and their underlying conceptions of reality. This theory postulates that men and women may have somewhat—or even greatly—differing "world structures," due to their contrasting positions in hierarchical societies. World structures are culturally specific systems of fundamental meanings, composed of (a) underlying assumptions and enduring basic classifications of reality and (b) the continually transformed understandings of ongoing events, which influence the apprehension of still other events. [2] As Edwin Ardener has noted:

> . . . what we are discussing is not founded *in* language, but in a language-like, sluggishly-moving continuum of social

perceptions of time and physical space, with language both expressing them and intruding into them through its own independent propensity towards change and restructuring.

[n.d. p. 11]

The immediacies of classification, object, and event are encoded and expressed, according to this perspective, through the "surface structures" of spoken language as well as other symbolic systems like art, dance, drama, ritual, and song. Individuals use a multiplicity of "idioms" to express and impress conceptions of reality in the face of the complexities of everyday life.

A problematic issue for the Ardeners is how underlying meanings are transformed into socially significant discourse in societies where gender makes an important, complicating difference in who speaks and who is heard. To the extent that community discourse is male-dominated, it generally embodies a distinctive masculinized idiom, which is not equivalently accessible to women or necessarily effective for the expression of women's values, perceptions, and needs. The result is a double bind. On the one hand, unless women are fluent in the dominant forms of discourse, they may not find a suitable forum for the expression of their alternative understandings of the world. On the other hand, if women embrace the dominant forms of discourse and portrayals of reality, they may find themselves operating in systems that do not accurately represent their own structural position. The Ardeners further suggest that such women may suffer increasing difficulty in generating the alternative understandings of reality that reflect their distinctive perceptions and experiences (S. Ardener 1975, p. xxi).

One solution to this dilemma is effective translation between the female and the dominant models of reality and their idioms of expression. In fact, translation becomes a major burden that women must bear in hierarchical societies.[3] Translation, however, is not simply a process of locating conceptual counterparts in different languages. Rather, moving between world structures into the dominant idiom is ultimately a *political* activity. In the process, women may face the necessity of censoring what might be "unacceptable statements" when cast in the dominant idiom. Or they may be forced to rejustify their own perceptions and desires within a novel patterning of values from the dominant framework (S. Ardener 1975, p. xv).

The Ardener perspective identifies several important implications for women's role as the translators of their understandings of reality into alternative idioms and frames of reference. First, women may be rendered culturally "mute" in the process. That is, the immense challenge of figuring out how to negotiate effectively between different models of reality and idioms for self-expression may simply overwhelm them. As a result, women may at times react with silence or a stumbling inarticulateness on those public matters that would logically have great significance for them. Second, as Edwin Ardener has said, ". . . because of the absence of a suitable code and because of a necessary indirectness rather than spontaneity of expression, women, more often than may be the case with men, might sometimes lack the facility to raise to a conscious level their unconscious thoughts" (S. Ardener 1975, p. xiv).

Third, women may find that their blocked expressions are best communicated outside the realm of public discourse in art, ritual, and dance where critical perceptions of the social order and alternative political commentaries may be expressed symbolically and, perhaps, non-verbally. This is not to say that the Ardeners see women as operating independently of the broader community. In fact, they argue that women's "counterpart models" of reality are not really alternative formulations born of a separate culture, but may well be shaped by, limited to, or derived from the structures

and idioms of the dominant culture. Women's culture is influenced by the broader system, at the very least in the
sense of being defined in contrast to it (S. Ardener 1975,
p. xii–xiii, xv).

This perspective raises new analytical issues for those doing cross-cultural research. It suggests that the full complexity of a community's value systems and social world
views has not necessarily been understood by studying the
dominant symbolism of rituals, political speeches, and
meetings of officially organized groups (or even their informal pre-meetings). By concentrating on the formal or informal variants of the *dominant* culture, other variations in
values and perceptions may be hidden, disguised, half-
expressed, or perhaps censored. The existence, scope, and
implications of distinctive structures and idioms will most
likely remain undiscovered unless scholars specifically ask
about and pursue possible differences.

Moreover, it is now clear that analysts have not completely exhausted the cultural construction of gender in
another society by examining images of the sexes or by
tracing sex roles and sexual divisions of work. Culturally-
created gender differences may also be manifested in the
patterning of communication, in significant differences in
women's and men's idioms for expression, and in the content of their messages. [4]

There is no doubt that the Ardeners have formulated a
model that poses very important questions. Its contribution
is in identifying the interplay of male and female communication systems as potentially reflecting and reinforcing
women's subordinate position. Perhaps its greatest weakness is the lack of a full-fledged political analysis of the process of muting. [5] Specifically, the Ardener model tends to
give preeminence to the symbolic dimension of dominance
at the expense of systematic considerations of power and
politics, social institutions, and the impact of material reali-

ties on the cultural construction of social meanings.[6] This singular emphasis is clear, for example, in E. Ardener's definition of dominance:

261

> *Dominance* occurs when one structure blocks the power of actualization of the other, so that it has no 'freedom of action.' That this approach is not simply a marxist one lies in our recognition that the articulation of world-structures does not rest only in their production base but at all levels of communication; that a structure is also a kind of language of many semiological elements, which specify all actions by its power of definition.
>
> [1975a, p. 25]

In our view, understanding dominance and muting requires a broader analysis of the political, economic, and institutional contexts in which reality is negotiated.[7] The issue is not just symbolic languages, but also power structures, modes of production, and social change.[8]

In sum, we are suggesting a reorientation of this perspective, from *mutedness* as a static condition to *muting* as a social and political process. The issue is not that women are simply less verbal than men but, rather, that their perceptions and evaluations may not reach community forums— whether formal or informal—in hierarchical societies. The political process of muting, the women's alternative responses, and the social-psychological experience of a muted individual are major themes that we will pursue in ethnographic case studies of two rural Peruvian communities.

Gender and Communication in Rural Peru

Since 1965 we have been studying two peasant settlements, which share similar Quechua-Spanish cultural backgrounds but practice contrasting economies and offer dis-

tinctive kinds of employment for their inhabitants. Despite
being located high in a remote corner of the department of
Lima, both towns have close ties to the urban coast and are
well integrated as rural outposts in national economics and
politics. Mayobamba is an agrarian community, where subsistence farming is combined with stock raising and petty
cash crop production. Chiuchin is a small trading center
with general stores, boarding houses, and regional offices of
government agencies.

In examining women's and men's lives in these towns,
we first wanted to determine if there were evidence that
women were collectively subject to muting. Then our task
was to determine if the patterns of muting were similar or
distinctive, and to account for variations. In this analysis we
ask such questions as: Do women hold values and understandings of reality that are distinct from the cultural understanding communicated through the dominant idioms
of town affairs? How do women communicate their values,
perceptions, and concerns? Are they structurally silenced?
Do they adopt dominant idioms as their own, become translators between idioms, or elaborate other symbolic media
through which to express themselves? In the following sections, we do not attempt an exhaustive analysis of muting
in the two settlements, but rather a characterization of the
major forms of muting in work and politics. Ours is not a
textual analysis as much as an exploration of the social environments in which cultural texts are created. [9]

Mayobamba: An Agrarian Community

Mayobamba is a community of 450 people located on the
crest of an 11,000 foot mountain range on the western
slopes of the Peruvian Andes northeast of Lima. Like neighboring agrarian communities, Mayobamba is inhabited by

people who maintain strong communal traditions, despite the increasing importance of private land and the cash economy. For example, land for the cultivation of the staple crop, potatoes, is held by the community as a whole. Rights to this land can be acquired only through formal community membership and are vested in the head of each household, called the *comunero*, who is generally the senior male. Everyone living in a household with a *comunero* has access to land for the cultivation of the subsistence crop.

In exchange for access to communal lands and irrigation water, the *comunero* must participate in communal labor projects. The work is quite time-consuming and includes participating in communal plantings to stock the town's treasury, repairing and extending irrigation works, serving as the community cow herder, and taking turns in the rotating offices of the local government. Community issues and decisions are formally discussed and decided on through assemblies of the town's *comuneros*.

On the face of it, Mayobamba is striking for its minimal sexual division of work. Both men and women are active in labor-intensive farming and herding, the mainstays of the local economy. The nuclear family is the focal point of production, with men and women sometimes working together and at other times apart in complementary tasks, making their way through the agricultural cycle without benefit of farm machinery.

Equally striking are the distinctive ways the sexes define and perceive their work. Men describe an unambiguous sexual division. *They* are the agriculturalists and herders while women, in the masculine view, remain at home, caring for children, mending and producing clothing, storing and allocating harvests, and preparing meals. Men explain that they are the ones who spend time in the fields, irrigating terraces, opening up new highland fields, plowing, and harvesting. In contrast, women consistently portray themselves as fully involved in agriculture, as active in all but a few tasks. [10]

Similar patterned gender differences can be found in communal forms of work. Sooner or later, all male heads of households are expected to take charge of the town's dairy herd for a year. The herd is of economic and symbolic importance to the people of Mayobamba. The animals belong jointly to the community, and excess stock is sold as the town needs money for communal purchases. The herd is also the focus of an annual religious festival when the fertility of the animals and, by extension, the community is celebrated. During the festival, the animals are brought into town by women and packed into the small central plaza, which is ringed by onlookers and town officials. There the herd is blessed by the patron saint, San Juan. Young women decorate their chosen animals with earrings of braided ribbons, while young men restrain the cattle. Men go on to demonstrate their strength by branding and trimming the horns of the uncooperative, thrashing cows. During the ceremony the official community herder accounts for births and deaths in the herd, and the responsibility for its welfare is transferred to the next herder.

Comuneros are openly relieved when their year as the community herder is completed because the work is time-consuming, demanding, and diverting from their subsistence agriculture. In fact, the position requires the entire family's labor to be carried out effectively. Men in the family take the herd to pasture in distant communal fields and make sure the animals do not stray into cultivated lands and ruin crops on the way. Women specialize in caring for and milking the cows when they are brought back to the communal fields adjacent to the town. During their year of service the herder's family benefits from the production of milk, part of which is processed into farmer's cheese. Also, milk can be bartered for part-time assistance in caring for

264

the herd. Yet the costs in time and effort are seen to out-
weigh the benefits, particularly since herders are responsible for any animals that are lost and must account as well
to the community officials for any deaths.

While only men as *comuneros* are publicly appointed as
community herders, their wives separately celebrate having
"passed the position," and express their own sense of hard
work and responsibility. During the festival for the communal *rodeo*, women who have participated as herders during
their husbands' official tours of duty bring the cows into the
plaza. On the way into town they sing a song whose light-
hearted, festive delivery does not overshadow its serious
theme:

> Count them yourself, patron saint,
> Count them yourself, San Juan.
> Perhaps one is missing in the transfer,
> Perhaps two.
> Neither have I sold them for my beer,
> Nor eaten them when I had no meat.
> Even though people talk about me,
> Why would they meet to censure me?[11]

Through their procession and in this song, women express in a different voice their fundamental involvement in
positions that the *comunero* system regards as solely men's
responsibility. The major theme of the song is a concern
about returning the herd to the community, and whether
there have been losses that might be interpreted as thefts.
What is particularly interesting in this case is that the
women elaborate a subtheme in the communal celebration
of fertility and continuity. Their songs name the very real
tension—recognized by both sexes as endemic to the communal system—of service in benefit of the community versus problematic if not illicit individual gain.

As we have illustrated here and analyzed in greater detail elsewhere, women and men effectively coordinate work at the same time as they have significantly different conceptions of its nature and scope (Bourque and Warren 1981a). Are women subject to muting? The answer to that question is undoubtedly "yes," in the sense that their conceptions of work and communal involvement are *not* taken into account by the decision-making structure of the town. Virtually all community decisions are made through official assemblies of *comuneros*, which select the issues that will reach the town's political agenda and allocate resources like communal land and water.

In the political arena, Mayobamba parallels Olivia Harris's account of the Laymi in the central Bolivian highlands:

> . . . [P]olitical activity and decision making are centered in the local assembly, in which all adult men participate. Women are rigorously excluded, and one reason frequently given for their absence was precisely their inability to speak. Adult women do join in decision making through informal means, but formal speech is commanded by men.
>
> [1980, p. 73]

As in the central Bolivian highlands, women in Mayobamba are structurally excluded from political assemblies where critical decisions are made about future patterns of leadership, community organization, and the communal system of service and resource distribution. Women have neither direct input on these issues nor the power to introduce additional concerns onto the community's political agenda.

Our argument here is that the Mayobamba assembly of male heads of household is a major forum where the dominant idiom of community affairs is reproduced. [12] Women, who have different conceptions of work and communal participation as well as their own phrasings of individual tensions within a communal system, are simply not given

266

a hearing. As a result their messages are silenced. That women are sometimes unhappy about this situation is clear from the frustration of older widows and single mothers who, under certain circumstances, are forced to contribute to communal work as female heads of household (*comuneras*). These women see themselves as victimized by decisions concerning work distribution, which are made by an assembly in which they have no voice. Mayobamba, then, is at present a community where women appear to be muted by exclusion from the major public forum. [13]

Do women find alternative ways to express their understandings of reality in agrarian communities like Mayobamba? Our research on the *communal rodeo* indicates that women use song as an idiom to express their otherwise muted commentaries about political affairs. [14] Women's offstage singing is also an integral part of the annual *private rodeos* for family herds. At these celebrations women sing among themselves a song that addresses the cows and their owner:

Mother cow, little woman,
One must dance on your day.
Owner without graciousness:
Where is the fine liquor?
With only corn *chicha*, we cannot celebrate.

Father bull, father bull.
Why do you sell him,
Stockraiser without manners?
You don't want to spend money;
But count money, yes, of course,
You miserable stockraiser.

Mother cow, mother cow,
Hide yourself, hide yourself.
Little woman, mother cow,

The buyer says he's coming.
Fog from *jatuhuanca*,
Conceal my little cow
The buyer says he's coming.[15]

Women explain that this song—in addition to criticizing any lack of generosity on the part of the host of the fiesta—expresses the distinctive attitudes the sexes have about the herds. Men are pictured as quick to sell private animals to make money. Women, who perceive the cows and their products as a crucial source of financial security, are portrayed as opposing sales. This quite accurately represents women's ambivalence about overcommitment to the cash economy at the expense of subsistence production.

How does women's music fit in with other songs in the community? In Mayobamba, most rituals are accompanied by songs, which are enjoyed especially for their jesting insults and sexual humor. For example, at the ritual for the cleaning of the irrigation works, men, dancing with an imitation fox, threaten to rob families unless they contribute coca, cigarettes, cheese, and rum for the festival. At the potato planting, the sexes tease each other about keeping up the pace and about their physical appearances as they work. Ploughmen with their hats plastered down over their faces in the rain are likened to mushrooms; women, bent over as they move along the rows to plant, are referred to as old condors. At the festival for making freeze-dried potatoes, men and women trade insulting verses about each others' unkempt appearances before dancing together late into the night.

Women's songs at the communal and private *rodeos* share the amusing tone of other songs as well as their veiled expression of underlying tensions. What is most interesting is that, when men and women sing together, themes of intersexual teasing and competitiveness prevail. When the sexes sing on their own they are quick to criticize individuals and families that are not generous in hosting others. What marks women's songs as distinctive, then, is that they go on to still another level of commentary about central conflicts in values between the family and the communal order or between the priorities of men and women in economics.[16]

Chiuchin: A Commercial Town

Chiuchin is a marketing settlement of 250 people located 3,500 feet below Mayobamba at 7,700 feet. The town is composed of merchants, many with roots in higher communities, who have taken advantage of the settlement's location as a gateway between the urbanized coast and the agrarian highlands. This is a magnetic, energetic center where trucks stop, migrants wait for transportation to and from the coast, and state employees—school teachers, national police, and agricultural extension agents—have regional offices. There is a great commercial and political vitality here despite the lack of electricity, piped water, sewage, and paved roads. Merchants in Chiuchin own and manage small general stores, restaurants, wholesale distribution outlets, boarding houses, and bakeries. Agricultural lands are limited in the valley bottom, and virtually no one makes a living entirely from agriculture or stock raising.

In Chiuchin, women are thoroughly involved in the commercial economy of the town. Both sexes own and manage businesses, as extended families, as couples, or on their own. Unlike the Mayobamba situation, women in Chiuchin have access to cash and can hire laborers or work as paid laborers for others.

Women shopkeepers benefit from opportunities to accumulate small amounts of capital, engage in independent commerce, and take an active role in local politics. In the commercial town, there is no *comunero* system of family representation in local government, no tradition of communal service or jointly held resources. Rather, *ad hoc* committees are convened when townspeople decide to pursue local issues and undertake public works. Without the political and financial support of male and female merchants, most projects are simply not feasible, since there are no communal resources and little or no assistance from regional or national governments. Women are not structurally excluded from politics by the system of family representation in local government, as they are in Mayobamba. In fact, Chiuchin women have gained access to the public forums of town meetings and *ad hoc* committees, and successful businesswomen have occupied administrative positions on important committees (Bourque and Warren 1980, 1981a, and 1981b).

In Chiuchin, we see a closer match of men's and women's conceptions of work, in contrast to the disjunctures we found in Mayobamba. When women differ from men on community matters in Chiuchin, it is in the evaluation and priority of what should be done when, rather than in the overall conception of what is basically valuable. In practice, differences in the priorities of men and women lend a political dynamism to the town; since, to accomplish anything major, energies and finances must be focused. As a result men and women are often involved in negotiations over their contrasting priorities for community development.

To pursue the Ardener terminology, women in Chiuchin have often found themselves forced to translate their priorities into the language of the dominant idiom. Specifically, the women have argued for local projects that would make their double day of commerce and domestic duties easier to accomplish. They have sought such additions as electric lighting to facilitate their housework in the evenings, piped water to their homes so that they would not have to carry water from public spigots or the river, a paved plaza where their children could play, and a public toilet. These projects are valued but given relatively low ranking on the town's agenda, while the women see them as of major significance for women's work and, by extension, for family welfare.

What is particularly interesting is that women are quite articulate about their own feelings of being silenced in this more fluid political system. They have gained access to decision-making bodies, yet are *not* supposed to speak up for themselves or to initiate ideas which might force the commitment of others, particularly men, in public meetings.

When Chiuchin women found themselves without an effective voice in the town's public forum and were increasingly unable to negotiate their own top priorities, they created a new forum for themselves, a *comité feminino* (women's committee) to deal with women's issues and community development. Within this committee, women's own framework for the justification of priorities is the basis for decision making. Thus, women in the commercial town have initiated a separate institutional forum in which to negotiate formerly muted issues (Bourque and Warren 1981b).

Our analysis finds significant contrasts in the patterns of muting in Mayobamba and Chiuchin. In the agrarian community, women are muted by a political structure that excludes them from the major public forum, the *comunero* assembly. There is suggestive evidence that women elaborate an alternative symbolic idiom, song, to express some of their reactions to the *comunero* system. This idiom, however, appears to be neither translated nor heard by the dominant political order. In contrast, in the commercial town, women have greater access to the public forum—in this case the *ad hoc* committees—but they are silenced with the anticipation that their evaluations might conflict with those expressed in the dominant idiom. Their ideal role in the dominant view is to be supportive of initiatives representing joint priorities, rather than to push ideas that represent their distinctive understandings of the community.[17] Women, however, have not always been satisfied with the resulting translations of their values to those of the dominant idiom. By creating a new organizational forum, the women's committee, the women have reasserted the public importance of their understandings of reality.

Does our analysis imply that all women in Chiuchin are strategic translators and negotiators between their own understanding of what is important and the priorities of the dominant idiom? Do all women become participants in organizations that focus on women's needs at home and work? Does the greater participation of a rural settlement in the cash economy inevitably weaken the muting of women's messages? The answer to each of these questions is "no," as we will show by focusing on a woman in Chiuchin who has become increasingly muted. Her case has special significance for our study of variations and changes in patterns of muting, because it allows us to examine the psychological and sociological dimensions of individual muting. This woman, Luz Gonzales, is an anomaly who reveals an organizational dimension to patterns of muting within the women's community.

Luz: A Silenced Woman in a Vocal Community

What was most striking to us about Luz, in the late 1970s, was that words were failing her, that she appeared to be losing the facility to express her own understanding of the problems that life presented her. She became increasingly passive just at a time when her family faced crises that called for definitive decisions.

The contrast with the Luz of four years earlier was dramatic. In the mid-1970s, she was an energetic, intelligent, assertive women in her early 30s. She supported her family by cultivating garden crops, collecting wild fruits in the hills above town, and selling her produce to regional travelers and local merchants. Her six young children assisted in the fields and at home. Her commonlaw husband, a bus driver who earned good money by local standards, was often absent. She was self-employed, however, and not greatly disturbed by this arrangement, which is not uncommon in rural trading centers.

By 1978 substantial changes had occurred in Luz's life. She had lost her entrepreneurial and domestic energies; she was at the end of another pregnancy, and abandoned by her husband. Instead of coming into town to sell produce, Luz remained at home, complaining of pain and isolation. She had lost the capacity to stand back from her problems and talk about her life and family as she had in the past. Rather she spoke to us of her situation in a narrowed series of laments: her older children did not care to help her; her husband viciously mistreated her when he came to town and rarely contributed to family finances; she was afraid of dying during the imminent delivery of her ninth child.[18] Increasingly she became passive and incapable of moving past these complaints to arrange or accept assistance for herself and her children.

Her isolation was real as she physically withdrew into silence, and no one appeared interested in visiting her. The townspeople did not rally to her side in crisis, rather they were highly critical of her inaction. They condemned her for having too many children for her own well-being; for self-destructive inactivity during pregnancy; and for having remained so long with her husband, whom people saw as a violent, dangerous man.

Why—in a town where women appear to have collectively resisted muting, both by negotiating within the dominant idiom and organizing outside it—was Luz so quiet about her needs and isolated from others who would have helped her? The answer, we believe, can be found on the one hand in Luz's sense of self as expressed in her autobiographical recollections, and on the other hand in the nature of rural economics and women's networks in the commercial town.

Luz's fragmentary descriptions of her youth incorporated two recurring themes. The first was an image of early self-reliance and assertive energy in business. In her youth she had worked hard to establish herself as an independent street vendor of hot snacks far away from Chiuchin in an urban trading center on the coast. The second theme was one of isolation and loneliness. She was orphaned as a young child, in a society in which kinship links are important both for economic survival and for a sense of social identity and belonging. Luz's strategy as an orphan was to make her own way in the world, to be self-employed in the risky, labor-intensive work of a street vendor. While she was successful in her own terms in the city, her values and strategies failed her when she moved back to town life in the Andes.

In the highlands, the penetration of market economics has increased class stratification and undermined self-employed merchants who lack capital. High national inflation and financial uncertainties have forced peasants to spread their risks in various business and agricultural ventures. In response, Chiuchin women have used a network strategy to diversify their access to economic resources. Local networks, in fact, have served as a conduit for recruiting women into the *comité feminino*.

While traditional communal values have not been adopted in the commercial town, there are nevertheless strong models of cooperation. Economic and kinship networks are continually used by rural women to mobilize mutual assistance in business, agriculture, and at home. Informal networks

are created and reaffirmed through multi-layered reciprocities of women who exchange labor, agricultural products,
commercial goods, medical knowledge, housing, and access to board and room for school children. Businesswomen
amass small amounts of capital by pooling resources with
close kin; poor women tie themselves into trading and employment networks to gain access to regular incomes and
mutual aid. These exchanges help women cope with their
double days of commercial and domestic duties and lessen
women's dependence on their husbands.[19] Friendship, social responsibility, and cooperation in group endeavors are
all expressed through the reciprocities of these network exchanges involving women. Of particular importance for our
understanding of Luz's problems is that female-centered
networks are generally quick to respond in crises such as
childbirth, sickness, or death in the family.

275

Why was Luz not tied into a network, which would have
provided assistance as part of an ongoing pattern of reciprocities? From our perspective, the answer to this question lies in the fact that networks, in this particular setting
in highland Peru, simply do not accommodate independent
women—women who choose to work only for themselves
and who fail to invest resources and efforts in network exchanges with others. As an impoverished woman without
close kin, Luz's logical place in a network would have been
as a wage laborer for women shopkeepers. Such positions
generally evolve into broader patterns of mutual assistance, buffering some of the differences of class. Luz, however, showed no interest in the option of working for other
women.[20]

At a more general level, the case of Luz highlights the
costs of network creation and participation for women.
While there is ample reason to celebrate the widened options and broadened security offered by this response to
women's needs, it is important to recognize that such net-

work solutions reflect the decision to invest scarce resources (i.e. time, energy), and therefore an assessment of the costs and advantages by the women involved. Women's evaluations of a network strategy may be affected by a range of considerations, including their own preferences for a more "independent" stance toward the world. Luz's case demonstrates the ways in which such desires for "independence" are socially and biographically shaped.

In our view, Luz's mutedness, demoralization, and passivity are not the result of her experiencing more serious problems than other impoverished women, rather, that she did not find access to Chiuchin women's solutions to these problems. A critical element of their solution has been an organized and collective response to the problem of muting. Women have struggled to negotiate and translate their priorities into the idiom of town politics, building on local networks to create a new forum for the expression of women's needs as they relate to work and community development. Luz appears not to have joined the mobilization of women in Chiuchin, perhaps because the forms of individualism and self-reliance that worked for her as an urban petty trader could not be successfully transplanted to Chiuchin. She is neither fluent in the new idiom nor a participant in the new forum and its organizational antecedent. So she is a doubly muted and terribly isolated individual. That her weak cries for help were not heard by the women of Chiuchin tells us a great deal about the collective and individual processes of muting. She was not silent; she was unheard, by a community that had generated different understandings, forms of social organization, and plans of action. Her case also underscores the fact that not all women are muted to the same extent. Just as political and economic structures affect the degree to which women are muted, individual women will experience and respond to muting in different fashions.

Conclusion

From our illustrative analysis, it is clear that most women in these peasant communities have successfully found a distinctive voice in the face of institutionalized muting. Through playful song and ritual, women in the agrarian community communicate their definitions of involvement in community service and perceptions of tensions in the communal social system. Through political activism in the *comité feminino*, women in the commercial town communicate their notions of women's work and community development.

It is appropriate to ask if we are dealing with gender or social status in these case studies (Borker 1980, pp. 28–29). In the agrarian community, gender appears to be the overriding consideration. Women who become *comuneras* do not gain the rights that male *comuneros* have. In the commercial town, there is a much more complicated interplay of status with gender. High-status women shopkeepers have gained access to the town's political arena; but both high- and low-status women have decided to work together, through the *comité*, on projects that are devalued by the men of the community.

The muting of women's alternative definitions of reality has provoked an active—though not necessarily system-confronting—response in both cases. How do these patterns fit in with what we know about cross-cultural variations in muting? One classic cross-cultural variant is represented by those cases where, despite great structural differences, there is a singular, dominant idiom that both genders employ. For example, Hilary Callen (1975) finds that the women in one mission of the British foreign service so internalized the dominant organization's notion of "dedication" to the diplomatic community, that they were unable to perceive the very real paradoxes of their status as diplomatic wives. This cultural system called on women to operate in idioms that obscured the realities of their position and, apparently, inhibited women's formulation of alternative models of their work world.

Neither Peruvian community represents such an extreme case. One problem facing the women of Mayobamba and Chiuchin is finding adequate idioms through which to express those aspects of their world structures that contrast with the dominant order. The contrast in structures ranges, in this case, from different conceptualizations of family and communal work, to distinctive priorities and frameworks for their justification. As we have discovered, the contrasts need not be major to be politically significant. A second problem is creating forums where they will be heard by a wider audience. In Mayobamba younger women witness the ritual participation and songs of the herdswomen, but the dominant idiom and forum for *comunero* politics remains unaffected. This situation parallels the findings of other anthropological studies of ritual, which conclude that ritual may serve as a storehouse for contrasting values and paradoxes without necessarily challenging the secular order (Turner 1969). This appears to be the case for Mayobamba.

It is clear, however, from Caroline Ifeka-Moller's work (1975) on the Igbo and Ibibio women's revolt in Nigeria, that ritually-derived symbolism can serve as a vehicle for protest by women unable to translate their alternative visions of reality into dominant idioms. In that case, women adapted and expanded traditional forms of social criticism and ritual symbolism associated with female fertility to protest changing colonial policy affecting women's status and cultural identity. Of particular significance was their use of powerful symbolic devices as catalysts for a broad-ranging, though short-term, political revolt in the face of colonial government policy.

As we have described in our Peruvian contrast, Chiuchin

women have been able to go a step further than their agrarian neighbors by creating a new forum for decision making, one which is specifically designed to be responsive to women's priorities. While their solution to muting is not as dramatic or symbolically focused as the Nigerian revolts, it is striking for its clear organizational base: women's networks that link individuals through reciprocal exchanges, so that they are able to balance their multiple economic and domestic roles in an uncertain cash economy. Women in Chiuchin now share experiences in a forum where their concerns about women's work predominate and new opportunities can be pursued for the translation of their ideas into action. For those who have not been a part of this political experiment, the cost may be greater vulnerability to acute isolation and passivity.

In applying the Ardener model to our rural Peruvian case studies, we have stressed process, context, and social structures. We have argued that, in addition to being an issue of idioms and perceptions, muting is an organizational and political phenomenon. As a result, we have talked at some length about the notion of political "forums," or the organizational context for the articulation and reproduction of idioms. In our view, this concept should be stressed in the analytical vocabulary of models dealing with gender and the politics of communication.[21]

In pursuing the sources and consequences of muting, we agree with the Ardeners that translation and integrative strategies pose major problems for those whose reality differs from the dominant world views and idioms. But we also suggest that, in many cases, separatist experiments may reflect attempts on the part of women to create forums where translation is not the major issue. As we have seen in Chiuchin and Mayobamba, even small arenas of separatism allow women the experience of operating and working within common frameworks and lend force to their alternative perceptions of work and community responsibility. Within these separate forums, women's alternative viewpoints are not, as they are elsewhere, assigned to "a non-real status, making them overlooked, muted, invisible," nor are women forced to "monitor their expressions in a way that men do not" (E. Ardener 1975a, p. 25; and Spender 1980, p. 81).[22] Yet, as we have seen in this analysis, separatism also leaves problematic the political issue of how women through their forums speak clearly to the dominant ideologies and institutions of the broader society.

Notes

This chapter has been written in the context of the lively interdisciplinary exchanges at the Smith College Project on Women and Social Change. In particular we would like to acknowledge the inspiration of Miriam Slater and the participants in the 1982 faculty seminar on the family, as well as Deidre David and her analysis of narrative voice. We would also like to thank Shirley and Edwin Ardener for their generous hospitality during our visits to Oxford and the Women's Studies Seminar in 1981 and 1982, and for their detailed reactions to our analysis during their visit to the U.S. in 1983. The authors, of course, are entirely responsible for the American translation of their framework. Questions and suggestions from Donna Divine, Penny Gill, Judith Shapiro, Suzanne Nash, Bill Powers, and participants in the doctoral and postdoctoral research seminars sponsored by Brown University's Pembroke Center and Princeton University's Program in Women's Studies were also helpful.

1. Our summary presentation of the Ardener perspective has been drawn from S. Ardener (1975a) and E. Ardener (1975a and b). We have self-consciously avoided the controversy surrounding how men and women distinctively bound their models of society, differentiating or merging their notions of the "wild" with "culture" (E. Ardener 1975a). This and the issue of whether there is a "biological" (in addition to a structural) basis for possible differences in male and female world structures have apparently discouraged the wide experimentation and refinement that the Ar-

dener perspective merits. Nor do we find E. Ardener's model for the development of male dominance convincing (1981, p. 18). See E. Ardener (1975 a and b); MacCormack (1980); and Ortner 1974) for key elements of the central debates. For a discussion that builds on the Ardener model of mutedness and discusses language use in the West (as well as reopening the biological debate in new terms), see Spender (1980).

281

2. S. Ardener's (1975a) phrasing of these distinctions stresses cultural models; E. Ardener's discussion moves in a more phenomenological direction:

> Once the classification exists, however, it is part of the total experience of unreflecting individuals. There is no 'arrow of causation' from behavior to category, since they cannot be separated. They form a 'simultaneity,' . . . that is, "a unit in total experience"
>
> [1983, pp. 6,10].

3. This, the Ardeners observe, women share with other structural subordinates. The degree to which sex, race, and class provide similar systems of muting is a central question posed by this framework, although gender has been the first focus of the Ardeners' research.

4. Showalter, in examining the Ardeners' model from a literary critic's point of view, stresses the importance of analyzing the "'double-voiced discourse' that always embodies the social, literary, and cultural heritages of both the muted and the dominant" (1981, p. 201).

5. Elshtain (1982) would also encourage work on muted languages, particularly those of the "private" sphere. Unfortunately she does not pursue the structural sources and consequences of muting or the politics of muting in the "public" sphere.

6. This is not an inevitable problem with this framework, as Ifeka-Moller (1975) demonstrates in her comprehensive analysis of the women's war in southeastern Nigeria.

7. E. Ardener (1971 and 1983) does not see his position as opposing materialists, but rather as encompassing materialist concerns by collapsing their non-symbolic/symbolic contrasts.

8. Clearly another significant issue, unexplored by the Ardener model, is the cultural shaping of speech styles. As Borker notes, "Skilled use of language may be a basis for power, merely a sign of power, or proof of powerlessness" (1980, p. 40). Borker's re-

view article (1980) cites as examples very different verbal strategies for men and women, striking contrasts in the cultural values associated with articulateness, and variations in the metaphorical or plain-speaking qualities of dominant idioms. Some of these ethnographic materials can be read as seriously challenging the Ardener approach, certainly to the extent that one might literally (and over narrowly, from our point of view) associate mutedness with verbal inarticulateness (Kramarae 1981, pp. 1–33). Gould (1981) provides a good case study of women's specialized linguistic roles and facilities as perpetuating a broader mutedness.

9. Those readers who seek additional details or further political, economic, and domestic background should consult our more comprehensive study (1981a).

10. In traditional and more isolated Andean communities, world views (Is it the dominant ideology in these cases?) stress the complementarity of male and female cultural principles and roles (see, for example, Harris 1978; and Isbell 1978). While generally recognized, complementarity is not stressed or symbolically elaborated to the same extent in Mayobamba and Chiuchin, both of which are heavily involved in the cash economy and national society due to their ties to the urbanized coast. For a closer examination of gender, religious symbolism, and complementarity, see Warren (n.d.).

11. In Spanish, the song goes:

Cuéntate, patrón del pueblo,
Cuéntate, San Juan.
Tal vez falta una en la entrega,
Tal vez faltan dos,
Ni he vendido por mi cerveza.
Ni he comido cuando faltaba carne.
Aunque me hablan, ¿para qué sesionan?

12. Our discussion of political agendas (Bourque and Warren 1981a, pp. 130–178) demonstrates the distinctive content of the dominant idiom. Clearly more analysis needs to be done to provide a symbolic analysis of the language of the dominant idiom.

13. Irvine (1979) gives examples of cultural variations in structuring of political meetings. She notes that restrictions on participation in formal meetings reflect a group's political ideology, but do not necessarily apply to off-stage contexts where decisions may be actually negotiated.

Many Andeanists claim that women influence communal decision making in private conversations with husbands between assemblies. A study of such conversations from the Ardener perspective might have interesting contributions to make on the
issue of translation between female and male meaning systems
and idioms. But for the older widows and independent single
mothers in Mayobamba who have *comunera* work responsibilities,
there is no husband or father to influence behind the scenes.

14. Ethnomusicologists like Merriam also note that "in song,
the individual or group can apparently express deep-seated feelings
not permissibly verbalized in other contexts" (1964, pp. 190–
192). Data from Brownrigg's unpublished study of Mayobamba
and our own fieldwork point to women's off-stage singing as a
regular part of community rituals. Brownrigg described song as
accompanying the *rodeos* of the town's cattle and sheep herds, as
well as the planting ceremonies for potatoes and corn (n.d., pp. 75,
77). Significantly, Harris finds that song is an important medium
for women in the Bolivian community of Laymi. There, women
can gain wide recognition as lyricists and are known to have
"greater command over words" relative to men who specialize in
instrumentation (1980, pp. 73–74). Women, however, stop com-
posing for fiestas and courtship after they marry.

15. In Spanish, the song goes:

Madre vaca, chica mujer,
Hay que bailar en tu día.
Dueño que no tiene gracia,
¿Dónde está el licor fino?
Con chicha no mas se celebra.

Padre toro, padre toro.
¿Por qué lo vendes,
Criandero malagracia?
No quieres gastar.
Para contar el dinero, sí,
Criandero miserable.

Madre vaca, madre vaca.
Escóndete, escóndete.
Chica mujer, madre vaca,
Ganadero dice que viene.
Nublina de jatuhuanca,
Tápalo a mi vaquita.
Ganadero dice que viene.

16. Whether women make a broader contribution to publicly aired music in Mayobamba is increasingly problematic, because musicians for town fiestas are now imported by urban migrants who want to demonstrate their economic success in Lima to their rural kin. The current directions of social change would appear to limit the development of music as a distinctive *public* idiom for women.

17. For a good comparative example of women's decision to enter community politics to argue for their own priorities, see Molnar (1982).

18. As S. Ardener pointed out to us, our presence allowed Luz to be heard by a broader audience and to recapture a situational articulateness. Her silence and silenced position were more profound vis-à-vis the community.

Luz's silence, however, is not an example of muting during a specific period in the life trajectory, as is categorically the case in Mongolia among women of childbearing age (Humphrey 1978) or in Bolivia among married women (see the Harris example cited in this paper).

19. For a broader discussion of women's networks and class in this region of rural Peru, see Bourque and Warren (1981a, pp. 135–149).

20. As Luz's life demonstrates, the process of muting is more complicated than is signified by those who hold that "words constantly ignored may eventually come to be unspoken and perhaps even unthought" (S. Ardener 1978, p. 20; and Kramarae 1981, p. 1).

21. This is not a novel term in the Ardener vocabulary (see S. Ardener 1978 and 1981), but the addition of a political analysis is our broadening of its significance.

22. Bloch (1971) finds significant differences in the styles of decision making for male-dominated community councils and women's specialized councils among the Merina and Madagascar. Clearly this kind of analysis would be a logical next step for the study of political forums in the commercial town of Chiuchin.

References

Ardener, Edwin. 1971. "New Anthropology and the Critics." *Man* 6:449–467.

284

————. 1975a. "Belief and the Problem of Women." In S. Ardener, ed. *Perceiving Women*, pp. 1–17. London: Malaby Press.

————. 1975b. "The Problem Revisited." In S. Ardener, ed. *Perceiving Women*, pp. 19–27. London: Malaby Press.

————. 1981. "The Problem of Dominance." *JASO* 2:116–121.

————. 1983. "Social Anthropology, Language and Reality." In R. Harris, ed. *Aspects of Language*, pp. 1–14. London: Pergamon Press.

————. n.d. "The Voice of Prophecy: Further Problems in the Analysis of Events," The Monroe Lecture, Edinburgh, Scotland [1975].

Ardener, Shirley. 1975a. "Introduction." In S. Ardener, ed. *Perceiving Women*, pp. vii–xxiii. London: Malaby Press.

————. 1975b. "Sexual Insult and Female Militancy." in S. Ardener, ed. *Perceiving Women*, pp. 29–54. London: Malaby Press.

Ardener, Shirley, ed. 1978. *Defining Females*. London: Croom and Helm.

————. 1981. *Women and Space*. London: Croom and Helm.

Bloch, Maurice. 1971. "Decision-Making in Councils Among the Merina." In A. Richards and A. Kuper, eds. *Councils in Action*. Cambridge, Mass.: Cambridge University Press.

Borker, Ruth. 1980. "Anthropology: Social and Cultural Perspective." In Sally McConnell-Genet et al., eds. *Women and Language in Literature and Society*, pp. 27–44. New York: Praeger.

Bourque, Susan C., and Kay B. Warren. 1981a. *Women of the Andes: Patriarchy and Social Change in Two Peruvian Towns*. Ann Arbor: University of Michigan Press.

————. 1981b. "Rural Women and Development Planning in Peru." In Naomi Black and Ann Cotrell, eds. *Women and World Change*. Beverly Hills: Sage.

Brownrigg, Leslie Ann. n.d. "Religion in Mayobamba." Unpublished manuscript, Cornell University and the Ministerio de Trabajo y Communidades.

Callan, Hilary. 1975. "The Premise of Dedication: Notes Towards an Ethnography of Diplomats' Wives." In S. Ardener, ed. *Perceiving Women*, pp. 87–104. London: Malaby Press.

Elshtain, Jean Bethke. 1982. "Feminist Discourse and Its Discontents: Language, Power, and Meaning." *Signs* 7:603–621.

Gould, Karen. 1981. "Setting Words Free: Feminist Writing in Quebec." *Signs* 6:617–642.

Harris, Olivia. 1978. "Complementarity and Conflict: An Andean View of Women and Men." In J. S. LaFontaine, ed. *Sex and Age as Principles of Social Differentiation*, pp. 21–40. New York: Academic Press.

———. 1980. "The Power of Signs: Gender, Culture, and the World in the Bolivian Andes." In Carol P. MacCormack and Marilyn Strathern, eds. *Nature, Culture, and Gender*, pp. 70–94. New York: Cambridge University Press.

Humphrey, Caroline. 1978. "Women, Taboo and the Suppression of Attention." In S. Ardener, ed. *Defining Females*, pp. 89–108. London: Croom and Helm.

Ifeka-Moller, Caroline. 1975. "Female Militancy and Colonial Revolt: The Women's War of 1929, Eastern Nigeria." In S. Ardener, ed. *Perceiving Women*, pp. 127–157. London: Malaby Press.

Isbell, Billie Jean. 1978. *To Defend Ourselves*. Austin: University of Texas Press.

Irvine, Judith. 1979. "Formality and Informality in Communicative Events." *American Anthropologist* 81 : 773–90.

Kramarae, Cheris. 1981. *Women and Men Speaking: Frameworks for Analysis*. Rowley: Newbury.

Lederman, Rena. 1980. "Who Speaks Here? Formality and the Politics of Gender in Mendi, Highland Papua New Guinea." *Journal of the Polynesian Society* (December) 89:4.

MacCormack, Carol. 1980. "Nature, Culture, and Gender: A Critique." In Carol MacCormack and Marilyn Strathern, eds. *Nature, Culture, and Gender*, pp. 1–24. New York: Cambridge University Press.

Merriam, Alan P. 1964. *The Anthropology of Music*. Chicago: Northwestern University Press.

Molnar, Augusta. 1982. "Women and Politics: Case of the Kham Magar of Western Nepal." *American Ethnologist* 9:485–502.

Ortner, Sherry. 1974. "Is Female to Male as Nature Is to Culture?" in M. Rosaldo and L. Lamphere, eds. *Women, Culture, and Society*. Palo Alto: Stanford University Press.

Showalter, Elaine. 1981. "Feminist Criticism in the Wilderness." *Critical Inquiry* 8 : 179–205.

Spender, Dale. 1980. *Man Made Language*. London: Routledge and Kegan Paul.

Turner, Victor. 1969. *The Ritual Process: Structure and Anti-Structure*. Chicago: Aldine.

Warren, Kay B. n.d. "When Cosmologies Lie: Gender, Value, and Power in the Andes." Unpublished manuscript.

Contributors

Martha Ackelsberg (Ph.D., Princeton) is an Associate Professor of Government at Smith College and a Principal Investigator with the Project of Women and Social Change. She has written on the politics of family life, women's political activism, and the Spanish anarchist movement; and spent the 1983–84 academic year as a Fellow of the Mary Ingraham Bunting Institute of Radcliffe College, working on *Strong Is What We Make Each Other*, a study of the social and political vision of the Spanish anarchist women's organization, Mujeres Libres.

Susan C. Bourque (Ph.D., Cornell) is Professor of Government at Smith College and a Principal Investigator with the Project on Women and Social Change. She is the author of *Cholification and the Campesino*, co-author of *Women of the Andes: Patriarchy and Social Change in Two Peruvian Towns* and of a number of articles on social policy and political change in Latin America. Her current research focuses on a comparative study of change in Peru and Guatemala.

Donna Robinson Divine (Ph.D., Columbia) is an Associate Professor in the Department of Government at Smith College and a Principal Investigator with the Project on Women and Social Change. Author of articles on Egyptian and Palestinian Arab social and political history, Israeli politics and Zionist history, she is currently completing *The Arab Awakening in Palestine: Social, Economic and Cultural Changes, 1839–1939*.

Stephen William Foster (Ph.D., Princeton) taught anthropology at Smith College (1980–1983) and now teaches in the Department of Anthropology, University of California, Berkeley. He lived in Morocco in 1974 and 1976 and is presently writing a book about Tangier.

Sue J. M. Freeman (Ph.D., Wisconsin) is Associate Professor of Education and Child Study at Smith College and a Principal Investigator with the Project on Women and Social Change. Having served as school psychologist and consultant to several school systems, she currently teaches courses in special education and maintains a part-time private clinical practice. Her research interests have been concerned with the psychological study of women's personal and professional development.

Penny Gill (Ph.D., Yale) is a Professor of Politics at Mount Holyoke College and a Principal Investigator with the Mount Holyoke Project on Gender and Context. She is continuing her interest in the social and political contexts of women's narratives with a study of Beguines, women of fourteenth-century Europe.

Diedrick Snoek (Ph.D., University of Michigan) is a Professor in the Department of Psychology at Smith College and a Principal Investigator with the Project on Women and Social Change. Author of articles and books in the field of social psychology, he is currently pursuing psychobiographical studies of women who became feminist activists in the 1970s and a study of attitude maintenance in graduates of women's colleges.

Kay Barbara Warren (Ph.D., Princeton) is Director of the Program in Women's Studies, Associate Professor of Anthropology at Princeton University, and a Principal Investigator with the Smith Project on Women and Social Change. She is the author of *The Symbolism of Subordina-*

tion: Indian Identity in a Guatemalan Town and the co-author of *Women of the Andes: Patriarchy and Social Change in Two Peruvian Towns.* Her current research interests also include comparative religious ethics, feminist theory and the social sciences, and gender and American corporations.

289

Index